McFootball

WEST DUNBARTONSHIRE LIBRARIES	
PRICE £16.95	SUPPLIER
LOCATION CL	CLSS 796.334
INVOICE DATE 5.3.04	
ACCESSION NUMBER CO2O236301	

McFootball

The Scottish heroes
of the English game

Norman Giller

ROBSON BOOKS

First published in Great Britain in 2003 by Robson Books, The Chrysalis Building, Bramley Road, London W10 6SP

An imprint of Chrysalis Books Group plc

Copyright © 2003 Norman Giller

The right of Norman Giller to be identified as the Author of the Work has been asserted by him in accordance with the Copyright, Designs and Patents Act 1988.

The author has made every reasonable effort to contact all copyright holders. Any errors that may have occurred are inadvertent and anyone who for any reason has not been contacted is invited to write to the publishers so that a full acknowledgement may be made in subsequent editions of this work.

British Library Cataloguing in Publication Data
A catalogue record for this title is available from the British Library.

ISBN 1 86105 690 7

All rights reserved. No part of this publication may be reproduced, stored in a retrieval system, or transmitted in any form or by any means, electronic, mechanical, photocopying, recording or otherwise, without the prior permission in writing of the publishers.

Typeset by SX Composing DTP, Rayleigh, Essex
Printed and bound in Great Britain by
Butler & Tanner Ltd, Frome and London

To the memory of
Sir Matt Busby,
Bill Shankly
and Jock Stein.
Giants of the game
who will never be
diminished by time.

PREVIOUS BOOKS BY NORMAN GILLER

Banks of England (with Gordon Banks)
The Glory and the Grief (with George Graham)
The Seventies Revisited (with Kevin Keegan) *Billy Wright: A Hero for All Seasons*
The Final Score (with Brian Moore) *ABC of Soccer Sense* (with Tommy Docherty)
The Rat Race (with Tommy Docherty) *Denis Compton: the Untold Stories*
The Book of Rugby Lists (with Gareth Edwards)
The Book of Tennis Lists (with John Newcombe)
The Book of Golf Lists TV Quiz Trivia Sports Quiz Trivia
Fighting for Peace (Barry McGuigan biography, with Peter Batt)
Know What I Mean (with Frank Bruno) *Eye of the Tiger* (with Frank Bruno)
From Zero to Hero (with Frank Bruno)
Mike Tyson Biography Mike Tyson, the Release of Power (with Reg Gutteridge)
World's Greatest Cricket Matches World's Greatest Football Matches
Golden Heroes (with Dennis Signy) *The Judge: 1,001 arguments settled*
The Judge Book of Sports Answers
Crown of Thorns, the World Heavyweight Championship (with Neil Duncanson)
The Marathon Kings The Golden Milers (with Sir Roger Bannister)
Olympic Heroes (with Brendan Foster)
Olympics Handbook 1980 Olympics Handbook 1984
Book of Cricket Lists (with Tom Graveney)
Top Ten Cricket Book (with Tom Graveney)
Cricket Heroes (with Eric Morecambe) *Big Fight Quiz Book TVIQ Puzzle Book*
Lucky the Fox (with Barbara Wright) *Gloria Hunniford's TV Challenge*
Watt's My Name (with Jim Watt)
My Most Memorable Fights (with Henry Cooper)
How to Box (with Henry Cooper) *Henry Cooper's 100 Greatest Boxers*
Comedy novels: *Carry On Doctor Carry On England Carry On Loving
Carry On Up the Khyber Carry On Abroad Carry On Henry*
A Stolen Life (novel) *Mike Baldwin: Mr Heartbreak* (novel) *Hitler's Last Victim* (novel)

In collaboration with Jimmy Greaves:
This One's On Me The Final (novel) *The Ball Game* (novel)
The Boss (novel) *The Second Half* (novel)
World Cup History GOALS! Stop the Game, I Want to Get On
Let's Be Honest (with Reg Gutteridge)
The Book of Football Lists Taking Sides
Sports Quiz Challenge Sports Quiz Challenge 2
It's a Funny Old Life Saint & Greavsie's World Cup Special
The Sixties Revisited Don't Shoot the Manager

Contents

Acknowledgements

Norman Giller wishes to thank publisher Jeremy Robson for having the good sense to commission this book for his impressive list, and Senior Editor Jane Donovan and her skilled editorial team at Robson Books for making sure I get my words, mostly, in the right order. Thanks in particular to Rob Dimery for his expert editing input, Ian Allen for his eagle eye, and Richard Mason for a perfectly tailored jacket. For the facts of the book, I have to thank first of all the many Scottish managers and players who have furnished me with memories and inspiration. Then there is a master statistician called Barry Hugman. I would not even have attempted to tackle the mammoth research job if he and his team of facts-and-figures fanatics had not produced such wonderful mines of information as the book of *Football League Players' Records*. My old press-box colleague Jack Rollin and his omniscient daughter, Glenda, helped me lay the foundation to *McFootball* with their procession of hugely informative *Rothmans and Sky Sports Football Yearbooks*, and I have dipped copiously into the many facts and figures published by the doyen of statesmen, Albert Sewell, of BBCTV and *News of the World Football Annual* fame. Albert and I have known and avoided each other for more than forty years. Website masters Peter Young (www.englandfootballonline.com) and Bob Dunning (www.bobdunning.net) provided encouragement and background facts and figures, for which both are famous. I was also given considerable help by the staff of the Collindale branch of the British Library, who kindly allowed me time and space in their archives section. For the photographs, I turned to the leading agency Popperfoto, and I thank my retiring but not shy old pal Monte Fresco, the king of sports photographers, for his advice and guidance. The Dream

Team final section would not have been possible without the army of visitors to the official website at www.macsoccer.co.uk and I thank them all for their votes and their enthusiastic support. Finally, my gratitude to my son and right-hand man, Michael, who is a sports factician like his old dad but, thank goodness, strengthened and steadied by the common sense he inherited from his mum.

Introduction:
by Norman Giller

This book has been written for those generations of supporters lucky to have been witnesses to the fact that Henrik Larsson and Andrei Kanchelskis are not the greatest 'Scottish' footballers of all time.

I am taking it upon myself as a Sassenach, and on behalf of millions of English football followers, to put on record a tribute to the Tartan Army of players and managers who have come south to enrich and embroider our game with their skill and leadership.

The reflex habit now is to look south to France for the best players to put the bite, the fight and the flair into English teams. We have switched our taste from the Highlands and the haggis to the Gallic and the garlic. The automatic reaction used to be to look north to Scotland, and our clubs happily plundered many of the best players from the Scottish game. And we wonder why Scottish fans detest us!

The Scottish influence on English football goes right to the roots and into the bones of our game. It took a Scot (William McGregor) to form the Football League, and another Scot (Lord Kinnaird) was the driving force behind the Football Association in its formative years.

All the best English teams back in Victorian times – when professional football was first finding its feet – were driven by Scottish players who brought on-the-ground passing skills to what was, by comparison, the crude English way of leathering the ball into the heavens. It took the Scots to bring heaven to our hell.

The book has been a long time coming. My first hero in football was a goalkeeper called Malcolm Finlayson, who played in goal for Millwall in the immediate post-war years. He had such a hold on me that, as an eight-year-old short-trousered schoolboy, I used to walk the length of Rotherhithe Tunnel from my East End home to see him performing his dare-devil saves down in the foreign land of South London, and when I walked back again I would usually have his autograph on my twopenny programme as pencilled proof that he and I had a special bond.

Malcolm talked in a strange tongue, which I later discovered to be a Scottish accent out of the Renfrewshire school. I used to stand behind his goal at The Den down in Cold Blow Lane, willing him to save the shots coming his way. He rarely disappointed me. I would watch him take off and dive across his goal, feeling as if I had a close-up view of Clark Kent suddenly turning into Superman.

Little did I know that sharing my hero worship on those same Millwall terraces was a young boy who used to be accompanied by his father, the local vicar. That boy grew up to be the Voice of Football, John Motson. Goodness knows what the language on those terraces used to do to his father's clerical ears. These were the pre-hooligan days when dockers ruled at The Den, and the most common 'f' word was not football.

I remember crying the day Millwall chose to sell Finlayson to Wolves as the successor to Bert 'The Cat' Williams. Now, more than fifty years on, I am in occasional correspondence with Malcolm, who became a stunningly successful businessman in the steel trade after winning back-to-back League championship medals with the Stan Cullis Wolves.

Let me share a story that Malcolm told me about his Millwall days which will get you in a laughing mood and better tempered to read (and hopefully buy) a book that is stacked with anecdotes as well as profiles on every post-war Scot who has been capped by his country while playing in England.

'The Millwall fans were in the Merseyside class for humour,' Malcolm recalled. 'I remember coming out on to the pitch after a losing first-half at the time of the German War Crimes Tribunal. "They hanged the wrong bloody eleven at Nuremberg," one of our supporters shouted. I could hardly play for laughing.'

As the following pages will testify, the Scots have given me lots of laughs to go with their football over the years. My credentials for writing this book, apart from a deep love and respect for all things Scottish, is that I have been in a privileged position of knowing personally many of the famed and feted

Anglo-Scots who have graced (and just occasionally) disgraced the English soccer scene. As chief football writer for the *Daily Express* in the 1960s through into the 1970s, my relationships with master managers such as Sir Matt Busby, Bill Shankly and Tommy Docherty crossed from professional associations into the field of friendship.

Players of the calibre of Denis Law, Billy Bremner, Frank McLintock and English Scot Bob Wilson became pals of mine off the pitch, and George Graham (with whom I collaborated on his autobiography *The Glory and the Grief*) continues to phone on a weekly basis to inquire about the health of my wife, who spends eleven hours a day on a dialysis machine. I toss this into the pot not for a sympathy vote, but 1) to show what a caring man George is and 2) to put on record my love and admiration for Eileen, who never ever complains about her lot, and encouraged me to pour myself into a book that has taken an enormous amount of research time that, rightfully, belonged to her.

Our game has not only been blessed with Scottish footballing skill, but also the finest and most fluent of Scottish wordsmiths. Among a procession of Scottish writers who have brought their beautifully constructed sentences to the English canvas, and with whom I have shared many a noggin, are poetic reporters and columnists of the quality and class of John Macadam, John Rafferty, Sam Leitch, Ian Archer, the Montgomerys – Ken and Alex – and, the king of them all, Hugh McIlvanney.

In bowing the knee to Hugh, I wonder what he will make of a Sassenach trying to capture the Scottish influence on English football? I have done my best with a vocabulary that would be considered just loose change to McIlvanney, who can call down phrases in the same sort of natural way that the likes of Alex James and Jim Baxter produced passes.

Hugh and his outstanding novelist brother, William, are to Scottish literature what the Charlton brothers are to football. Relatively speaking, they are untouchable and this book would have been much better coming from the McIlvanney pen. I just hope I have done his heroes justice.

The compiling of this book gives me the chance to ease my conscience by making a public apology to Peter Marinello, who joined the exodus of Scottish players to England only to be pushed off that capricious tightrope called fame. I apologise to him for being part of the charade that helped wreck his career in England almost before it had started. The boy of Italian descent but Scottish parentage made an early name for himself as a flying winger with Hibernian. Arsenal bought him for £100,000 in a bold bid to bring width and invention to the team that was on its way to the League and FA Cup double in 1970–71.

In his debut at Old Trafford, fly-away Peter scored the sort of dream solo goal that was the copyright of Manchester United idol George Best. The media got carried away with it to the extent that the *Daily Express*, the paper with which I was earning my daily bread, signed him up as a £100-a-week guest columnist. The fact that his wife-to-be's uncle, Jim Murray, was features editor helped seal the deal.

I was assigned to be Peter's ghostwriter, and went along with my paymasters by putting ridiculous statements into the naive young Scot's mouth. This was the bland leading the blind. I turned him into a cross between a Beatle and a Best, making him sound like a West End playboy when, in truth, he hardly knew one side of London from the other. It bred resentment in the Arsenal dressing-room, where there were players picking up less for playing the game than Peter was getting for his newspaper column (it was also £20 a week more than I was earning as a staffman!).

The Milk Marketing Board jumped on the bandwagon almost before the wheels had made one revolution by signing him for a nationwide poster campaign. The pretty-boy Marinello face was everywhere. He was, almost literally, a footballer who was running before he could walk. Peter was fast enough to catch pigeons, but tactics might just as well have been a packet of mints for all he knew. Arsenal were a carefully choreographed side, and hard as coach Don Howe tried he just could not get Peter to pick up the codes. We looked on in agony as he tried and failed to play solos in a finely tuned orchestra.

He was a thoroughly pleasant and likeable boy, but completely out of his depth in the First Division, and not helped by the fact that some Arsenal players were choosing not to let him have the ball. It all ended in tears, of course, and after just 38 League appearances he continued his career down the scale with Portsmouth, Motherwell and Fulham. I am not proud of the part I played in his rise and fall. Had Don Howe got hold of him away from the publicity glare I am convinced he would have turned him into a winger almost in the Best class. But the media, with me as one of the chief culprits, scorched him with our spotlight. Sorry, Pete.

Now that I am out of the confessional, let me caution you that I will be painting myself into several of the major chapters in the first half of the book, when I concentrate on the pioneers and the managers who have made most impact on the English soccer stage. I hope my appearances do not irritate you, but it helps me bring you closer to the men who have brought so much pleasure and pride into our game. Hitchcock used to appear in his films, now I am writing myself into my books. Time to hang up the quill?

In the second half, I bring together for the first time in one volume complete profiles and statistical facts and figures on every post-war Anglo-Scottish footballer who has been capped for his country while playing in England. I also make references to many of the outstanding players who were ignored by the Scottish selectors, often almost as punishment for taking the English shilling.

The final section of the book was made possible by the army of people who kindly visited the website – www.macsoccer.co.uk – that I have set up. They took part in a poll to select their favourite post-war Anglo-Scottish footballers, and the players many of them voted for feature in the 'Dream Team' chapter. My thanks to all those who participated in the poll, English and Scots alike.

All of us should take it as a duty to find the young Scots who look on Henrik Larsson as the greatest of all 'Scottish' players. Entice them away from their Play Stations and Gameboys, and encourage them to play the auld game that their ancestors mastered as 'tanner baw' players, a reference to the little sixpenny balls from Woolworths that Scottish boys invariably had at their feet on their way to and from school.

The influx of foreign footballers to Scottish – and English – clubs has taken away from the current generation both the incentive and the opportunity to become local heroes. Scottish team manager Berti Vogts, once an exceptional German footballer, knows all about the traditions of the game. He must feel like a prospector who has arrived after the Gold Rush has finished. Vogts has had to scrabble around reserve team matches and tap into the ancestry of English-born players to try to discover footballers fit to wear the Scottish blue.

I contacted Graham Leggat, a fine Anglo-Scottish player of the fifties and sixties, to tell him about my *McFootball* project. He is now the respected voice of soccer on Canadian television, and his long-range view was, 'I just hope your book helps rekindle the old spirit in pulling on the Scottish jersey. I just cannot believe how the standards have fallen. It is so sad.'

We need to tell the young generation of Scots of their proud past and of how English football, for at least its first hundred years, would not have been nearly as successful and as satisfying without the strong Scottish influence.

The Scottish spirit and soul would be very welcome back in our game. As Robert Burns once said, 'Kick the bastards before they kick you.' Oh no, sorry, it was Kenny Burns.

Here's tae ye. Wha's like ye?

PART ONE

Chapter One

The Pioneers

If a forensic scientist had been able to study English football in its embryonic state, he would have found Scottish fingerprints all over it; or, to be more accurate with my metaphor, Scottish footprints.

It was a Scot, William McGregor, who founded the Football League, and another Scot, Lord Kinnaird – unwillingly born among the Auld Enemy in England – who was a major driving force behind the Football Association in its formative years.

McGregor's influence on the English game can be measured in fathoms. Football was on the brink of uncivil war when he applied sound Scottish logic and inspiring powers of leadership to introduce an unashamedly professional competition.

The Football Association was founded in 1863 (traditionalists will insist you never call it the English FA . . . it is THE Football Association, because it was the first). It was run by amateurs for amateurs, and the mere mention of the word 'professional' could cause apoplexy in the gentlemen's clubs in London where the FA hierarchy were generally to be found.

Northern clubs considered the game more working class than down in the South, where most teams were of the old-school variety or linked to universities and military associations. Players 'oop North' could not afford to take time off from their jobs in the mills and the mines, and their chairmen introduced broken-time payments to compensate them for lost wages.

It was the most contentious issue in sport in the 1880s, and there was a north-south divide between those in favour of amateurism and those who silently and surreptitiously supported 'shamateurism' – paying players undisclosed money to represent their clubs. Among the earliest Scots to have benefited from finding money tucked into their boots were almost certainly Fergus Suter and James Love, who helped virtually unknown Lancashire club Darwen take the leading team of the time, Old Etonians, to two replays before losing a fourth-round FA Cup tie in 1879.

The Old Etonians, heaving with 'hons' and full of noble intent, were far too gentlemanly to say anything publicly, but in private the question was being asked: 'What has encouraged two exceptional players from Partick to up sticks and move to Darwen?' The view was that it could only have been the promise of payment.

Despite widespread opposition, professionalism was finally allowed in English football in 1885. There were huge protests from the still-amateur Scots when nineteen-year-old Blackburn half-back Jimmy Forrest became the first professional to play for England, and what had become the annual fixture between England and Scotland was in danger of being called off because of the strongly held belief that amateurs and professionals should not mix (cricket provides an accurate reflection of the times in that professional players were not allowed to use the same dressing-room, or even the same entrance to the field, as the 'gentlemen' cricketers).

This was the backdrop to some serious and creative thinking by Aston Villa director William McGregor, who recognised that professionalism was here to stay and that extra competition was needed to boost income that came exclusively from FA Cup ties and friendly fixtures.

Born in Braco, Perthshire, in 1847, McGregor had come to England in the footsteps of his brother, Peter, to seek his fortune at the age of 23. He and his wife, Jessie, ran a draper's shop at 301 Summer Lane, Aston, in the heart of England, and it was here that he quietly planned the revolution that was to change the face of English football forever.

He had been drawn to the newly formed Aston Villa club by the presence of three Scottish players, including club captain George Ramsay, who was 'a demon dribbler'. After seeing how a crowd-pleaser like Ramsay could attract huge attendances, McGregor composed the following historic letter in March 1888, handwritten and delivered to four carefully selected club chairmen, plus his Villa colleagues:

Every year it is becoming more and more difficult for football clubs of any standing to meet their friendly engagements and even arrange friendly matches. The consequence is that at the last moment, through cup-tie interference, clubs are compelled to take on teams who will not attract the public.

I beg to tender the following suggestion as a means of getting over the difficulty: that ten or twelve of the most prominent clubs in England combine to arrange home-and-away fixtures each season, the said fixtures to be arranged at a friendly conference about the same time as the International Conference.

This combination might be known as the Association Football Union, and could be managed by representatives from each club. Of course, this is in no way to interfere with the National Association; even the suggested matches might be played under cup-tie rules. However, this is a detail.

My object in writing to you at present is merely to draw your attention to the subject, and to suggest a friendly conference to discuss the matter more fully. I would take it as a favour if you would kindly think the matter over, and make whatever suggestions you deem necessary.

I am only writing to the following – Blackburn Rovers, Bolton Wanderers, Preston North End, West Bromwich Albion and Aston Villa, and would like to hear what other clubs you would suggest.

I am, yours very truly, William McGregor (Aston Villa F.C.)

P.S. – How would Friday, 23rd March, 1888, suit for the friendly conference at Anderton's Hotel, London?

McGregor confided in his good friend, Joe Tillotson, who ran a small café close to his draper's shop and was a keen Aston Villa supporter. Together, they worked out how a league could be run on similar lines to the baseball league that was up and running with huge success in the United States.

A teetotaller and deeply religious, McGregor had a demeanour that acquaintances variously described as 'trustworthy', 'inspirational', and 'deeply sincere'. He was portly, looked benevolent and had a bush of a white beard that gave him the appearance of a Father Christmas. The present he gave to English football was a structure that provided the foundation for the game as we know it today.

The turn-out at the meeting in Anderton's Hotel in Fleet Street exceeded McGregor's expectations, and he found himself preaching to the converted with his rich Scottish tones that carried the sounds of Perthshire through the Victorian hotel and which would reverberate throughout the land. Representatives were present from Aston Villa, Burnley, Blackburn Rovers, Derby County, Notts County, Stoke, West Bromwich Albion and Wolverhampton Wanderers. It was agreed to hold another meeting at the Royal Hotel in Manchester on 17 April 1888, with Accrington, Bolton, Everton and Preston North End invited to take part.

These were the twelve clubs who agreed to launch the Football League in September 1888. McGregor argued against calling it the English League because deep down he wanted the competition to eventually embrace clubs from his homeland of Scotland. This did not seem such a distant dream because top Scottish club Queen's Park had been leading challengers for the FA Cup.

McGregor, 'Father of the Football League' and its first president, had not bothered to invite any southern clubs to participate because the opposition to professionalism emanating from London was so strong. There was quiet rage in the corridors of power at the Football Association over what was seen as the spread of a poison that could prove contagious.

Among the leading spokesmen for the Football Association was a man who had become a footballing legend in his own lifetime, Lord Kinnaird, who as A (Arthur) F (Fitzgerald) Kinnaird had played in nine FA Cup finals with the Wanderers and Old Etonians, finishing on the winning side five times.

The eleventh Baron of Inchture, and elected High Commissioner to the Church of Scotland in 1907, Kinnaird was born in Paddington in 1847 – the same year as McGregor – but considered himself Scottish to the core.

He was distinctive on the football field because of a red beard, exceptional speed and energy and a warrior-like approach to the game; this in an era when hacking was part and painful parcel of the game. His wife once said to a team-mate, 'I am worried that Arthur will one day come home with a broken leg.' The friend nodded his agreement. 'Yes,' he said. 'I wonder who it will belong to?' The anecdote is no doubt apocryphal, but it illustrates his competitiveness. One true story that shows he had personality to go with his talent is that he celebrated collecting his fifth and final FA Cup winners' medal in 1882 by standing on his head in front of the main stand at The Oval.

Kinnaird played for an England XI in the first unofficial international match against Scotland in 1870, but chose to play for Scotland in the second official game three years later. His service to the Football Association, which stretched to 55 years and included a prolonged spell as president, was marked in an extraordinary way. In 1911 the FA Cup was presented to Kinnaird, and a new trophy ordered. Now there's one for a trivia quiz: 'Who is the only Scot to have won the FA Cup outright?'

He worked in tandem with English 'Father of Football' C W (Charles) Alcock, to bring stability and organisation to the spread of association football – shortened in the universities to 'soccer' to differentiate from the rival game of 'rugger' that was the preferred pastime in several southern strongholds.

Kinnaird, a banker by profession, was an amateur sportsman from the tip of his toes to the top of his aristocratic head, and he was appalled by the swing towards professionalism. It was a view shared north of the border, where the Scottish Football Association – formed in 1873 – was strenuously opposed to pay for play. They looked on in growing fury and frustration as the English clubs continually raided their teams for players to help them make an impact in the new Football League.

A procession of top Scottish players were tempted into England by offers of jobs to go with cash payments for playing on Saturdays. The Scottish press were unmerciful with their criticism of anybody taking 'the English bribes' and accused them of being 'traitorous mercenaries'.

The Scottish FA punished the players by refusing to select them for international matches, but eventually gave in after a run of six matches against England without a victory. They started to have annual trial matches between Scottish-based players and Anglo-Scottish teams to find the best combination with which to face the Auld Enemy.

In a bid to stop their best players being poached, several Scottish clubs resorted to the sort of under-the-counter payments that had been rife in England. When Hibernian won the Scottish Cup in 1887, runners-up Dumbarton hired a private detective to probe what they were convinced was professionalism by their opponents. He uncovered the fact that Hibs had paid one of their players a £1 broken-time payment for missing three days from his work as a stonemason, for which his weekly wage was ten shillings.

Faced with these sort of disclosures, the Scottish FA slowly capitu-
lated and finally gave a reluctant green light for professionalism in 1893,
but by then many of their best players had 'emigrated' south of the
border, where their cultured, all-on-the-floor passing game of football
was much in demand.

An example of the bribery being used to magnetise the Scottish players
south is that in 1889 England's oldest League club, Notts County, offered
Third Lanark centre-forward James Oswald not only a salary of £160 a
season but also a tobacconist's shop with £500 of stock. As he was on a wage
of 36s for a 54-hour week as a fitter, he took the bait and scored 55 goals in
95 League appearances for Notts County before returning to Scotland in
1892 to play for St Bernard's and then Rangers.

All the major English sides had the tartan touch. Preston, 'The
Invincibles', who won the first League championship without a single defeat
and also captured the FA Cup without conceding a goal, had Scotland
stamped all the way through them.

The Ross brothers from Edinburgh, Nick and Jimmy, were the heart and
soul of the team – Nick a defender who could kick the ball the length of the
pitch, and Jimmy a right winger with a crashing shot. George 'Geordie'
Drummond was another Edinburgh man. He scored 36 goals in 139 League
games for Proud Preston, who had emerged from the North End Cricket
Club in 1881.

Glaswegian Jack Gordon had the distinction of scoring the first goal in
the Football League in Preston's 1–1 draw at Wolverhampton on the first
day of the first season, 8 September 1888 (some record books claim this
cannot be correct because the match against Wolves kicked off later than the
other fixtures).

Attacking centre-half David Russell, born and raised in Airdrie, put
the punch into Preston with performances that earned him six Scottish
caps and the reputation for being the hardest man in the League. He
tackled like a clap of thunder, and was described by one Victorian sportswriter as charging upfield 'like a wild, hungry and ferocious animal in
search of a meal'.

Aston Villa surpassed Preston in the trophy-winning stakes, and it was
the 'demon dribbler' Ramsay – now in charge as manager-secretary – who
motivated them during what were golden years for the Birmingham club.

The quiet Scot, a former clerk in a brass foundry, guided Villa to six FA Cups and six League championships between 1884 and 1920.

He helped them develop from a club playing on the sloping pastures of Aston Park to being kings of the castle at Villa Park, where at the turn of the century they were one of the most famous and feted clubs in the world. 'Mr Loyalty' served Villa for an astonishing stretch of 59 years.

Ramsay put much of his faith on the sturdy shoulders of fellow Scot Jimmy Cowan, from Jamestown. He was a driving centre-half, like Preston's David Russell, but more composed on the ball and a supreme passer in the true Scottish style. A single-minded character, he once got suspended by the club for taking time off to secretly prepare for the 1896 New Year's Day Powderhall Sprint, which was then the most prized professional handicap sprint race in Europe.

Not noted for his sprint speed on the pitch, he went home to the Highlands to train after telling Villa that he had damaged his back. He worked on perfecting his start and stride pattern, and kept everything quiet so that he would be allowed as big a yardage advantage as possible over the off-scratch professional sprinters. The handicappers awarded him a twelve-and-a-half-yard start to a race run over a flat grass course of 130 yards. The only people who knew of his secret preparations were a small group of gamblers from Birmingham, and they travelled to the Powderhall meeting in Scotland to see him win the race with a yard to spare over his nearest rival. They took the bookmakers for several hundred pounds, of which a percentage was paid to the canny Cowan. One of the Birmingham betting syndicate failed to get paid out. The bookmaker took off quicker than Cowan had finished the race when he realised he was on the wrong end of a sting.

Aston Villa's biggest rivals during this golden age were Sunderland, who leaned heavily on the skilled contributions from Scottish players after they had replaced relegated Stoke in the League at the start of the 1890–91 season. They had been formed as the Sunderland and District Teachers' Association Football Club by Scottish schoolmaster James Allan in 1879, but quickly became Sunderland AFC when players from outside the teaching profession clamoured to join.

The north-east club made mass signings of Scots, promising them work in the local shipyards to supplement their football wage of 25s a week. They were also paid a £10 signing-on bonus and were given club houses in which to live free of rent. Ironically, the club founder James Allan disagreed with this form of recruitment and he led a breakaway group in 1888, creating a rival amateur club called Sunderland Albion.

But it was the club that Allan left behind that prospered and flourished. Boosted by the powerhouse performances of centre-forward John Campbell, the trickery of inside-right Jimmy Millar and the midfield drive of captain Hugh Wilson – all Scots, of course – Sunderland were almost unbeatable at home, and gave second best to a visiting team only once in their first six seasons in the League. They won the League championship three times in four years in the 1890s and again in 1902, always with sides packed with Scots.

Following one of their victories over Aston Villa, 'Father of the League' William McGregor told the Sunderland chairman, 'Your team have all the talents.' It was a quote picked up by the newspapers and from then on the Sunderland side became known as 'The Team of All the Talents'.

Best known of the Sunderland Scots was goalkeeper Edward ('Teddy' or 'Ned') Doig, who was rated to have the safest pair of hands in the game. When signed from Arbroath along with his brother, Robert, he played before his seven-day registration had been cleared. Sunderland were fined £50 and had two points deducted.

Doig, who had previously played just one game for Lancashire giants Blackburn, became a much-loved personality at the back of the Sunderland defence across a span of fourteen seasons and 417 League games before winding down his career with Liverpool.

He was quite a character. While he was being chaired off after a series of match-winning saves in an international against England, a female spectator from his hometown of Arbroath called out: 'Gie me a lock o' your hair "Ned", tae tak hame tae Arbroath.'

Doig removed his goalkeeper's cap to reveal his famously bald dome. 'I'm awfu' sorry I canna oblige, madam,' he said. 'Ye will have tae make do with taking ma best wishes tae them at hame.'

The Team of All the Talents had the following Scots challenging for places: John Campbell (Renton), John Harvie (Renton), Davy Hannah (Renton), John Auld (Third Lanark), John Spence (Airdrieonians), Will Gibson (Cambuslang), Tom Porteous (Kilmarnock), John Smith (Kilmarnock),

John Scott (Albion Rovers), James Gillespie (Greenock Morton), and, of course, the one and only Ted Doig (Arbroath). If anybody shouted John on the pitch, six heads would turn!

The team was reinforced in 1890 by the arrival of exceptional marksman Jimmy Millar, from Awnbank, and Hughie Wilson, a driving half-back from Newmilns. Wilson was renowned for his long one-handed throw bowled into the goalmouth before one-handed throws were banned, and Millar weighed in with 79 goals in 140 League games.

Newcastle United were having to live in the shadow of their neighbours Sunderland, but started to make up ground when they signed as their first manager-secretary Frank Watt, who had made a name for himself as an outstanding administrator with the East Edinburgh Football Association. He served Newcastle with distinction for 37 years from 1895 and laid the foundation to their triumphs of the 1920s. Watt encouraged the importing of a procession of skilled Scots, and he more than anybody else was responsible for bringing the indomitable Hughie Gallacher to Gallowgate from Airdrie.

The most stark evidence of how English clubs were relying on Scottish players came when Liverpool made their debut as a League club in 1893 after Everton had famously walked out on Anfield landlord John Houlding. He responded by forming Liverpool Football Club, and kicked off with a team containing ten Scots and an English goalkeeper by the name of McOwen! (This record was beaten in April 1955, when Scottish manager Walter Galbraith selected eleven Scots for Accrington Stanley in their Football League match against York City.)

It was a Scottish visionary, William McGregor, who pioneered the Football League, and now it was the Scottish players who were decorating and dictating the English game with their artistry and, let's be frank, their aggression and not a little arrogance. It was a wonderful cocktail that brought the scent of the heather to English football.

A great Anglo-Scottish tradition had started, and it would be carried on by a conveyor belt of exceptional players and unmatchable managers. The following chapters will spotlight and honour the best of them.

Chapter Two

Jimmy McMullan and the Wembley Wizards

There is one momentous match that brings into focus the status and standing of Anglo-Scottish footballers in the 1920s, when England were attempting to build on the foundation of being the 'Old Masters' of football. Enter the Wembley Wizards.

The date 31 March 1928 – when the Scots played England off the park on the way to a 5–1 victory – deserves to be engraved in gold lettering in the annals of Scottish football history.

It marked the second visit of Scotland to Wembley Stadium, built for the Empire Games of 1924. England's national stadium. For the Scots it was like being challenged to tumble the walls of Jericho, and it was estimated that twenty thousand made the trek south to cheer on the boys in blue.

Earlier in the day Cambridge had won the Boat Race with ease, leaving the Oxford crew labouring in their wake over the Putney–Mortlake course. Nobody would have guessed that in the afternoon England's footballers would be sunk without trace.

There had been a mixture of despair and derision when the Scottish selectors announced their team . . . despair, because the side included eight Anglo-Scots, and derision because the tallest of the five forwards stood just 5ft 7in.

The Scottish newspapers were unmerciful in their criticism of the selectors. How could they ignore so many home-based footballing masters, who had not sold their soul to English clubs for thirty pieces of silver? Who was going to stop the tall, heavily built English defenders from winning everything in the air? Music-hall comedians in England wondered aloud on stage whether the Scots would be bringing Snow White with them to go with the dwarfs in Scotland's team (they were not shackled by politically correct restrictions in those days).

The critics had overlooked the little matter that thoroughbred Scottish footballers, brought up on the traditional passing game, rarely believed in playing the ball above knee height. This was, and always has been, the appeal of Scottish football. They play to feet as they follow the old creed, 'It's fitba' not heedba'.'

On paper, it was difficult to see how the wee Scots would be able to unhinge an England team that boasted exceptional players such as Huddersfield skipper and right-back Roy Goodall, West Ham goalkeeper Ted Hufton – then considered as good as any custodian in the world – rocketing Arsenal winger Joe Hulme, Birmingham's barnstorming Joe Bradford, and the king of Goodison William 'Dixie' Dean, who was coming to the close of a season in which he managed the extraordinary feat of scoring a record 60 First Division goals. But this was to be a match in which even the Dean of football was forced to take a back seat.

I am able to bring a personal flavour to this reconstruction of a game and an era in which the Anglo-Scots were supreme. Fast-forward from 1928 to 1963, and to a vicious English winter when the country was buried under snow that virtually wiped out two months of the football season. I was earning my daily bread with a late, lamented national newspaper called the *Daily Herald* (which in 1964 became the broadsheet *Sun*, with the tabloid version just a twinkle in Rupert Murdoch's eye).

As there was no football action to report in that snowbound season we filled blank pages by recalling great matches of days gone by under the title *Game of My Life*. I tracked down an elderly Scottish gentleman called Jimmy McMullan, who was living in retirement in Sheffield, close to the Hillsborough ground where he had once been the manager of Sheffield Wednesday.

Any self-respecting Scot with proper knowledge of Scottish football history will tell you that McMullan captained that team of Wembley Wizards in what was, without doubt, the game of his life.

He was a specialist left-half, an elegant, thoughtful player whose precise passes steered Manchester City to the Second Division championship and two FA Cup finals. By the time I came into his life he was 68 and more than happy to be reminded of a magical match that was played two days after his 33rd birthday.

'It was the nearest thing you will ever see to perfection on a football field,' he recalled in a Scottish burr that still carried the echoes of his formative years in his hometown of Denny in Stirlingshire. 'We were a team of wee men but with hearts as big as buckets, and with footballers as skilful as have ever played the game.'

This was not an old man being deceived by a fading memory. The Scottish forward line read: Alec Jackson (Huddersfield), Jimmy Dunn (Hibernian), Hughie Gallacher (Newcastle), Alex James (Preston) and Alan Morton (Rangers). Jackson, at five foot seven, was the tallest of them, Morton, at five foot four, the smallest; but each of the players carved out careers that made them giants of the game.

A quick and quirky right winger, Jackson helped Huddersfield to their third successive League championship; Dunn joined Everton to play alongside Dean in the 1933 FA Cup-winning team; Gallacher and James became legends whom I will explore in the next two chapters, and Morton was the original 'Wee Blue Devil' about whom Rangers fans wrote ballads to mark his fantastic feats.

Skipper McMullan was himself only five foot five, leading out the smallest team ever to play in an international match at Wembley (and that, I have little doubt, includes schoolboy internationals!).

'The night before the game,' McMullan recalled, 'I said to the lads, "When you go to bed pray for rain." Our prayers were answered and there was a downpour that made the pitch just that little bit slippery. I knew we had the forwards who would make life hell for the English defenders trying to turn on a wet surface.'

Rain was still falling when Scotland took the lead in the third minute, just seconds after England had gone close to scoring. Huddersfield left winger Billy Smith cracked a low shot against the base of a Scottish post. McMullan collected the rebound, released the ball to James who exchanged passes with Dunn before pushing it into the path of Morton out on the left wing. He raced down the touchline and then lofted the ball into the goalmouth. Alec Jackson came galloping in from the right wing to head the ball into the net. The vertically challenged men had snatched the lead with a headed goal! It was one of the few times they played the ball above ankle height.

'That was just the confidence booster we needed,' said McMullan, suddenly warmed by the 35-year-old memory. 'We started to pass the ball around as if we owned the place, and the England defenders were panicking.'

Alex James conjured a solo goal a minute before half-time, gliding past three England defenders before scoring with a low shot from just outside the penalty area while everybody, including his team-mates, expected a pass.

'The timing of the goal could not have been better for us,' McMullan told me. 'It was a marvellous piece of individual brilliance by Alex. I remember that the only time he got ruffled that day was when the skip arrived carrying our new kit. The shorts were too brief for him because his liking for baggy shorts had become an obsession. We had to send an official back to the team hotel to get him the right sort of long shorts. At half-time we decided we would just keep pushing the ball around to feet. The English were making the mistake of marking our wingers with their wing-halves, and this gave our inside-forwards freedom on which they thrived.'

There was a swagger and cockiness in the way the Scots played in the second half, and just about everything they tried on a soaking-wet surface came off. Their ecstatic supporters made Wembley sound like Hampden as their blue-shirted heroes stitched together multi-pass movements as if embroidering a giant tapestry.

In the 65th minute Alec Jackson scored a carbon copy of his first goal, and almost immediately Alex James made it 4–0 when he steered the ball home after Hughie Gallacher had powered through the middle of the demoralised England defence.

Jackson completed his hat-trick five minutes from the end with a spectacular mid-air shot after Morton had once again mercilessly gunned past defenders tackling thin air.

Huddersfield marksman Bob Kelly hammered in a last-minute free-kick from fully forty yards to give England some sort of consolation, but it was like arriving at a party after the last drink had been poured and it was the Scots who had helped themselves to the sweet wine of victory.

'The scenes afterwards were unbelievable,' said the winning captain, enjoying his memory carpet-ride back to the greatest day of his life. 'The pitch was suddenly engulfed with Scottish supporters, who tried to carry us off as if we were trophies. I shook hands with every player in the dressing-room and congratulated them on being part of the greatest team performance I had ever seen. The only thing that has come close to it is Hungary's display against England at Wembley in 1953 when they won 6–3. I was so proud to be part of it. On that day I can say without fear of contradiction that Scotland were the best team in the world.'

The Scottish newspapers, so disappointed and disillusioned when the team was first announced, went into raptures. 'The success of the Scots,' trumpeted the *Glasgow Herald*, 'was primarily another demonstration that Scottish skill, science and trickery will prevail against the less attractive and simpler methods of the English style in which speed and brute force are relied upon as major factors. Want of height was looked upon as a handicap to the Scots attack but the Scottish forwards had ability and skill of such high degree as to make their physical shortcomings of little consequence.'

The *Daily Record* continued the anthem of acclaim: 'Came the second-half and an exhibition of football that was as perfect as perfect can be. Every man touched his highest pinnacle. Every man became part of an efficient machine that moved with a rhythm, power and speed that crushed the Saxons. There was never any sign of selfishness. Their power and virility were amazing.'

An English view came from the pages of the *Daily Mail*: 'On the evidence of this performance, Scotland can lay claims to be considered the greatest team in the world. They are little men with big hearts and talent that knows no bounds. The inferiority of the England side was so marked that the confusion and bewilderment of the individual players, against the science, skill and pace of Scotland's dazzling team, became positively ludicrous.'

For a final word I turn to the modest, unassuming little man who led the Wembley Wizards to that glorious victory on 31 March 1928, the Scottish skipper Jimmy McMullan:

'My abiding memory is of seeing Hughie Gallacher sent crashing by an unnecessarily wild tackle early in the game,' McMullan said, his eyes half closed as he brought up the incident on his memory screen. 'Hughie had a wild temper and I was worried that he was going to retaliate. But as he pulled himself up he winked at me and said, "Don't worry, skip. I'll get my own back with fitba'." That was when I knew this was going to be our day.'

Ah, Hughie Gallacher. Now there was character and a half, and he gets my full attention in the next chapter.

Chapter Three

Hughie Gallacher:
The Cursed Genius

Of all the Anglo-Scottish footballers featured in these pages, nobody was more talented than Hughie Kilpatrick Gallacher; sadly, nobody was as tragic. He could control just about everything on the football pitch, but in his private life he stumbled from one crisis to another. It reached a chilling climax when Gallacher committed suicide by stepping into the path of an Edinburgh express train the day before he was due to appear in court on a charge of ill-treating his son. He was 54 years old.

For the purposes of a football book like this, it is necessary that I separate the footballer from the man; but there are unavoidable instances when I need to pinpoint private matters that affected not only his playing career but also his personality.

One thing that everybody who witnessed Gallacher in action agreed on – spectator, team-mate or opponent – is that he was the *complete* centre-forward. He was compact, quick, had natural positional instinct, dribbled like a winger, could control the ball and shoot with either foot and, despite standing only five foot five inches, managed to beat much taller defenders in the air. Hughie led the line like a conductor, pointing to where he wanted the ball delivered and then completing the orchestration by being there when it arrived. God help the team-mate who did not meet his perfectionist standards. He could deliver volleys of abuse like a gunfighter, shooting from the lip.

Some startling statistics to support Hughie's claim that he deserved the best service from those around him: he scored 387 goals in 543 League games (only Jimmy McGrory, 410, and Arthur Rowley, 434, found the net more times), and in nineteen international appearances for Scotland between 1923 and 1935 he scored 22 goals. Few players in the world have bettered a goal a game in the international arena.

Gallacher came from the footballing hotbed of Lanarkshire, a rich industrial vein of the West of Scotland that has had a bigger impact on the English soccer scene than any other. The local football pitches – green treasure islands decorating the bleak coalfields – produced in Sir Matt Busby, Bill Shankly and Jock Stein three of the greatest managers in the history of the game, and in Gallacher and his schoolboy team-mate Alex James two of the greatest players ever to lace a pair of football boots.

It is a toss of a coin whether Gallacher or James was the finest of the Lanarkshire lads who rose from the challenge of their childhood to find footballing fame in the first half of a twentieth century that provided few escape routes for anybody caught in the poverty trap.

Gallacher was born in the mining village of Bellshill on 2 February 1903, with the sounds of Ireland in his ears. His father, Matthew Gallacher, was a farming Ulsterman who had emigrated across the Irish Sea to the West of Scotland to scrape a living on a strip of land surrounded by coalfields.

Strangely, for a man who was to become arguably the greatest centre-forward of all time, Gallacher started his football life as a schoolboy goalkeeper. His was the classic case of the goalkeeper turned poacher. He later played centre-half and inside-left before finding that it was the number 9 shirt that fitted him best of all. He captained the school team that, for one season, included another wee footballing genius in the shape of Alex James, who was a year ahead of him.

The world was at war when Gallacher left school at fourteen in 1917, and he was put to work in a munitions factory at Mossend. A year later, following the Armistice, he transferred to the pits, labouring at the coal face. I am one of those southern softies who has no conception of how hard this life could be (I have the smooth hands of a writer whose hardest manual labour has been pounding keyboards for nearly half a century, but you should see the blisters on my brain!). The mining experience toughened Gallacher physically, and gave him the mental motivation to use football as an escape route from the punishment of the pits.

While starring in amateur football as a teenager with Tannochside Athletic, Hattonrigg Thistle and Bellshill Athletic, Gallacher considered a career as a professional boxer. He was a regular on the punchbags at the renowned Hamilton fight academy that produced British champions Johnny Brown and Tommy Milligan. This love of fighting often spilled over into his football, and his aggression got him into constant trouble with referees.

Before he could test his boxing prowess in the professional ring, Gallacher was signed by Queen of the South, who had been attracted by his performance for Scotland against Ireland in a 1920 junior international. He headed a dramatic last-gasp winner from ten yards that persuaded them to give him a £6-a-week contract, £4 more than he was getting for working down the mine.

I now need to make my first intrusion into Hughie's privacy to reveal how fate conspired to burden him with a bitterness that was never far from the surface for the rest of his life. He went against the wishes of his family at the age of seventeen and married a girl he had met while she was working in the office at the local pit. She was Annie McIlvaney, from a Roman Catholic family. Hughie's father belonged to the Orange Order. They were trying to cross a religious divide that in those bigoted days was several bridges too far.

They first of all lived in rented rooms, and then he with his parents and she with hers. No marriage could survive such strains, and their union was then dealt a mortal blow. Their first baby, a son called Hughie, died within months of his birth.

Exactly the same tragic thing happened forty years later to another goal-scoring genius called Jimmy Greaves, who was compared throughout his career with Gallacher. Jimmy and his wife, Irene, lost their first child, James Junior, to a cot death. Jimmy later turned to the crutch of alcohol to combat his personal gremlins, but had the character to beat the bottle. Gallacher, too, looked for answers to life's problems in the bottom of a glass and found only more problems.

His marriage inevitably came apart after briefly being given a breath of life with the birth of a daughter. The Gallachers separated acrimoniously in 1923, by which time Hughie was laying the foundation to his footballing legend as a prolific goal-scorer with Airdrieonians.

Airdrie signed him on a bumper £9-a-week contract after he had recovered from a life-threatening bout of double pneumonia that put him on his back in a Dumfries hospital. He showed the illness had not robbed him of his sharpness, skill and strength on the football field, and he helped Airdrie win the Scottish Cup in 1924, and bulged the net with 91 goals in 111 games.

Scouts for English clubs were sending urgent 'come and get him' signals to their bosses south of the border, and it was Newcastle who made a £6,500 offer that Airdrie could not refuse, despite angry demonstrations by their supporters.

Newcastle's fans were unimpressed by their first sight of the little man in the famous black-and-white striped shirt that made him look like a baby zebra. But by the time the final whistle signalled the end of his debut against Everton at St James' Park on 8 December 1925, he was a giant in their eyes and they were Gallacher disciples. He scored two goals and made a third for Stan Seymour in a thrilling 3–3 draw. A player by the name of Dixie Dean scored a hat-trick for Everton.

Gallacher, cocky to the point of arrogant, had so much to say for himself on and off the pitch that the Newcastle management decided he would make an ideal captain, an appointment that caused enormous controversy. Many considered him too young, too headstrong, too temperamental and too much of a bullying type of character to get the best out of his team-mates. Many were proved wrong. In his first season as skipper, Gallacher lifted the 1926–27 League championship trophy, providing atomic action to go with his leadership. He led by example, scoring 36 goals in 38 matches.

Nothing could have been better for the morale of the fanatical football followers on Tyneside, where the year of the General Strike and mass unemployment were biting deep. They even forgave Gallacher his brashness and off-the-pitch playboy antics as he lived life with the accelerator to the floor. He dressed like a dandy in the latest London fashions, often sporting spats and a white trilby, and he also liked to play the gentleman by wearing a black bowler and carrying a tightly rolled umbrella. But he far from acted the gentleman as he threw money across the bar in local pubs, doing his best to drink Newcastle dry.

He had several fall-outs with the Newcastle directors over his lifestyle, but always had the final word on the pitch, where his goals did all the talking. These were the heady days when he was young enough to run off his excesses in training, where he could match any of his team-mates in laps of the pitch and demanding exercise routines.

Hughie was a ladies' man and got himself into the headlines when he fell for Hannah Anderson, the seventeen-year-old daughter of the landlord of one of his favourite pubs in Gateshead. Forgetting to tell her that he was still officially married, he had a run-in with her brother when the news was revealed. Their angry confrontation finished with them both appearing in court, where they were bound over to keep the peace.

His long-running battle against officialdom hit a new low when he was suspended for two months after an infamous clash with a prominent referee, Arthur Fogg. During a match against Huddersfield on an icebound pitch, Gallacher felt the referee had failed to give him at least two blatant penalties after he had been tackled off the ball. He let fly with a torrent of abuse as the final whistle blew and the referee asked for his name. 'If ye don't know who I am ye've no reet being on the pitch,' Hughie told him. 'Anyway, what's YOUR name?'

'Fogg,' the referee replied.

'Aye,' said Hughie, 'and you've been in a fog all afternoon.'

It did not end there. Gallacher followed the referee into his dressing-room and attempted to push him into the bath.

Fogg refereed two more matches in which Hughie played. Each time he scored five goals as his version of a two-fingered salute to the official. 'He'll know who I am now,' he told team-mates.

Rumours that Gallacher had a drink problem gathered strength when he was sent off for 'acting in a drunk and disorderly manner' during a tour match in Budapest. The Football Association disciplinary committee rather generously accepted his explanation that, because it had been such a hot day, he had washed his mouth out with whisky and water. The saying 'If you believe that, you'll believe anything' comes to mind.

The Newcastle board ran out of patience with Gallacher's behaviour, and behind his back arranged for him to be sold to Chelsea for £10,000 in May 1930. He returned home to Bellshill to rest after playing for Scotland against France in Paris, where he tasted Parisian nightlife to the full. His parents woke him from a deep sleep to tell him there were 'London people' on the doorstep.

The Chelsea directors, who had called to negotiate transfer terms, were deliberately kept on tenterhooks for hours. Finally, he agreed to a deal that gave him the best contract in football, including what was rumoured as the sweetener of a cash-in-hand payment.

Gallacher needed every penny he could get his hands on. He and the publican's daughter had secretly kept their affair going, and now she held him to a promise to marry her. She followed him to London, and Gallacher had to shell out what was in those days a fortune – £4,000 – to divorce his first wife. It made him virtually penniless.

Andy Cunningham, the former Rangers goal master, had taken over as Newcastle manager, and he sincerely wished Gallacher good luck when he called into St James' Park to collect his boots. 'I'll do well wherever I play,' Hughie told him with typical arrogance.

Newcastle's fans were furious that their hero had been sold after scoring 160 League goals in five seasons. When he returned to Tyneside for the first time as a Chelsea player there was a club record crowd of 68,386 shoe-horned into the ground, and it was estimated that another twenty thousand would-be spectators were locked out. They all wanted to see the living legend called Gallacher.

Chelsea bought him as a partner for Alec Jackson in a bid to recreate at least part of the Wembley Wizards of 1928, but by now Gallacher had abused his body too many times and was rarely able to produce peak performances for the London club.

Placing him in the King's Road was like letting a starving man loose at a banquet. There were horrific stories of him being thrown out of pubs and being picked up off the pavement in a legless condition. Yet he still had enough natural skill and ability to make himself a threat to defences, and he scored 72 League goals in just over four seasons at Stamford Bridge.

He was capped only once while with Chelsea, a 3–0 defeat by England at Wembley in 1934. Shortly after, he joined Derby County for £3,000, and part of the deal was that his new club cleared debts that had piled up while he was 'lost' in London.

Gallacher played a final time for Scotland – a 2–0 victory over England in front of 130,000 spectators at Hampden in April 1935. But his career was now on a distinct downhill slide, and after scoring 38 League goals in two seasons with Derby he moved quickly through take-the-money-and-run stints with Notts County, Grimsby and Gateshead.

While with Grimsby he was banned from driving for a year after being found guilty of being drunk at the wheel. The great football hero was now at rock bottom, bankrupt both financially and of goals, which by his startling standards had virtually dried up.

His League career ended with the outbreak of the Second World War, and he spent the war years as an assistant in the ambulance service in Gateshead. He was warmed by recollections of a career in which there were momentous moments. Pressed to select his greatest goal, he plumped for the one against Wales at Tynecastle Park in Edinburgh in 1925 when he dribbled the ball from deep in his own half, ghosting past a queue of defenders before lobbing the ball over the oncoming goalkeeper. Running it close in his memory bank was a goal against Birmingham when he finished a maze of a run by calculatingly slipping the ball through the legs of great England goalkeeper Harry Hibbs. Then there was one for Airdrie when he took the ball the length of the pitch, beating man after man, and then feigning to shoot. As the goalkeeper dived he casually walked the ball into the other side of the goal. Oh yes, he could play a bit.

In the immediate post-war years he struggled to get enough money together to look after his wife Hannah and their three sons Hugh, Thomas and Matthew. Freelance work as a sports journalist gave him a decent income until his outspoken views led to Newcastle supremo Stan Seymour, his old team-mate, barring him from the club where he had been the original number nine idol of Tyneside. Included among his comments were rambling thoughts about the rigging of match results, unsubstantiated allegations that were to rebound on him later.

The curse that seemed to shadow Gallacher throughout his life struck again in 1951 when his wife, Hannah, died, leaving him to bring up his three sons alone.

Working in a Gateshead factory to earn sufficient money to live, he was still a slave of alcohol. One day in a drunken rage in the summer of 1957 he threw an ashtray at his youngest son, eight-year-old Matthew. It hit him in the head and cut him.

A neighbour called the police and Gallacher was arrested and charged with assault, ill-treatment and neglect. Just the previous week he had heard that he was going to have to face a probe into his comments about match-fixing.

On the evening of Tuesday 11 June 1957 – the eve of his court appearance – he walked to Dead Man's Railway Crossing at Low Fell near his home in Gateshead, and deliberately stepped into the path of the Edinburgh to York express.

An eyewitness told the inquest that Gallacher had brushed past him as he stepped towards the crossing. 'He said sorry,' the witness revealed.

'Sorry' was the last word from a man who had touched the heights and the depths in a rollercoaster life during which he proved he was a footballer of unsurpassed ability and a person with an overload of human failings.

In the summer of 2002, the *Newcastle Evening Chronicle* – that always reliable source of all things Geordie – had a remarkable interview with Gallacher's son, Hugh Junior, who had just completed his RAF service at the time of the ashtray-throwing incident. He said that he considered himself responsible for his father's suicide because in a fit of anger he had told him he never wanted anything to do with him again.

He considered that the final breaking point for his father, and he carried the guilt ever after. 'I want to place on record,' said Hugh Junior, 'that my father always tried to do right by his family, and was nothing like the person painted in the newspaper reports of the incident with Matthew. It was the only time he ever physically hurt him, and I think he threw the ashtray to frighten him rather than hurt him. We all said things in temper, and it was a domestic situation that just got out of hand. It was ridiculous that he was charged with ill-treatment and neglect. My family are enormously proud of all that my father achieved as a footballer, and he deserves to be remembered as a decent man as well as a great player.'

Let's be charitable, and think of him as an Anglo-Scot who brought pleasure to thousands with the wonderful football skill learned on the playing fields of Lanarkshire, a son of whom the West of Scotland can always be proud. There will never be another like him.

Chapter Four

Alex James:
The Emperor in Baggy Shorts

Tom Webster, a supreme sports cartoonist who specialised in turning heroes of the sports arena into comical figures, caricatured Alex James in baggy shorts that came down past his knees. When James saw the cartoon published in the *Daily Mail* in 1925 he was impressed rather than irked, and decided to adopt the image.

From then on, James became famous and instantly identifiable by the length of his baggy shorts, and shirt cuffs buttoned at the wrist. Standing only five foot five inches tall, he looked an almost Chaplinesque character, but he was even more distinguishable because of his footballing skill. He was up there with the very best players of his generation; an army of pre-war Arsenal supporters would have argued that he was *the* best of them all.

Like his schoolmate Hughie Gallacher, James first fashioned his skills on the pitches of Lanarkshire. Born in Mossend on 14 September 1901, he went to the same Bellshill Academy school as Gallacher, and in the first half of his career was, like Hughie, a goal-scoring machine.

But it is as a schemer rather than a scorer that James is remembered, changing his style to midfield playmaker during his golden days as the baggy-trousered Emperor of Highbury. He also switched faces, from clowning entertainer to serious field marshal.

Alex had kicked off his professional career with Raith Rovers after labouring at a steelworks during the First World War, when his football was confined to amateur appearances with local sides Brandon, Orbiston Celtic and Glasgow Ashfield. He had a trial with Motherwell before settling at

Stark's Park, where he was the finest of the forward line that became known as 'Fife's Famous Five' – Bell, Miller, Jennings, James and Archibald. His contribution was 27 goals in exactly 100 League matches before he was persuaded to join Preston for £3,250 in September 1925.

Preston were then pushing to get out of the Second Division and turned to a platoon of Scottish players to try to regain the old glory days of The Invincibles. James made his debut on a dry, bumpy pitch at Middlesbrough, and Preston were pulverised 5–1.

James had a tongue that could be as cutting as his feet. 'Ye'd better be gieing me a ticket back home,' he told the Preston directors after the game. 'I canna play fitba' wi' the baw up in the air most of the time.'

He had come out of a forward line that played the game the classic Scottish way, with passes along the ground. The kick and rush of the English Second Division was not at all to his taste, and it took him time to settle at Preston. He finally brought them round to his style and what was, in comparison, scientific soccer.

James set his stall out to be a showman at Deepdale, playing conjuring tricks with the ball and often settling for walking the ball into the net rather than shooting it as he played to the crowd. He teased and tormented opponents, sometimes sitting on the ball as if hatching it, and dribbling the ball past baffled defenders as if they were not there. Despite his apparent casual, clowning approach he still managed to score 53 goals in 146 League appearances for the Lancashire club. The Preston supporters loved him and his cheeky, often cocky approach to the game, but Alex became disillusioned following a dispute with the Preston directors over whether he should be released to play for Scotland.

There was hardly a major club in the country that was not keen to sign him after his two goals had helped the Wembley Wizards to their amazing 5–1 defeat of England in 1928. Preston agreed to sell him to Manchester City, but James refused to make the move after looking round Maine Road and inspecting club houses. Rumours quickly circulated that he had been 'tapped' by another club.

Within a month he had agreed to join Arsenal for the surprisingly low fee of £8,750. Highbury manager Herbert Chapman anticipated there would be an inquiry into the transfer and refused to clinch the deal until the League had satisfied themselves that everything was above board.

Once James was installed at Arsenal, there were raised eyebrows when it was revealed that on top of his maximum £8-a-week football wages he would receive a further £250 a year as 'a sports demonstrator' at the Selfridges store in the West End.

Chapman made it clear to James that he had signed him as the chief orchestrator of the team, not as its comedian. 'Cut out the circus tricks until we're three goals up,' he warned after James had made a less than spectacular start to his Arsenal career. He was briefly dropped because his fitness was not considered up to Highbury standards. Alex was inclined to put on weight, which went against the Chapman creed of having a team of footballing athletes.

But once he settled into the Arsenal way of doing things, he quickly became the idolised Emperor of Highbury. He was an outstanding tactician, who had the confidence and vision to change the way the team was playing while the game was in progress rather than wait until dressing-room discussion.

He patrolled the left side of the midfield, taking defences apart with raking passes that nearly always found a team-mate, and he could make faster opponents look cumbersome with his shuffling style that featured astonishing changes of pace. His speciality was a disguised diagonal ball inside the full-backs into the path of wingers Joe Hulme and Cliff Bastin. If there had been a statistical assessment of goal assists in those days, they would have shown that there was rarely an Arsenal goal movement that did not have a James touch somewhere along the way.

'Alex had such a thick Scottish accent that I hardly ever understood a word he uttered,' 'Boy' Bastin said. 'But I never had problems under-standing him on the pitch. He was The Master who could pass the ball with either foot to an exact spot anywhere on the pitch.'

Chapman gave him his head and built the Arsenal side around him, and James was a key player in helping the Gunners win four First Division championships in five years, the last three in a row, with the FA Cup captured in 1930 and 1936.

It was the 1930 FA Cup final in which James carved himself a lasting place in the hearts of Arsenal fans. Chapman's previous club, Huddersfield Town, provided the opposition, and James scored the first goal and made the second to set the Gunners on the way to a 2–0 victory that gave the club the confidence and motivation to monopolise the 1930s.

Amazingly, Scotland selected him only eight times. His ability should have been rewarded with a cupboardful of caps. There were several theories as to why he was not an automatic choice for Scotland, chiefly that the selectors were concerned about his desire to be the boss. He had a self-confidence that could be almost unnerving.

Alex, always shrewdly looking to supplement his income from football, earned extra money by putting his name to a regular newspaper column. Roy Ullyett, a genius of a sports cartoonist on the London *Evening Star*, took over from Tom Webster as the man who liked to capture James on a sketch pad, and the pair of them became inseparable companions.

I later became Roy's colleague on the *Daily Express* and many years later collaborated with him on his autobiography, *While There's Still Lead in My Pencil*. We devoted a chapter to his close friendship with James. 'Alex was a wonderful wee man but not the best of influences on me,' Roy revealed. 'I was a young man new to the fleshpots of London, and Alex became my guide and mentor. He introduced me to the nightclub circuit, and used to regularly take me to an afternoon drinking haunt in Covent Garden. "We'll just go for a quick wee dram," he would say. Invariably he would get legless and then rely on me to drive him home. This was commonplace on a Thursday, with a First Division match just forty-eight hours away. But on the Saturday he would play a blinder, and I quickly realised that alcohol to Alex was like petrol in his engine. He was something of a playboy who was fastidious about his appearance, and always shrewd enough to talk Selfridges into keeping his wardrobe up to date!'

Roy was his regular partner on the golf course. 'Alex was always immaculately turned out and used to wear baggy plus fours,' he recalled. 'He played a beautiful game of golf and could easily have made it as a professional. We used to play at South Herts Golf Club, and he was so careful with his money that he would not buy wooden tees. He would dig up a small mound on the tee with his heel and then drive off. One particular day on the first hole he had just driven off when an elderly man in an ankle-length raincoat approached us from the direction of the clubhouse, holding up his hand like a traffic policeman. "Young man," he boomed, "I know who you are, and you should know better than to tee the ball up like that. Always use a peg. You will get a much better drive, and do less damage to the tee." Alex turned to me and winked. "It's not often ye get a free lesson from Harry Vardon," he said. Yes, it was the legendary man who invented the Vardon golf grip who shouted the advice.'

Alex made no secret of his love of the nightlife. 'It's better for me to be in a nightclub enjoying masel' than in bed struggling to sleep,' he said, with strange logic. 'But I wouldnee advise it fer all fitballers, only those who can handle it.'

Chapman tried to turn a blind eye to the James lifestyle, and went out of his way to give the temperamental maestro preferential treatment. He allowed him extra hours in bed on match days so that Alex could rest limbs that had taken many damaging tackles and were continually aching from attacks of rheumatism.

There were several times when Chapman and James had explosive encounters, and neither the legendary manager nor the legendary footballer would give ground. Trainer Tom Whittaker used to have to act as peacemaker, and would talk them into agreeing that the club must come first at all times.

Their most famous bust-up came over a contract dispute. James threatened never to play for Arsenal again, and Chapman told him he should go away and think things through. 'I'll tell you what we'll do,' he told Alex. 'The club will pay for you to go on a cruise while you deliberate over your future.'

James considered this an acceptable goodwill gesture, that is until he arrived at the London docks to start his cruise. He had been booked on a banana boat! Alex saw the funny side of the joke, shook hands with Chapman and agreed terms.

When Chapman died suddenly in 1934 James was one of the pallbearers, which squashed stories that he despised the Arsenal manager.

The influence of James on the great Arsenal team of the thirties is that in 231 League games he was on the losing side only 30 times. He confined himself to making rather than taking goals, yet still managed to get on the scoresheet 26 times.

Recurring injuries forced his retirement in 1937, and he kept in touch with the game as a sports journalist and in the immediate post-war years had a spell as Arsenal coach. George Allison, who succeeded Herbert Chapman as Arsenal manager, said of James: 'His greatness lay not only in his outstanding skill as an individual player but in his ability to bring the best out of other players. He was that rarity, an exceptional individualist who could turn himself into a team player. There have been few players in the history of the game to match him.'

Alex James, the Emperor in Baggy Shorts, died of cancer in 1953 at the age of 51, but his name will always live on in the annals of football as a genius of a player and as a showman supreme.

Chapter Five

Sir Matt Busby:
Father of Football

We now come face to face with the man who, perhaps beyond argument, had a bigger influence on English football than any Scot before or since. Arise, Sir Matt Busby.

To this point in my navigation through Anglo-Scottish football history I have focused on legendary Scots of whom I have only heard or read. In the cases of Hughie Gallacher and Alex James, my eyewitness statements are restricted to seeing them in fleeting moments, flitting across the screen in black-and-white newsreels that do no justice to their immense ability.

With Matt Busby it is a different story. I got to know him well, and sat at his feet on many memorable occasions listening to his philosophy on football and life. To be in his presence was more like having an audience than a conversation. There was something almost papal in his manner and bearing, and he was treated with a reverence and respect that is usually reserved for royalty and heads of state.

When I was juggling words as a young, starry-eyed football reporter on the *Daily Express* in the 1960s we had a special rapport with Matt. We considered him 'one of ours' because, for years, he took the Beaverbrook shilling for widely read columns that were ghosted by a fine Manchester sports journalist called Bill Fryer.

Whenever Matt brought his Manchester United team to London to play, it was the tradition on the eve of the game for me to accompany colourful *Express* columnist Desmond 'The Man in the Brown Bowler' Hackett to welcome him at the Russell Hotel in Holborn. Des would be in charge of the hospitality, while I would be responsible for collecting any worthwhile thoughts for the next morning's back page. 'I'll get the champagne, you get the quotes,' was a typical Hackett aside.

A relaxed Busby was a wonderful raconteur. He had a bagpipes accent with a strong West of Scotland tone, and to the untrained English ear could sometimes be almost unintelligible, as he himself would admit. 'I remember when I was playing with Liverpool in the 1930s,' he said, 'and there was a national census. In those days they used to do it by sending people to your door to ask questions. When I told the young lady what I did for a living, she wrote down "fruit boiler".'

It was as a manager rather than a player that Busby planted a smile on the face of English football, putting Manchester United on the world map not only because of their trophy collection but also because of the style and panache with which their success was achieved. It was all done playing the Scottish way.

The fact that he was nearly killed in a plane crash that, in 1958, cost the lives of eight of one of his finest teams – the Busby Babes – added tragedy to the tapestry of a life that lifted him into the land of legend. You would have thought his experiences could not have existed outside the imagination of a Hollywood screenwriter.

The trophies he won while boss at Old Trafford are lasting testimony to his talent: FA Cup winners in 1948 and 1963 (runners-up in 1957 and 1958), League champions in 1952, 1956, 1957, 1965 and 1967 (six times runners-up) and unforgettable winners of the European Cup at Wembley in 1968, when you could have paddled in the tears of emotion.

In the 1980s I devised a series screened by ITV called *Who's the Greatest?* I worked on it with presenter Brian Moore and producer John D Taylor. In their wisdom, ITV decided not to go ahead with a second series that was going to include a programme featuring Sir Matt Busby against Bob Paisley for the crown of 'greatest manager'.

I can now share with you a question-and-answer session that I had with Sir Matt in preparation for the biographical section of the programme that was never produced. He was by then in his mid-seventies, with a memory recall still as quick and sharp as a Scottish salmon-fisherman's reflexes.

Where and when were you born?

May 26th, 1909, at Old Orbiston, which was down the road from the mining village of Bellshill. Alex James and Hughie Gallacher came from the same area. Now if you're going to throw about that overused and misleading word 'great' then they should be right at the top of your list. They were magnificent footballers. Magnificent. Their worth in today's transfer market would be in millions and millions.

What sort of childhood did you have?

To say it was grim would be an understatement. My father and three uncles were all killed in the First World War, and so my earliest memories are of my mother and most of the other women in our family grieving. I was a wee lad in short trousers and did not fully understand what all the grief was about, but to this day I could cry at the thought of the cost of that war to my family. It was absolutely senseless.

How did you get into football?

I left school as early as possible to help my mother and my three younger sisters cope, and I worked at the local coal pit. They were the hardest days of my life. I just can't begin to describe how miserable it was to go down into the blackness of the pit. It was as if you were turned into a rat scurrying underground. The only thing to brighten our lives then was fitba'. I followed a pal of mine, Frank Rogers, to Denny Hibernian. I had no plans to make a career in the game, and was all set to emigrate to America with my mother when Manchester City offered me a trial. I played in a Central League match against Burnley, and made a good enough impression for City to offer me terms of £5 a week in the season and £4 in the summer. Well, it was better than the pits. *Anything* was better than the pits.

What were the highlights of playing for Manchester City?

It has to be the two back-to-back FA Cup finals. We were well caned 3–0 by Dixie Dean's Everton at Wembley in 1933. That was the first final in which numbered shirts were worn. It will come as a surprise to many City fans to know that we wore scarlet shirts, and ours were numbered from 12 to 22. I wore number 15 at left-half, which became my specialist position after I had started out as a forward. We were back at Wembley a year later and beat Portsmouth 2–1. I remember there was a thunder-and-lightning storm, Stanley Rous was the referee, King George the Fifth presented the Cup, and at the end our young goalkeeper Frank Swift went into a dead faint.

[Sir Matt paused for a few moments and reflected in respectful silence following his mention of Frank Swift, one of the all-time great goal-keepers who died in the Munich air crash while travelling as a *News of the World* reporter.]

Why did you leave Manchester City?
I just felt it was time for a change. The edge had gone off my game at City and I thought I needed a new challenge. I joined Liverpool in February 1936 and stayed with them until war broke out. That meant my League playing career was finished when I was barely thirty, but I couldn't complain. I'd had a good shout and there were a lot of younger chaps who lost the best years of their career to the war. The only major disappointment I had in my playing career, apart from not winning a League championship medal, is that Scotland picked me only the once. That was in a 3–2 win against Wales at Aberdeen in 1934. To be honest, I thought I deserved more caps but those were the days when some selectors considered you a traitor if you dared cross the border to earn your living in England. I had the consolation of playing quite a few times for my country in wartime internationals, and I also skippered the side.

When did you realise that management was where your future lay?
I always knew in my bones that one day I'd like to try my hand at managing, but first of all I felt I would coach. I coached and organised teams while serving in the Army as a physical training instructor, and as a company sergeant-major got a lot of man-management experience. Towards the end of the war Liverpool got in touch with me and asked if I'd return to Anfield as first-team coach on my demobilisation on a five-year contract. There were several other offers, but the one that appealed to me most of all was a letter from Louis Rocca, that wonderful Manchester United scout, telling me that Mr James Gibson, the chairman at Old Trafford, wanted to see me about the managerial vacancy at the club.

The rest is history. Busby took over as Manchester United manager in February 1945, literally rebuilding the club from the ruins left behind by Hitler's *Luftwaffe*. There was a deep bomb crater at the heart of the Old Trafford pitch and the stands had been blitzed. Busby, toughened by his former life down the pits, found the challenge facing him at United appealing rather than appalling.

In his first public statement of intent when he became £15-a-week manager, Busby said: 'I am determined that United will provide the footballing public with the best in the game. We will develop the finest young players.' He then provided dynamic action to go with his words.

An instinctive judge of a player, Busby set up a nationwide scouting network that sometimes operated close to the borders of scandal as he went all out to attract the most promising young talent to Old Trafford. There were tales of illegal inducements being made to youngsters and their parents, but whispering it and proving it were two different things.

If Busby could not find them, he was never afraid to go out and buy the players to keep United at the top. As a builder and as a buyer, his judgement of football and footballers was supreme. He was made a Freeman of the City of Manchester in 1967, but in the eyes of the ordinary men and women in the street Matt Busby had earned the freedom of Manchester years earlier.

A devout Roman Catholic, a committed family man, and usually a gentleman of the first order, Busby occasionally showed a merciless side to his character in the way he moved players out the moment he realised they were no longer right for United. In all his calculations the club came first, second and third. He took time off only for regular games of golf, which he played with true Scottish skill and zeal. I once caddied for *Daily Express* sports cartoonist Roy Ullyett, a single-handicap golfer, in a friendly match with Matt, who played as competitively as if it were a Cup final. Hardly a hole went by without Matt beguiling us with stories from his world of football, but once on the green he gave all his concentration and attention to getting 'the wee rascal' – his name for the ball – down the hole in a bid to win the half-a-crown being gambled on each green.

He could be stubborn and fiercely independent to the point of bloody-mindedness in the all-consuming cause of United. It was typical of him that he went against the wishes of the Football League in 1956 when he accepted an invitation for United to take part in the European Cup, a competition that the insular League chiefs blindly believed should remain beneath the consideration of their clubs. How ironic that the lure of Europe was to bring him the grimmest and greatest days of his life.

If I am to probe for weaknesses while painting this portrait of Sir Matt, it has to be admitted that he was often not as firm a disciplinarian with his star players as he might have been. He believed in treating them like men, but some of them hit the headlines when they betrayed his trust and behaved like petulant juveniles. Matt sensed that to have shackled his players with, say, the sort of Stan Cullis-style military discipline at Wolves, he might have stifled their natural flair and, in some cases, pure genius.

On the pitch, he liked to give these individualists the freedom to play off the cuff within the framework of loosely formulated team tactics. Off the pitch, he trusted them to go their own way. It was not always the right way. Even as far back as the Busby Babes, there was head-shaking criticism of the behaviour of some of the Old Trafford stars, who were accused in the most disparaging way of the time as 'behaving like Teddy Boys'.

Busby had a relationship with his players that was as close as you can get to that between a father and his sons. It was a two-way street, with loyalty, respect and devotion flowing both ways between manager and players. My omniscient former Fleet Street colleague David Miller wrote a beautifully composed biography of Busby called, fittingly, *Father of Football*. It was a title that summed him up perfectly, but there was also something of the Godfather about him. Like all the best managers, he was a nice man who could show a nasty edge if anybody or anything trespassed on his turf and tried to come between him and his players. We in the media were allowed to be close but not too close. When his 1963 FA Cup final skipper Noel Cantwell went into management, he famously advised him, 'Treat the press as you would the police.'

After his retirement as United manager and his elevation to the board and later the club Presidency, he could not help but cast a giant shadow over those who followed him. A procession of very good managers tried and failed to match his astonishing achievements. Not until the arrival of another Scot, Alex Ferguson, did anybody manage to meet his standards of supremacy.

* * *

Busby, making full use of his innate Scottish organisational sense, moulded and managed three majestic teams during his glorious 25-year reign at Old Trafford. Many old pros in the game consider the first Busby-built team to have been his best. That side's impressive impact on the immediate post-war years gives powerful weight to the argument. In the six years following the war United captured the League championship once (1951–52), were runners-up four times and won a classic FA Cup final against Blackpool at Wembley in 1948. This was the team skippered by Gentleman Johnny Carey and featuring the fabulous forward line of Jimmy 'Old Bones' Delaney, Johnny Morris, Jack Rowley, Stan Pearson and Charlie Mitten. Delaney (his profile features in the Players' section) was a battle-hardened Scot whom Busby considered, at £4,000, one of his greatest ever buys.

With Delaney performing baffling tricks out on the wings, that 1940s Busby team rattled in goals with Gatling-gun regularity and lured massive crowds to Maine Road, the ground they shared with Manchester City for three years while bomb-damaged Old Trafford was being recon-structed. They pulled in a League record attendance of 82,950 for a First Division match against Arsenal on 17 January 1948, and have retained a special place in the hearts of all followers of what was an exciting and adventurous footballing period, when scoring goals took priority over trying to stop them.

Twenty years after their memorable FA Cup triumph against a Blackpool side inspired by the two Stanleys – Matthews and Mortensen – Busby was back at Wembley with his third great United team; this time for a European Cup final victory over Benfica on one of the most emotive and moving nights in the history of British football.

This was the mesmerising era of George Best, Bobby Charlton and great Scot Denis Law (who missed the final because of injury), arguably the finest trio of British forwards ever accumulated in one club attack. Busby, and his right-hand man Jimmy Murphy, motivated promising youngsters Brian Kidd and John Aston into producing new peak performances, while in midfield polished Paddy Crerand, an attack architect out of the traditional Scottish school, was the lightning to the thunder of Nobby 'The Toothless Tiger' Stiles. They brought a perfect balance to the orchestrations of conductor-in-chief Bobby Charlton. Goalkeeper Alex Stepney handled with care at the back of a defence toughened by the presence of big Bill

Foulkes and the versatile David Sadler, and strengthened by the determination of Irish full-back partners Shay Brennan and Tony Dunne.

You had to be around ten years earlier to fully understand and appreciate why United's European Cup final victory against Benfica had such deep significance; and that brings me to the second and potentially the greatest of the Manchester United teams that Matt Busby built – the incomparable Busby Babes.

They won the League championship in 1955–56 by an overwhelming margin of 11 points, this when there were just two points for a victory. Never had the title been captured so conclusively and never by a younger team, with an average age of under 23. They took the title again the following season, this time by eight points.

While their main rivals, Wolves, were having equal success with the controversial long-ball game, United were performing with more style and sophistication. There was latitude as well as longitude to their lines of attack, and Busby actively encouraged his players to make progress with the ball at their feet. Busby wanted it the Scottish way. Wolves, in contrast, took the direct route to the penalty area, and the evidence that it was working for them is that they topped 100 goals in the First Division for four successive seasons. The Cullis Cubs against the Busby Babes was one of the most thrilling soccer serials of the twentieth century, but it ended in appalling tragedy.

The young United team had developed into one of the most exciting and explosive combinations in world football, yet were still short of their full power and potential when cruelly decimated by the horrific Munich air disaster of 6 February 1958. United players Geoff Bent, Roger Byrne, Eddie Colman, Duncan Edwards, Mark Jones, David Pegg, Tommy Taylor and Liam Whelan were among those killed in Munich on the way home from a successful European Cup quarter-final match against Red Star Belgrade. The heart had been ripped out of the team, but the legend of the Busby Babes lives on in the minds and memories of all those lucky enough to have seen these young Saturday Giants in action.

The most fitting epitaph for these magnificent footballers and fine young men whose lives were so sadly cut short in Munich came from the pen of Laurence Binyon, whose famous 'Poem for the Fallen' was reproduced in the United match programme of 19 February 1958:

They shall grow not old
As we that are left grow old.
Age shall not weary them
nor the years condemn.
At the going down of the sun,
and in the morning
We will remember them.

Sir Matt, knighted in the Queen's Birthday Honours list of June 1968, outlived by 36 years the Busby Babes who perished at Munich. The European Cup triumph had been like a personal monument to the memory of that great team.

The Busby Babes were something quite unique. They were artists; the rest were artisans. They were a stringed orchestra; the rest buskers. I make no excuse for waxing lyrical. This was the effect that the Busby Babes had on anybody lucky enough to see them in action. They made even the most jaundiced football reporters look for new descriptive phrases.

More than any of Sir Matt's teams, the Babes reflected the image he had in his mind of how the game could and should be played. On the day that the team died in the snow and slush of Munich airport, a beautiful flower was crushed before reaching its full bloom, but it had grown and flourished sufficiently for us to know and appreciate that it had been impregnated with a touch of magic. I will be accused of hyperbole; of getting carried away into the land of exaggeration and overstatement. But I know that every word is true.

Sir Matt himself told me in that understated way of his: 'They were a very special team. Aye, very special.'

And Sir Matt Busby was a very special man and manager. Aye, very special.

Chapter Six

Bill Shankly:
Man of the People

While Matt Busby was invariably surrounded by a papal-like aura, Bill Shankly preferred to be known as 'the man of the people'. Busby was revered and respected; Shanks was loved – particularly on the red side of Liverpool, where he was expected to walk rather than ferry across the Mersey.

It is difficult not to draw comparisons between Sir Matt and Shanks. Both came out of horrendously difficult childhoods in the West of Scotland to find their fame first as players and then as managers in the north-west of England. Shanks was a right-half, Busby a left-half, and they played in tandem for Scotland in wartime internationals. They later became managerial gods just 35 miles apart.

Shanks would be high on my list of 'most unforgettable characters' I have met on this mortal coil. There were three things he would like to have achieved away from his complete obsession with football: 1) to have been middleweight boxing champion of the world; 2) to have portrayed Jimmy Cagney on screen ('Look at me ma, top of the world'); and 3) to have been a Labour prime minister at 10 Downing Street.

I once wrote in a football match report for the *Daily Express* that Shanks had inspired his team with a half-time talk that was Churchillian in its content and delivery. 'If ye must liken me to a politician,' he boomed down the phone in his heavy Ayrshire accent, 'I'd much rather it were Keir Hardie!' (Scottish founder of the Labour Party).

Shankly, I swear, became more Scottish the longer he was away from his homeland. He had his own unique way of talking that influenced an army of

41

impersonators, but nobody could quite get the way he dropped words like hand-grenades. When wanting to make a point there was a barely discernible pause between each syllable of the key word, and the sentence would end with an 'aye' like a vocal exclamation mark.

'The referee today was di-a-bol-i-cal. Aye. Di-a-bol-i-cal.'

He would see that you were noting down his quote, and then – proving that he was one of the early spin doctors – he would add, 'Now it doesn't do for me to be saying that. YOU saw it. YOU write it. I will not say anything about him having left his guide dog in the dressing-room. I'll leave that to YOU.'

Another referee slaughtered, and Shanks making sure that the media were the messengers and his hands clean.

What an experience to interview him! He liked to stand and arrange himself in front of you with his feet apart, almost in a boxing stance and as if modelled on his look-alike screen idol James Cagney when delivering his rat-a-tat-tat gangster lines in *White Heat*. Shanks had his hair cut prison-warder short, and intimidated his interviewers with a pugnacious look that made you think twice about asking a question that might be considered awkward. His unblinking stare was like one his boxing hero Jack Dempsey might have used when eyeballing the likes of Gene Tunney. 'Come on then, hit me with your best shot,' he might have been saying. It took a brave man to risk asking him anything in the least bit controversial. I must have interviewed him more than a hundred times without once feeling I had got the better of him. It was usually a case of 'ref stopped fight' to save me from further punishment from the fastest tongue in the west. He had the knack of telling you exactly what he wanted to and no more. Shanks knew when he had made a telling point, and would immediately repeat it just in case your shorthand was not up to it. 'This wee man Kevin Keegan is going to be an awesome force, aye an awesome force,' was a typical quote. He could make Liverpool players sound as if they had come down from Mount Olympus, and opponents seem as insignificant as if they belonged in the gutter.

Like most reporters who managed to get within listening distance of him, I had a great affection for Shanks but I have to say he was the worst loser I have ever known. He could rarely find a gracious thing to say for the winners. Following a 5–1 embarrassment in Europe against Ajax, including a hat-trick from an 'unknown' youngster called Johan Cruyff, Shanks growled: 'Och, we just got frustrated against their defensive tactics.'

Bill Shankly was shaped by his early experiences and environment that made him always want to be a winner after starting out at the back of the pack. Born in the mining village of Glenbuck, Ayrshire, on 2 September 1913, he grew up as one of ten children in the depression years when just surviving was a day-to-day challenge. 'I left school without an education and had to use my brains to get where I am today,' Shankly once famously said, unwittingly feeding those of us who collected his quotes for dinner-party and bar-room anecdotes.

He used football as the launching pad to get away from his impoverished background, and jumped at a 1929 offer to join Carlisle United. This rescued him from a daily slog in the pits. Bob Shankly, one of his four footballing brothers, also became a respected manager but stayed north of the border. Bill was a human dynamo of a right-half, feeding the attack with intelligent passes and helping out in defence with thundering tackles. What gave him the edge on players with equal ability is that he was a fitness fanatic, teetotal, a non-smoker and a man who went on lone training runs after team training. It was a conditioning regime that he followed throughout his career.

Shanks had his best playing days at Preston, winning five Scotland caps in a distinguished career during which his peak years were lost to the war. He played in back-to-back FA Cup finals with Preston, finishing a loser against Sunderland in 1937 and then a winner in 1938 when fellow-Scot George Mutch scored a last-minute penalty to sink Huddersfield.

After serving with the RAF during the war and guesting for Arsenal, he had four memorable years in support of Pride of Preston Tom Finney ('The greatest thing on two feet', was the Shanks assessment) before hanging up his boots to become Carlisle manager in 1949. Shankly handed his number 4 Preston shirt to his successor Tommy Docherty with the words: 'All you have to do is put this on and it will do the running around for you.'

He served his managerial apprenticeship with Carlisle, Grimsby, Workington and Huddersfield, where he introduced a young Scottish lad called Denis Law to the English football scene. Then the hour and the man came together when he took over at Anfield on 1 December 1959.

The arrival of Shankly provided the spark that ignited a Liverpool fire that continues to blaze fiercely to this day. Shanks and Liverpool were made for each other. He was a producer and a showman in search of a stage big enough for his ideas and mega-watt personality. Liverpool was a club on its knees, urgently in need of somebody to project and propel them back to football's top table where they belonged.

When Shankly took over as manager they were depressed and stagnating down in the Second Division after an unbroken 49-year run in the First. He had found his stage. Liverpool had found their saviour. Shanks led them to promotion as Second Division champions in 1962 and laid such solid foundations that they have since rarely been out of the hunt for major honours.

Just about the time that Shankly was breathing life into Liverpool, four mop-haired Merseyside pop musicians were starting to 'yeah-yeah-yeah' their way to fame as a group called The Beatles. A music and football revolution had started in Liverpool that was to have an enormous impact on the unsuspecting outside world. The Anfield Kop choir had a foot in both camps as they joined the soccer and the singing revolution. Their 'ee-aye-adio' chants inspired new sounds and sights on the terraces of clubs throughout the country as the first wave of Shankly's Red Army – playing the famous Scottish passing game – marched off with two League titles and the FA Cup between 1964 and 1966.

The torch of triumph has been carried on by subsequent Liverpool teams, but it was the Shankly-built side of the swinging sixties that lit the flame.

Shanks had a Keir Hardie – I almost said Churchillian – gift for motivating men. He could be hard, humorous, stern, soothing, ruthless, ranting, and, above all, demanding – all this in the space of a ten-minute pre-match team talk during which he would inspire his players to go beyond the call of duty. His Scottish growl of a voice could be as uplifting to the Liverpool players as the bagpipes to the Gordon Highlanders on their way into battle.

He was dedicated to football in general and to Liverpool in particular, capturing everybody who played for him with his infectious mood. Shanks was never a one-man band. He just happened to blow his own trumpet (or should I say bagpipes?) louder than most because he appreciated the importance of publicity both for pulling in spectators and for propaganda purposes.

Nobody knew better than Shankly the importance of having a good backroom team of knowledgeable and loyal assistants. His two most trusted aides were Bob Paisley and Joe Fagan, both of whom were to prove in later years that the Shankly magic for getting the best out of Liverpool players had rubbed off on them.

Spending Liverpool's money boldly but wisely, Shanks operated in the transfer market with fine judgement. He always had an eye on the Scottish scene and bought players of the quality and calibre of Ian St John, Ron Yeats and Willie Stevenson, and he promoted Ayrshire goalkeeper Tommy Lawrence from the reserves. He mixed them into a cocktail with English players Roger Hunt, Gordon Milne, Peter Thompson, Geoff Strong, Jimmy Melia, Gerry Byrne, Ian Callaghan, Tommy Smith, Chris Lawler and Emlyn Hughes. It was a heady concoction of Scottish will and skill and English endeavour and enterprise.

Liverpool clinched the League championship in 1963–64 with a crushing 5–0 victory over Arsenal in the final crucial match of the season at Anfield. They left no doubts about their superiority two years later when winning the title by a margin of six points from runners-up Leeds. In that championship season Shanks used only fourteen players.

An extra-time goal by Ian St John lifted Liverpool to their first ever FA Cup final victory over Don Revie's Leeds at Wembley in 1965, and the following season they carried England's challenge for the European Cup Winner's Cup all the way to the final and an extra-time defeat by Borussia Dortmund.

Shanks then began to build the new Liverpool, buying goalkeeper Ray Clemence from Scunthorpe, full-back Alec Lindsay from Bury, centre-half Larry Lloyd from Bristol Rovers, and big John Toshack from Cardiff. Two young university graduates, Steve Heighway and Brian Hall, proved themselves masters of the soccer arts and helped the Merseysiders reach the 1971 FA Cup final at Wembley, where they went down to an extra-time defeat by double-winning Arsenal.

Then, for the unbelievable bargain price of £35,000, Shankly snapped up Kevin Keegan from Scunthorpe. It was the vital last piece in his jigsaw, and it was Keegan's two goals that helped give Liverpool a 3–0 FA Cup final victory over Newcastle at Wembley in 1974.

Shanks was always a man of surprises, but none came bigger than his announcement in the summer of 1974 that he was retiring and handing over the relay torch to Bob Paisley who – building on the Shankly foundations – led Liverpool through their golden age of total domination in Europe.

Those of us close to Shanks knew that he had got the timing wrong. He thought he was getting off at the top of the mountain, but the success that followed at Anfield immediately after his departure proved that he had abandoned the climb with the most rewarding moments still to come. Sadly, there was a bitterness in him during his last years as he reflected on what might have been. But I prefer to remember Shanks as the occasionally mischievous, often amusing, and always magnificent manager who pumped the pride back into Liverpool Football Club.

He left behind not only a legacy of a great team but enough anecdotal material to fill several books. Here are just a few of the Shanklyisms that merit retelling:

At a presentation dinner, Shanks was being lauded by a speaker who told the audience: 'Bill will always be remembered as a great manager, but let us not forget that he was also a great player. Many of you here will be too young to have seen him in action, but I can tell you that he was the finest half-back Preston ever had.' From the top table came the shout, 'Aye, he's right ye know.' It was Shanks doing the seconding!

Phil Thompson was so skinny when he joined Liverpool as a young lad from school that Shanks ordered, 'Put him on a steak diet. I've seen more flesh on a sparrow.' A year or so later Phil told Shanks that he was planning to get married. 'Married?' boomed Shanks. 'My God, we've bred a monster.'

Shankly hated holidays abroad because there was nobody with whom he could talk football apart from his long-suffering, lovely wife Nessie. He came back from one overseas holiday admitting it had been better than he had expected. 'We got up a team in the hotel and beat the waiters,' he said.

For years it was rumoured that Shankly had taken Nessie on a visit to watch Rochdale reserves on their wedding anniversary. Finally, Shankly issued a denial, saying with a poker face, 'As if I would have got married in the football season. It was Nessie's birthday.'

Always conscious of the great rivalry with Everton, Shanks once said: 'There are two great sides on Merseyside . . . Liverpool and Liverpool reserves.'

Asked by the barber if he would like anything off the top in 1970, he said, 'Aye, Everton.'

The Liverpool team were staying near Lake Como on the eve of a European Cup semi-final against Inter Milan. The players had just gone to bed when a bell started ringing in a nearby monastery. Shanks, convinced it was a plot to keep them awake, picked up his bedside telephone and rang the interpreter, who was staying in the same hotel.

'What's that ringing?' Shanks demanded.

'It's the monastery bell, Mr Shankly,' explained the bewildered interpreter.

'Well, ring the head monk and tell him I want it stopped this minute,' snapped Shanks, slamming down the receiver.

The interpreter called back a few minutes later and said, 'I'm sorry, Mr Shankly, but the bell-ringing has some holy significance and I cannot get it stopped.'

Shanks thought for a moment, and then said, 'Ring the head monk back and tell him to put a bloody bandage around his damned bell.'

A reporter likened then Sheffield United schemer Tony Currie to Tom Finney in Shankly's hearing. 'Aye, you're right,' he said. 'He is very nearly in Tom's class, but let's remember that Tom is now nearly sixty.'

England international left-back Bob McNab was being shown around Anfield by Shanks who had agreed terms for his transfer from Huddersfield. 'You'll be joining the greatest club in the world, son,' Shanks said, with his usual gift for understatement. 'We've got the best players, the best fans, the best facilities. You're a quality player and this is the right club for you.' After all his sales talk, Shanks was surprised to hear McNab say that he wanted time to think things over. Two days later, Bob telephoned Shanks from Highbury to tell him that he had decided to sign for Arsenal. 'Och,' said Shanks. 'They're welcome to you. You never could play the game anyway. I only wanted you for our reserves . . .'

Shanks was less than happy when a match at Orient was called off because of a waterlogged pitch. He sought out the groundsman and told him, 'The trouble with this ground is that you've got just ordinary grass. Come up to Anfield and see our pitch. We've got *professional* grass.'

Booking into a hotel in the United States, he put alongside 'home address' on the registration form: 'Anfield.'

Told by a referee that a player had not been offside because he was not interfering with play, Shanks responded: 'If he's not interfering with play what the bloody hell is he doing on the pitch?'

Shanks used to take part in the training matches while manager, and played every game as competitively as if it were a Cup final. Chris Lawler, new to the club and very shy and uncommunicative, was standing watching a five-a-side match when Bill insisted he had scored before the ball had been kicked off the line.
   'Chris, son,' he said, 'You saw that. Was that shot of mine over the line?'
   Honest Chris said, 'No, boss. It was cleared.'
   Bill put his hands on his hips and gave his best James Cagney pose. 'That's the first words ye've spoken since ye've been here and it's a lie,' said Shanks.

Ian St John says that he was once discussing tactics with Shanks, who told him, 'If you're not sure what to do with the ball, just pop it in the net and we'll discuss your options afterwards.'

Following a contract dispute with Anfield Iron Man Tommy Smith, Shanks said: 'He could start a riot in a graveyard.'

Introducing giant new signing Ron Yeats, he told the press: 'He's a colossus. Come and walk round him and inspect him for yourself.'

Yeats became captain, and after a defeat in a match Shanks asked him what he had called when he tossed the coin before the kick-off.
   'Heads,' said Yeats.

'Och,' said Shanks, with a shake of his head. 'You should have called tails.'

A posse of Italian journalists were shouting questions at Shanks after a controversial match in Milan. He watched the interpreter fielding the questions and then said, 'Tell them that whatever they're saying, I disagree with them.'

Finally, perhaps his most famous quote of all: 'Some people believe football is a matter of life and death. I'm very disappointed with that attitude. It's much more important than that.'

After his much-mourned death from a heart attack in 1981, Liverpool erected the Shankly Gates at Anfield as a permanent memorial to the man who made the club what it is today. His ashes were scattered over the pitch.

There will always be a corner of an English field that is for ever Scottish, and for ever Shankly's – the man of the people.

Chapter Seven

Tommy Docherty:
Anything for a Laugh

The irrepressible Tommy Docherty did not collect nearly as many trophies and titles as his countrymen Matt Busby and Bill Shankly, but he outdistanced each of them for tittle-tattle column inches on the front as well as the back pages. If you think that's an exaggeration, go to the British newspaper library at Collindale and count the references that come up when you tap the name of The Doc into the computer. The man is a walking, talking headline maker.

Docherty made news wherever he went, and he went to a lot of places. As he once famously said, he had more clubs than Jack Nicklaus. Let's count them: he played with distinction for Celtic, Preston and Arsenal before starting a managerial career with Chelsea, followed by adventurous assignments with Rotherham, Queen's Park Rangers (twice), Aston Villa, Oporto in Portugal, Hull City, Glasgow as Scotland manager, Manchester United, Derby County, Sydney Olympic, Preston, South Melbourne, Wolves, and, finally, Altrincham. I make that sixteen clubs. If he took as many on the golf course he would get disqualified.

Yes, he had more clubs than Nicklaus, but he did not have a swinging time at all of them. Excuse the supposed pun. I have been put into comedy mode by just the thought of The Doc.

Half the time, Bill Shankly did not know he was being funny. Tommy Docherty, by contrast, was usually intentionally hilarious and played it for laughs even at the gravest moments in his rollercoaster career. Here's an example you will find hard to believe:

I was at Tommy's side when his Manchester United world was falling down around his ears. We were collaborating together on a book called *The Rat Race*, in which he was pointing the finger at all that was wrong with football in general and club chairmen and directors in particular. We were all set to go to print when Tommy got himself sacked by United for falling in love with Mary Brown, the wife of the club physiotherapist, Laurie Brown.

An extra chapter was needed and Tommy gave me the background to the love affair that ended his marriage to his wife of 27 years, Agnes, and propelled him into a second marriage with Mary. 'When Mary and I gave the news to her husband Laurie that we had fallen hopelessly in love,' The Doc told me, 'he was standing in his kitchen with a bread knife in his hand. I decided to lighten the moment by saying, "While you've got that in your hand, Laurie, do us a favour and cut me a sandwich."'

Only The Doc could be that outrageous. Only The Doc would have shared the story. He just could not resist being the conduit for anecdotes that were usually hilariously, sometimes hideously, funny.

There is an absurd punchline to the Mary Brown Affair that winded both of us. Without a word to me, Tommy, who was then desperate for cash to fund his chaotic domestic life, went and sold his story to the *Daily Mirror*, which killed the book stone dead. Desperate for cash to fuel my own domestic life, I went to the *Sun* and sold my version of what was then the biggest scandal in football. Because I knew exactly what was in the manuscript in the possession of the *Mirror* I was able to keep the *Sun* a step ahead with the headlines. It infuriated the *Mirror*, and Tommy was persuaded to have a writ served on me. I sent him a telegram that read, 'The Rat Race has now become the Writ Race. See you in court.'

Tommy being Tommy, he saw the funny side of things. We kissed and made up, and he eventually followed the advice I had given him years earlier and became a stand-up comedian. I had always told him that he should have been on stage at the Glasgow Empire because he was a non-stop joke machine. Now, in his seventies, he is one of the funniest after-dinner speakers in the land. Catch him if you can. You will not hear his like again.

But for all his bubbling humour, Tommy took his football seriously. We collaborated on a book called *The ABC of Soccer Sense*, in which he showed he had a grasp of modern football tactics that was second to none. His problem was that he had such an explosive, self-detonating personality that he too often fell out with key players before he could get them to perform the way he wanted.

I could fill the book with Docherty fall-out stories. There was the time at Chelsea when he sent home eight players from Blackpool for breaking a late-night curfew, and he had a long-running battle with his skipper Terry Venables before selling him to Tottenham after telling me, 'Only one of us can manage Chelsea, and it's not going to be him.'

His later adventures included being involved in a breadroll-throwing incident on board a plane carrying the Chelsea team . . . having vicious personality clashes with Scottish Manchester United stars Willie Morgan, Lou Macari and Denis Law (the Morgan incident finished up as a court case, with Tommy being accused and cleared of perjury) . . . dropping and transfer-listing Scotland captain and vice-captain Bruce Rioch and Don Masson at Derby County . . . buying and selling more players than possibly any other manager in history (I told him he should have had a revolving door fitted to the entrance of each of his clubs).

I could go on and on with the controversy collection, but I believe I have got the message across that The Doc was a character of earthquaking moods. When he wasn't making jokes he was invariably making enemies. One thing's for sure, there was not a dull moment when Tommy was around and I was one of dozens of football reporters grateful for the stories he continually dropped into our laptops.

Like Busby and Shankly before him, Tommy had a tough start in life. Born on the hard side of Glasgow on 24 August 1928, he was just nine when his father died during the 1930s Depression. He vowed to do all he could to help his mother bring up his two sisters, and he left school as soon as he could to first of all work as a labourer and then in a bakery, where he started each morning at four o'clock.

He had been a useful schoolboy footballer with St Mark's and then the St Paul's Boys' Guild, and on Saturdays idolised Celtic from the Parkhead terraces. It was not until he was called up for National Service with the Highland Light Infantry that he blossomed into a player who took the eye. While serving in the Middle East as a physical training instructor, he played in the Third Infantry Division team and news quickly filtered back to Britain that the Army had a new footballing find. By the time of his demob in 1948 he had clubs queuing to sign him, including Celtic, Sheffield Wednesday, Newcastle, Middlesbrough and Manchester United.

'It was no race,' The Doc told me. 'Celtic were the team I had dreamed of playing for, and when the great Jimmy McGrory called at my home to ask me to sign I knew all the managers and scouts sitting outside in their cars waiting to talk to me were wasting their time.'

At Celtic, Tommy was coached by Jimmy Hogan, renowned for laying the foundation to the football played in the 1950s by the exceptional Hungarian and Austrian sides. 'I learned more from him about football tactics than any other person in the game,' he said.

He had barely been at Celtic a year when Preston came hunting for a successor in midfield to Bill Shankly, who was planning to hang up his boots to start a new life as a manager. Tommy, all five foot seven inches of him, later learned that the Celtic chairman agreed that he could be sold because he considered him too short to make the grade.

The Doc walked tall for the rest of his playing career, following Shanks into the number 4 Preston and Scotland shirts. He was a player in the Shankly mould, full of tenacity and skill and fit enough to run marathons. Talkative Tommy drove his teams on from midfield, forcing Finney-fuelled Preston to the 1954 FA Cup final and skippering Scotland eight times while winning 25 caps in an era when Anglos were not the flavour of the month with the selectors.

Tommy spent nearly nine years serving Preston, and also serving customers in the café he shrewdly owned near the Deepdale ground. But he was not everybody's cup of tea. Once, after he had been booked for a foul against Burnley, the Preston chairman said, 'We should put Docherty on tranquillisers. He has got too much energy and runs around like a wild horse. He needs calming down.'

The Doc had several run-ins with the Preston board, and made six transfer requests including one following a dispute over the fact that his club house did not have an inside toilet.

The final breaking point came when Preston refused to take him on a summer tour to South Africa just before the 1958 World Cup finals in Sweden. He captained Scotland in the World Cup, and then immediately on his return demanded a transfer. Preston made him train on his own and with the reserves. He was portrayed as the 'Deepdale Outcast' and he was at last relieved when autocratic Preston boss Cliff Britton agreed to sell him to Arsenal for £27,000. He was new Arsenal manager George Swindin's first signing.

Only after he had moved to Highbury did The Doc hear that Matt Busby had also wanted him as he set about rebuilding Manchester United after the Munich disaster. 'I would have walked barefoot across glass to play for Matt, who had been my manager when I was playing for Scotland,' said Tommy.

He hardly set the Gunners ablaze in what was a transitional period for the North London club, and a broken ankle took the edge off his game and hurried his desire to switch to coaching. In 1961, the year football's maximum wage was lifted, he wound down his career as player-coach of a young Chelsea side, and he became their manager on 2 January 1962. It was the start of the real Tommy Docherty adventure.

It is a fair assessment that Tommy's managerial career had more downs than ups. He took Chelsea down into the Second Division, and then – leaning heavily on Scottish imports – brought them straight up again before capturing the 1965 League Cup. He later led Chelsea to the 1967 FA Cup final, in which they were beaten 2–1 by Dave Mackay-motivated Tottenham. Within six months he jumped from Stamford Bridge before he was pushed after a series of extraordinary bust-ups with the Chelsea board.

He then appeared in the football outpost of Rotherham, spending the club's money like a repentant miser and promising that Rotherham would be fashioned into a major club. They were relegated to the Third Division at the end of his first season.

Next stop Queen's Park Rangers, and The Doc hardly had time to catch his breath before walking out on the West London club after just 28 days following a disagreement with chairman Jim Gregory over a transfer deal.

Within two weeks he was installed as manager of fallen giants Aston Villa, vowing to recapture their former glories. He was sacked by chairman 'Deadly' Doug Ellis on 19 January 1970, with Villa jammed at the bottom of the Second Division after he had bought and sold enough players to fill a cattle truck. The Doc came out with one of his classic quotes after his departure from Villa Park: 'Doug Ellis told me that he was right behind me. I said I preferred it if he were in front of me where I could see him.'

Never one to be anything less than surprising, The Doc next popped up in Portugal as manager of Oporto. He learned the lingo and gave Oporto the full Docherty all-change treatment before retreating for home in 1971 and the job of assistant manager to Terry Neill at Hull City (The Twin Tongues of Hull; you risked grievous harm to the eardrums if ever you engaged them both in conversation).

Tommy then landed the job that I thought suited him best: manager of Scotland. By not having day-to-day involvement with the players, there was less risk of those personality clashes for which he had become infamous. Scotland lost only three of twelve matches under his stewardship, and there seemed a new maturity in The Doc that promised good things for both himself and his country.

But just as we started to kid ourselves that he might put together a Scottish team that could actually make a telling challenge for the World Cup, the unpredictable Docherty roared back to the surface. In the New Year of 1972 Frank O'Farrell parted company with Manchester United, and the man they turned to as their new manager was our Tommy. It was the one club challenge The Doc could not refuse and he dropped the Scottish reins to return to the English League.

Suddenly, Old Trafford began to resemble a Glasgow bus station terminus. Tommy wore out the Manchester United chequebook as he splashed £420,000 – a fortune in the 1970s – in surrounding himself with countrymen. Scots Alex Forsyth (Partick), George Graham (Arsenal, appointed captain), Lou Macari (Celtic), Stewart Houston (Brentford), Jim McCalliog (Wolves) and Jim Holton, a big, raw-boned centre-half from Shrewsbury, signed as The Doc turned Man United into MacUnited.

The result: disaster. United were relegated, the goal that helped clinch their downward spiral coming from ex-King of Old Trafford Denis Law, who had fallen foul of Jekyll and Hyde Docherty and been allowed to move to Manchester City on a free transfer. The Doc had also burned his fingers in the furnace that was George Best, failing miserably in an attempt to bring the wayward genius back into the United fold.

While everybody waited for Tommy's blood to soak the boardroom carpet he got on with the job of bringing United straight back up again in swaggering style as Second Division champions. Then he led them to back-to-back FA Cup finals, first a startling defeat by Lawrie McMenemy's

Southampton and then in 1977 a glorious victory over Liverpool . . . by which time Tommy had fallen for Mary and was about to fall from grace at Old Trafford.

The next ten years were relatively gruesome for Tommy in football but good for him domestically. He and Mary settled down to a strong marriage, and she kept him sane and sensible as he tried and failed to conjure managerial magic on a whirlwind round of moves that took him from Derby to QPR again, and to two abortive attempts to make it in Australia either side of a disappointing stop-over back at one of his first loves, Preston.

The Docherty rocket finally came to earth in 1987 at Altrincham, a non-League setting that could not possibly accommodate his giant personality for long. He climbed off the football bandwagon, disillusioned and disappointed by the way the game was going.

Then, at long last, Tommy found the stage that had beckoned him throughout his anything-for-a-laugh life. He became a popular radio broadcaster, hilarious after-dinner speaker, and a reviewer of football who could pour acid on any players or teams who were not playing the way Tommy always liked to try to make his teams play: with style and with the emphasis on entertainment.

Provided you found Tommy's Dr Jekyll rather than his Mr Hyde, he always – as with the best music-hall comedians – liked to leave you laughing. I closed the previous chapter with Shanklyisms. Now come the Dochertys . . .

Told by a chairman that one hundred thousand wouldn't buy his centre-forward, Tommy replied: 'Aye, and I'm one of those hundred thousand.'

When Ray Wilkins was skipper at Manchester United, Tommy told radio listeners: 'The only time he goes forward is when he has to toss the coin.'

One morning during The Doc's spell in charge at Old Trafford, he walked into the medical room to find striker Stuart Pearson on the treatment table. 'What's wrong with you?' he asked.

'I've got a bad back,' said Pearson.

'Not to worry, son,' said The Doc. 'Manchester City have got two bad backs.'

Tommy was once asked if, while he was manager at Man United, he got any death threats. 'Only the one,' he replied, with a deadpan face. 'A supporter wrote to me and threatened that if I picked goalkeeper Paddy Roche again, he'd kill himself.'

Docherty can be devastating in his criticism of some current managers. 'They're so negative these days,' he said, 'that they should be working for Kodak.'

The Doc was on a shortlist of two for his first coaching job in football at Chelsea. He told the Stamford Bridge directors: 'If you appoint the other man you won't get a coach . . . you'll get a hearse.' They fell about laughing and gave him the job.

During his headline-hitting romance with Mary Brown that led to his departure from United, Tommy said that he was stopped in the street by an Old Trafford fan who told him: 'If you win the Cup for us again next season, Tom, you can run off with *my* missus.'

When taking over as Wolves manager in the bleak mid-1980s at Molineux he said, 'I have just opened the trophy cabinet and two Japanese prisoners of war came out.'

Talking scornfully about cricket and cricketers: 'Och, that's the only game where players can actually put on weight while playing.'

After Mark Wright had limped off during a match, Tommy said: 'He's so injury-prone he'd pull a muscle appearing on *A Question of Sport*.'

Talking of an England full-back: 'I've seen milk turn faster.'

The Doc on football club directors: 'An ideal board would be made up of just three directors – two dead and the other dying.'

Making an after-dinner speech at a time when George Best was making news for one of his drunken escapades: 'I'm sorry George could not be with us here tonight. He was launching a ship in Belfast and wouldn't let go of the bottle. We tried to get Ron Atkinson as a substitute, but he's in mourning for his hair stylist who died . . . in 1956.'

If only Tommy had learned to bite his tongue more often, I think he could have been a manager to rival Busby and Shankly in the trophy race. But football without the Docherty tongue would have been like Billy Connolly without his jokes – a lot less entertaining.

Thanks for the laughs, Tom. You didn't win the Writ Race, but you do win the Wit Race.

Chapter Eight

Jock Stein: The Miracle Worker

Jock Stein, the man to whom many bowed the knee as the master of all managers, spent just 44 days as an Anglo when fleetingly and frustratingly in charge of Leeds. But it was his outstanding achievements north of the border that helped to send a wind of change roaring through the English game. Jock showed us how to win in Europe.

Stein, a former Celtic centre-half and captain, always passionately believed that football should be played with a positive attitude. He demanded an attacking approach at Parkhead where Celtic – the team that Jock built – provided testimony to his enormous talent as a supreme creator.

Celtic's record under his mesmerising management was remarkable to the point of miraculous. In his first six full seasons in charge at Parkhead, the Glasgow club won six Scottish League titles and lost only seventeen out of 204 League games while scoring 597 goals. They reached five Scottish FA Cup finals, winning three; and they won five out of six League Cup finals. It was consistency on a Bradmanesque scale. And not a foreign player in sight. Amazingly, the eleven players who brought home the European Cup – the first British triumph in the tournament – were all born within a 30-mile radius of Glasgow.

There were dismissive remarks heard south of the border that the Scottish League was not a real test of a team's quality, but these sort of sniping comments were silenced as Celtic set out to achieve new standards in Europe. They barnstormed into the final with a brand of exciting, attacking football that put to shame those clubs becoming addicted to the drug of defensive football that paralysed so many games in the mid-to-late sixties.

In the final in Lisbon they came head-to-head with the great architects of defence-dominated football, Internazionale Milan, who captured the European Cup in successive seasons in 1964 and 1965 from the springboard of their stifling *catenaccio* defensive system.

Argentinian coach Helenio Herrera had built a human fortress around the Inter goal and then relied on three or four jet-paced forwards to make maximum capital out of carefully constructed counter-attacks. It was ruthlessly efficient; mind-numbingly boring. Celtic's style and attitude was the exact opposite. They were geared for flair and adventure. The simple tactic was: attack, attack and then attack again.

Every journey has to start with the first step, every revolution with the first bullet, every romance with the first kiss. Jock's first step was to create a team in his own image – that of a larger-than-life character who liked to entertain and be magnanimous in victory and defeat. The first bullet in the revolution was fired at the heart of the teams who were frightened to try anything daring on the pitch. And the first kiss was that metaphorically delivered to the thousands who packed Paradise Park every week to start a love affair that reached an extraordinary peak in Lisbon.

Jock's team was to become as well known and as greatly admired south of the border as north. There was not an English manager who did not take at least one opportunity to watch them play to see what they could learn.

Ronnie Simpson, son of a former Rangers captain, was Celtic's man-for-all-seasons goalkeeper. He provided a safe-as-houses last line of defence, and torpedoed the slur that Scottish goalkeepers cannot even catch colds. Ronnie had won two FA Cup-winners' medals with Newcastle in 1952 and 1955. Over a decade later at the age of 36 he was still as agile and alert as ever.

Jim Craig, iron-man skipper Billy McNeill, John Clark and power-shooting left-back Tommy Gemmill made up a formidable back line in front of Simpson. They were all encouraged to keep pushing forward as auxiliary attackers. Their tackling was man's-game tough but rarely strayed towards the cynical or violent.

Taking responsibility for the supply of passes from the midfield engine room in Celtic's 4–2–4 formation were the skilful and competitive Bertie

Auld and the industrious and inventive Bobby Murdoch. Bertie had left Parkhead to become an unsung Anglo with Birmingham City until called back home by the shrewd Stein, who knew he could produce the passes that would help make the team tick. Bobby Murdoch, later to ply his trade with Middlesbrough, was the heart of the team, a driving, determined player who appeared to have been equipped with an extra set of lungs.

The four-man firing line was one of the most effective goal machines in football. Jinking Jimmy Johnstone was unstoppable on his day as a quick and clever right winger who could destroy defences with his dribbling, darting runs. Bobby Lennox patrolled the left wing with a mixture of cunning and power, cutting in to shoot or to feed delicate passes to central strikers Willie Wallace and Steve Chalmers.

The 1967 European Cup final was a contest between Inter Milan's negative, smothering tactics and the up-and-at-'em cavalier charges of Celtic. Neutrals hoped that the positive would beat the negative. I give the match full coverage here because of the effect it had on the attitudes of coaches and players throughout Europe.

The Inter Milan method was tried and tested. They liked to search for a quick score and then sit back and barricade their goal behind a fortress defence. So it was no surprise to Celtic when the Italians opened with a burst of attacking football that could have come out of the Jock Stein manual.

Sandro Mazzola, Inter's key player following the late withdrawal of injured schemer Luis Suarez, headed against Ronnie Simpson's legs in the opening raid.

Then, in the seventh minute, Mazzola triggered an attack that led to the early goal on which Inter had set their sights. He put Corso clear on the left with a penetrating pass. The wingman released the ball to Cappellini, who was in the process of trying to shoot when a crunching Jim Craig tackle knocked him off the ball. It was judged a foul by German referee Tschenscher, and Mazzola coolly scored from the penalty spot.

It had been a magnificent opening spell by the Italians, but by force of habit they shelved their attacking talents and pulled all but two forwards back to guard their goal. It was an invitation to Celtic to attack. This was like asking Nureyev to dance or Tommy Docherty to tell a joke. They simply could not resist the invitation.

The Scottish champions pushed full-backs Craig and Gemmill forward on virtually permanent duty as extra wingers, and the Inter defensive wall buckled and bent under an avalanche of attacks.

Goalkeeper Sarti made a procession of brilliant saves, and when he was beaten the woodwork came to his rescue as first Auld and then Gemmill hammered shots against the bar. Any other team might have surrendered with broken hearts as the Milan goal miraculously survived the onslaught, but skipper McNeill kept brandishing his fist as he urged his team-mates to greater efforts. The word 'surrender' was not part of the Celtic vocabulary.

At last, after an hour of sustained attack, Celtic were rewarded with an equaliser and it was the exclusive creation of overlapping full-backs Craig and Gemmill.

First of all Craig brought the ball forward along the right side of the pitch. The retreating Italian defenders tightly marked virtually every player in a green-hooped shirt, but there was one man that they missed. Craig spotted Gemmill coming through on the left side like the Flying Scot express train and angled a pass into his path. Sarti had managed to stop everything to date, but no goalkeeper on earth could have saved Gemmill's scorching shot that was smashed high into the net from 20 yards.

Propelled by panic, Inter tried to get their attacking instincts working but they were so accustomed to back-pedalling that they could not lift the pace or alter the pattern of their play.

Celtic, urged on from the touchline by the composed figure of Big Jock, maintained their momentum and created the winning goal they so richly deserved six minutes from the end of an emotion-draining match. Gemmill came pounding forward along the left touchline. The Italians were not sure whether to mark his team-mates or to try to block his route to goal in case he was tempted to take another pot shot.

Caught in two minds, they gave too much room to Bobby Murdoch, who accepted a pass from Gemmill and unleashed a shot. The diving Sarti was confident he had the ball covered, but Steve Chalmers managed to deflect it out of his reach for a winning goal that made Celtic the first British winners of the premier prize in club football.

At the final whistle thousands of Celtic fans came chasing on to the pitch to parade their heroes like trophies. Jock Stein waited anxiously in the dressing-room, counting his players as they battled their way through the thronging supporters on a night that Lisbon belonged to Glasgow. Scottish football folklore has it that half the pitch was carried home to Glasgow as delirious fans collected souvenirs of what was then the greatest club triumph in British – let alone Scottish – football history.

Following on behind the last of the Celtic players was Liverpool's beaming manager Bill Shankly, one of the few people who could put his record up against his old Scottish pal Stein. As he entered the dressing-room Shankly summed up Stein's achievement with one of his typically direct and appropriate statements. 'John,' he boomed, using Stein's Christian name, 'You've just become bloody immortal.'

For six years, Celtic were the Great Untouchables, winning everything in sight apart from an infamous world championship match with Racing Club of Buenos Aires in which tempers and tantrums overruled the talent of both teams. Their ugly encounter in Argentina could have been staged under world professional wrestling rules, except there was nothing fake about the feuding and the fouling.

In 1970 they won the unofficial crown as champions of Britain when they conquered formidable Football League champions Leeds United in the semi-final of the European Cup. In the final they were narrowly beaten 2–1 by Feyenoord after extra time, with Gemmill scoring their goal.

Celtic mastermind John 'Jock' Stein was an amiable yet exhilarating person to meet. He was known throughout the game as the 'Big Man', and it was a description that sat comfortably on his broad shoulders.

Visiting him in his Parkhead office was an experience to treasure, and he put himself out to be friendly and forthcoming to quote-hungry journalists, be they Scottish or English. He had a wide, rouge-cheeked face that had a rugged warrior quality about it that would have looked at home on the shoulders of a heavyweight boxer. His thick black hair was combed back in tidal waves that baldies like Jimmy Delaney and Archie Gemmill would have killed for. A handshake delivered with a crush was a silent code signalling sincerity, and he would instantly offer a drink from a well-stocked cocktail cabinet from which he never ever touched a drop. 'I've never seen the point in drinking alcohol,' he said. 'Life provides enough of an adrenaline rush for me.'

Like his close friends Matt Busby and Bill Shankly, Jock grew up in the coalmining area of the West of Scotland that was a gold mine of footballing talent. He was born in Burnbank, Lanarkshire, on 1 October 1922, and had to work harder than most before he escaped the misery of the coalfields.

I once had the Big Man to myself for an hour when he answered readers' questions for a weekly 1970s Sports Forum column that I wrote for the *Daily Express*. His answers had to be heavily edited for the limited space of my column, but now I can give them in full to help paint in his background and give an insight into his footballing philosophy:

Is it true that you worked in the coalmines while still playing professional football?
I first went down the pits when I was barely sixteen years old, first of all working with the ponies and then going to the coal face. I used to be down there in the dark – it was blacker than black – for eight hours a day, and I did that for eleven years. My only respite was Saturdays, when I played part-time for Albion Rovers. This was during the war, and right up until 1950. If there's anybody who tells you that life on earth is hard, tell them to try working under the earth in the pits. It's the hardest toil there is and I think miners are the greatest, bravest and most undervalued group of workers in the world. Whenever I hear young footballers of today grumbling about their lot, I can't help but tell them they should count their lucky stars they are not having to work down the mines.

When did you become a full-time professional footballer?
Not until I was 27. I tried my luck in the Welsh league with Llanelli but never really felt at home there, mainly because the house I had kept going in Hamilton was twice broken into by burglars and this unsettled me. In fact I was so fed up, I was ready to pack the game in. Then Celtic came in for me and asked if I would join the club, helping out with the reserves and bringing along the youngsters. I jumped at the chance, and never once regretted it.

How did you come to the famously Catholic club Celtic when you were a Protestant?
I have never allowed myself to be dragged into that Catholic/Protestant nonsense, and I am not going to start now. I never enquire after a person's religion. I just look to find the man within the man. When I sign a player I do not wish to know about where he worships, but I do want to know

whether he has the heart and soul for the great game of football. I have no time for bigotry in any shape or form.

What did you achieve with Celtic as a player?
I got into the first-team literally by accident. Both Celtic's first-choice centre-halves got injured early in my first season at Parkhead. I was called into the middle of the defence in emergency, and did well enough not only to keep my place but to be appointed captain. The highlight of my playing days was when I led Celtic to the League and Cup double in 1953–54. Then a busted ankle in 1955 virtually ended my playing career, and to this day it has left me with a limp.

How did you get into management?
I was on the coaching staff at Celtic when Dunfermline Athletic offered me their manager's job in 1960. They looked certain to be relegated when I arrived and my brief was to prepare them for a promotion push the following season. The players responded wonderfully to my suggestions and we won six games on the trot to avoid relegation. The following season we managed to capture the Scottish Cup, beating Celtic in the final. I think that made people sit up and take notice! I then moved on to Hibernian to learn more about all aspects of management before going back to Celtic as manager in 1965.

How confident were you that you could beat mighty Inter Milan in the 1967 European Cup final?
I don't wish to sound big-headed, but I had no doubts whatsoever. There was not a prouder man on God's earth than me the night we won the Cup in Lisbon. Winning was important, aye, but it was the way that we won that filled me with satisfaction. We did it by playing football. Pure, beautiful, inventive, positive football. There was not a negative thought in our heads. Inter played into our hands. It was so sad to see such gifted players as they had shackled by a system that restricted their freedom to think and to act. Our fans would never accept that sort of sterile approach. Our objective has always been to win with style.

Celtic's European Cup triumph was a victory for football, and the game started to come out of its dark tunnel of defence down which it had been taken by teams like Inter and scores (or should I say scoreless?) of impersonators. Now they started to try to play the Celtic way.

A little bit of name-dropping here to help me convey Jock's popularity and standing in the game. I was in Monte Carlo scriptwriting the 2003 Laureus World Sports Academy Awards show, and I was discussing with Rod Stewart and his stunning girlfriend, Penny 'Lady Longlegs' Lancaster, how they wanted to introduce a section on the 2002 World Cup finals. I casually said that Jock Stein would have been pleased to see the attacking football that featured in the tournament.

At the mention of Jock's name, Rod fell to his knees and crossed himself. 'You are talking God there,' he said. 'There has not been a better manager in the history of the game.'

He looked at his beautiful companion and said, 'Their 1967 European Cup victory was the greatest performance by a British club side, ever. Ain't that right, Penny?'

'Uh, well,' she said, stifling a laugh, 'I wasn't even born then.'

Rod the Rascal said, 'Well just take my word for it.'

He then instructed, 'Write that line in the script. Let the world know how great Jock Stein and his Celtic team were. And put that line in for Penny to say she wasn't even born then. That'll raise a few eyebrows!'

On the night of the show, watched by a 280 million worldwide audience, Rod dropped to his knees again as he mentioned Celtic and Jock Stein in the same breath.

Thirty-six years on, the name of the Big Man was still magic on the lips.

Sadly, the Stein reign at Parkhead ended in acrimony. The board tried to move him upstairs when he wanted only to be among his players, and in 1978 he at last gave in to the many overtures to move south when he agreed to take over from Jimmy Armfield at Leeds. Those of us who knew him well realised it was the right move at the wrong time. He joined the English league at least eight years too late. Jock was 55, had survived a car crash that almost killed him in the summer of 1975, and there had been warning signs that his heart was not as strong as it used to be. Bad news for a man who was all heart.

Stein had been at Elland Road for only an uncomfortable couple of months when he was enticed back to his beloved Scotland to take charge of the national team. He had immediate success by steering them to the 1982 World Cup finals in Spain, where they were eliminated on goal difference.

Three years later he tragically died 'in harness' aged 62. He collapsed in the players' tunnel moments after Scotland had eliminated Wales from the World Cup in a qualifying match in Cardiff. The spectators were still applauding the teams off as he passed away. He died with the roar of the crowd in his ears. A light had gone out in British football. The game had lost one of its most majestic managers.

Jock had been rewarded with a CBE after Celtic's European Cup victory. Many wondered why he did not receive the knighthood that came Matt Busby's way a year later after Manchester United had followed Celtic as kings of Europe.

But Jock never once questioned it. He was far too dignified to get involved in that sort of petty nonsense, and he was also genuinely delighted for the honour bestowed on a precious friend.

Jock Stein, the Big Man, was a big man in every way.

Chapter Nine

Jimmy Leadbetter:
England's World Cup Hero!

There will be eyebrows raised and heads scratched over Jimmy Leadbetter getting such prominence in this tribute to great Anglo–Scottish footballers and managers – he did not get to kick a ball for the Scottish international team or select a single side. Stop a hundred people in the street, and I will bet ninety-nine of them will not be able to say who he is. Many would probably guess he was an old rhythm and blues singer. No, not Leadbelly. *Leadbetter*.

As the comedians would say, Jimmy was hardly a household name in his own household. Yet I can reveal that his influence on English football went so deep that he could claim at least part of the credit for England winning the World Cup in 1966 (a triumph that brought unbounded joy to so many of our Scottish friends!).

I can almost hear people saying, 'Jimmy Who?' You will need a thorough knowledge of domestic English football to know anything at all about the wee man, who was born in Edinburgh on 15 July 1928. He was signed for Chelsea from his local club Edinburgh Thistle in 1949 by manager Billy Birrell, and was quickly shipped out to Brighton when Ted Drake took over as boss at Stamford Bridge. He played three matches for Chelsea, and 107 games for Brighton before joining Ipswich Town in the Third Division South in June 1957 for £1,750, a fee that accurately reflected the modest impact he had made on the English league.

He arrived at Portman Road a month ahead of Ipswich Town's new manager, a former England right-back by the name of Alf Ramsey, who had recently retired from playing at the age of 35. All of Ramsey's football had been played at the top level and, along with most others, he had no idea who Leadbetter was or what he could do on a football pitch. (Just for the record, Alf would have been equally blank about Leadbelly.)

Anybody meeting Jimmy for the first time would have thought they were in the company of somebody who had just come off a hunger strike. His wiry, scrawny physique earned him the affectionate nickname 'Sticks', and his legs were bandy and looked like corkscrews. He was round-shouldered, had a deadpan Stan Laurel face, and tended to shuffle around the pitch in an almost apologetic way. One thing was in his favour: he had a left foot that could have opened safe doors.

There was absolutely nothing in his footballing history to suggest that he was the man who could inspire a revolutionary and world-beating idea in the mind of Ramsey the visionary.

Ipswich gained promotion as Third Division South champions in 1956–57, with Leadbetter operating as a conventional left winger. He was still basically an outside-left when Ramsey steered Ipswich up from the Second Division as champions in 1960–61.

Ramsey knew in his heart that his team needed to be original and radical if they were to challenge the big guns of the First Division, where his old Tottenham team had just created history by becoming the first side of the twentieth century to win the League and FA Cup double. Arsenal, Wolves, Burnley and Matt Busby's Manchester United were other teams that, on paper, looked much too powerful for the Ipswich combination of veterans, misfits and discards.

Not for nothing was Alf known as 'The General' when playing for the push-and-run Spurs, who won the Second and First Division championships in successive years – 1949–50 and 1950–51. Now he was about to show just why he has gone down in history as one of the greatest of all tacticians, and it was unheralded Scotsman Jimmy Leadbetter who was going to be the key man in his plans.

In practice sessions on a training pitch behind the Portman Road stand, Alf introduced a system that involved Jimmy playing in a deep-lying role. He was instructed to forget his instincts to raid down the touchline, and to concentrate on finding twin strikers Ray Crawford and Ted Phillips or right-winger Roy 'The Rocket' Stephenson with passes from midfield, rather than the usual crosses from near the corner flag.

Ranged across the midfield to the right of Leadbetter were two fellow Scots, a classy schemer called Doug Moran – bought by Alf from Falkirk for £12,500 in the summer of 1961 – and Edinburgh-born midfield anchorman Bill Baxter, who had just finished his National Service.

Ramsey had been a magnificent number 2 for Southampton, Tottenham and England, and he knew better than anybody that the right-backs in the First Division would be confused and bemused when they found they did not have a winger to mark.

The plan worked so well that Ipswich won the League championship at the first time of asking as defences struggled to fathom how to counter a team playing without a left winger.

Alf the General had out-thought them all, winning the title with a team that did not have nearly as many outstanding players as a dozen of the sides below them. Leadbetter simply sat deep to collect the ball from defence and then sprayed passes into the path of Crawford, Phillips or Stephenson with his magic wand of a left foot. He had an assist role in dozens of goals as Phillips (33 goals) and Crawford (28) pounded defences.

It was the prototype of the formation that four years later was to win Ramsey and England the greatest prize of all, the World Cup. By then it had been labelled 4–3–3.

Little Jimmy Leadbetter – the 'Wizened Wizard' – was the man who made it work for Ipswich, but he did not get the credit he deserved for his contribution. There were not the massive financial rewards players collect today. His weekly wage would not have paid David Beckham's hairdressing bill. Before the 1960s were out, Jimmy was reduced to selling newspapers in the street in Ipswich for a living. Leadbelly's blues would have been appropriate.

But there was no bitterness in this pleasant, modest and agreeable man. 'I got three championship medals with Ipswich in seven years,' he told me once, when I stopped to buy an Ipswich *Evening Star* from him on the way to Portman Road to report a match. 'Alf was responsible for that because of his tactical knowledge. There was nobody to touch him for being able to read a game. I loved every second of my career under Alf, and the League title was just the icing on the cake. When Alf left us for the England job I *knew* he would come up with the tactics to win it.'

I once asked Sir Alf how highly he rated Jimmy. He looked into space, measuring his response before replying, 'He was very, very good at doing what he was told.'

Ramsey, infamously, was no lover of the Scots in general (he made an exception in Jimmy's case). I was alongside Alf when he arrived at Glasgow airport for a Scotland–England international match at Hampden Park. Larger-than-life *Scottish Daily Express* reporter Jim Rodger was on the tarmac waiting to greet the team. Only Jim, wider than a barn door, could have talked himself past security to get there. He held out a hand as Alf approached. 'Welcome to Scotland, Sir Alf,' he said.

Alf gave him his famed and feared cold-eye stare, ignored the outstretched hand and said: 'You must be f***ing joking.'

Perhaps Alf's dislike of the Scots had something to do with the chasings he used to be given by Liverpool's great Scottish outside-left Billy Liddell.

Ramsey got his revenge by doing away with wingers completely, and Jimmy Leadbetter was the unlikely hero who proved to Alf that his plan would work.

And now, more than forty years on, I am giving Jimmy the recognition he deserves. He was the Scot who helped England win the World Cup! Leadbelly? No, Leadbetter!

Chapter Ten

Dave Mackay:
The Ace of Hearts

There are three footballing faces of Dave Mackay that have remained as a lasting memory long after the man who was a warrior of a player and a worrier of a manager sheathed his sword.

First there was Mackay the buccaneering midfield hero of the splendid Spurs Double-winning side of 1960–61, who provided the piracy to the poetry of Danny Blanchflower. That was as good an English club team as I have ever seen grace a football field, and it played to a strong Scottish beat.

Handling with care in goal was Bill Brown, who joined Tottenham from Dundee in the same 1958–59 season that Bill Nicholson stepped up from coach to manager at White Hart Lane. He was not just plain Bill Brown. His glorious full name was William Dallas Fyfe Brown, and he proudly wore the Scottish international jersey in 28 international matches. Only an uncertainty about leaving his line to collect crosses stopped him being rated as good a goalkeeper as his magnificent successor between the Tottenham posts, Pat Jennings. Nobody – not even his club-mate Jimmy Greaves – made jokes about Scottish goalkeepers not being trusted with the china while Bill was around.

Making the team tick from midfield alongside skipper Blanchflower was John White, who was born in Musselburgh, Lothian. He features grandly in the Players' Profiles section, but suffice to say that any professional who operated in the First Division in the early 1960s will tell you that he was a prince of footballers. John used to make things happen almost without anybody realising that he was the one who had made the vital pass, or the unseen run that had unhinged a defence. He was a softly-softly assassin, and was perfectly nicknamed The Ghost of White Hart Lane. His star was at its zenith when he was tragically killed by a bolt of lightning while sheltering under a tree on a golf course in the summer of 1964.

Then there was Mackay! Bill Nicholson bought him almost as an afterthought in March 1959 after being beaten by deadly rivals Arsenal for the signature of Welsh international Mel Charles. He paid Hearts £30,000 for Dave's signature. If he had shelled out ten times as much he would still have been getting a bargain. His value in today's transfer market would be upwards of £20 million. For any young reader trying to get a picture of him imagine Roy Keane mixed and shaken with Bryan Robson and you have got him. Yes, he was that good, that powerful, that inspiring.

Born in Edinburgh on 14 November 1934, Mackay had the choice of following his father into the print industry as a linotype operator or taking up a career in football after attracting a queue of clubs with his performances for the Scottish international schools team. His mind was made up for him when Hearts, the team he had always supported, invited him to play for them. He became the heart of the Hearts team that challenged the two giants, Celtic and Rangers, for domestic supremacy in the 1950s. He collected Scottish League Cup, Scottish Cup and Scottish League championship medals before being persuaded to bring his talent and his tenacity to Tottenham.

Mackay stood around five foot nine, but because of a barrel chest and a desire to be involved in every bit of action, opponents and spectators got the impression that he was a giant. Anybody tackled by Dave felt that he was with them for the next seven days, and he had the stamina to run all day. He was not just about power. He also had considerable skill to go with his strength, and could drill a first-time left-footed pass through to a team-mate with wonderful precision. I can think of few players who had such presence on a football field. You could almost feel the ground shudder as he made his intrepid runs in support of his forwards.

If he had a fault, it was that he would sometimes recklessly forget his marking duties because he was so intent on huffing and puffing and blowing the opposition defence down. This was never more obvious than at Wembley in 1961 when he was absent without leave in the England half while behind him the Auld Enemy were helping themselves to goals by the bucketful. Scotland were beaten 9–3 in a match in which hapless goalkeeper

Frank Haffey passed into comedy folklore. To this day, you can turn a Scot purple by saying when asked the time, 'It's nearly ten past Haffey.'

Mackay was deeply scarred by the defeat, and people were well advised not to mention it in his hearing for years afterwards. It came in the season that he was playing a key role in helping Tottenham become the first club of the twentieth century to win the First Division championship and the FA Cup in the same season.

It was achieved with beautifully patterned football choreographed by Bill Nicholson, one of the few English managers who could look the likes of Busby, Shankly and Stein in the eye. Bill Nick admired Scottish football and Scottish players, and used to spend so much time over the border on scouting missions that his wife, Darkie, used to joke that he should wear a kilt.

I used to spend regular Sunday mornings with Bill in his White Hart Lane office, tapping him for tales and memories of his great life in the game. He would be at the ground seven days a week, and to keep in touch lived in a modest house just around the corner where Darkie could judge by the crowd's roar on match days what sort of mood he would be in on his return home.

I once asked Bill what the attraction was of Scottish players. He tapped his heart and then his head. 'It's all here,' he said. 'They have a great will to win, and they play a thinking game. I have never been let down by any player I have bought from a Scottish club.'

The impressive list includes internationals Brown, White, Mackay, Alan Gilzean and Jimmy Robertson. To get Bill to let go of a firm opinion for public consumption was like getting a certain Iraqi information minister to tell the truth, but he did happily admit that Dave Mackay had been his greatest buy. 'He was a phenomenal player,' he said. 'Attack, defend, scheme, score, he could do it all. Above all he was a great leader on the pitch, and his team-mates would raise their game at the sight of him brandishing his fist.'

Jimmy Greaves, who collected FA Cup-winners' medals with Mackay in 1962 and 1967, told me: 'You could almost hear the skirl of the pipes as he stuck out his barrel chest and led us into battle. There were times when he frightened me to death with his up-and-at-'em attitude. And I was on *his* side. I remember when we became the first British team to win a major

European trophy [the Cup Winners' Cup in 1963], Dave failed a late fitness
test for the final. You would have thought we'd had a death in the family.
We lost all our confidence, and it was only a great team-talk by our skipper
Danny Blanchflower that lifted us out of our depression. We then went out
and won the Cup for Dave.'

I have introduced the first Mackay face: the buccaneering midfield
player. Next came the grim, determined face of the disciplined central
defender and sweeper. He became known as 'The Miracle Man' after twice
making comebacks following the breaking of his leg, and he defied all the
medical odds by leading Tottenham to the FA Cup in 1967.

In those days 'King David' used to hold court in the saloon bar of the Bell
and Hare pub after home Tottenham matches. Every move and every kick
of each game was analysed while Dave sat at his barstool leading either the
celebrations or the inquests. The drinking school was as hard as it could get,
with Alan Gilzean and Greavsie challenging Mackay for which of them had
the hollowest legs. I was among the trusted press men allowed on the
periphery, and heaven help any one of us who 1) quoted anything that was
uttered in the pub in our newspapers, and 2) even worse, failed to get a
round in.

None of us had the courage to tell Mackay to his face that the edge was
going off his game after he had reached the pinnacle of driving Spurs to
Wembley within a year of being told his career was virtually over. While we
were wondering and worrying about how he was going to survive as
Tottenham's midfield marauder, a young manager in the north Midlands
was mapping out his future. Enter, Brian Clough.

It was Cloughie, in a seven-hour session of non-stop talking, who
persuaded Dave to leave London, give up his midfield position, let go of his
partnership in a tie-manufacturing company and join him in what was, for
Mackay, the unlikely football outpost of Derby County.

Cloughie handed Mackay the captaincy, and gave him the job of nursing
along his young Derby team from a position at the back of the defence
alongside promising centre-half Roy McFarland. It was a stroke of genius,
and added years and cheers to the Mackay playing career. He turned from
soldier into stroller, dictating the pattern of play from his own penalty area.
Even in this more sedate role, he was just as dominating and demanding a
personality. His leadership was a key reason for Derby winning the 1968–69

Second Division championship and he was elected joint-winner, with Manchester City's Tony Book, of the Footballer of the Year trophy, a prize he had deserved to win on his own years earlier.

By the time Derby won the League championship in 1971–72 Mackay had moved on to Swindon to show his third footballing face, this time as a manager who did not find the transition easy. Playing the game came as naturally to Dave as breathing, but management called for a patience and tolerance that were not part of the Mackay make-up.

After 25 games as Swindon's player-boss, he moved on to Nottingham Forest as manager in 1972 before being seduced into taking over the reins at Derby County, from where Brian Clough and his partner Peter Taylor had departed in a cloud of controversy. Mackay had stepped into a political minefield and did not enjoy his return, despite capturing the League championship in 1974–75 with a team largely left behind by Cloughie.

He departed the following year for a season in charge at Walsall before disappearing to the Middle East, where it was hard to imagine the King of the Bell and Hare in 'dry' surroundings. But his coaching out there was greatly admired and appreciated over a span of nine years before he came home for a wind-down spell as manager at Doncaster Rovers.

I return to my old mate Greavsie for the perfect summing-up of Mackay's impact at the peak of his playing career: 'There were many exceptional players in that outstanding Spurs side of the 1960s, but there is no doubt in my mind that the most influential of them all was Dave Mackay. He was quite simply the greatest professional I ever played with or against. If ever he was missing from the Tottenham team, the rest of us had to work twice as hard to make up for it. We always used to say that Dave was responsible for the bad pitch at White Hart Lane because he flattened every single blade of grass in search of the ball and of victory. Winning wasn't just everything to Dave. It was the only thing. Many a time I had reason to look up to the sky and say a silent prayer of thanks that he was with me and not against me.'

That was Dave Mackay, the ace of Hearts.

Chapter Eleven

Denis Law:
The True King

I am from the generation that gets a Manchester United red mist come down when I hear Eric Cantona described as The King of Old Trafford. That title belonged to only one man. Bend the knee to Denis Law.

When, in the early 1960s, I first met Denis in person away from the football pitch I fully expected to get a shock as we shook hands. He was *that* electric as a striker. Law had the quickest reflexes of any British player I have ever seen.

'Denis the Menace' – an obvious yet fitting nickname – was the showman and the swordsman in the celebrated Best-Charlton-Law trio that dismantled defences in such stunning style. George Best was the genius, Bobby Charlton the commander, and Law the executioner.

He would score with a rapier thrust, turning a half chance into a goal in the blinking of an eye. Then the showman would emerge, his right arm punched into the air and held there in a salute that spawned a procession of imitators (Allan Clarke and Rodney Marsh were just two who admitted copying their idol in the way they autographed goals).

A straw-haired assassin who was pencil slim and built for speed, he had an uncanny ability to hover in the air when heading the ball. He stood five feet nine inches, but could make much taller defenders seem about as mobile as lampposts as he soared above them. As well as doing conventional things well at lightning speed, the Electric Heel was a master of the hook shot and the overhead bicycle kick. He was extrovert, flamboyant, provocative and spectacular, and never ever dull. How dare they try to take away his title of The King!

His temper was as quick as his reflexes, and he was often in trouble with referees for retaliating. I once saw him involved in a full-blooded fist fight with Arsenal centre-half Ian Ure at Old Trafford. Both got their marching orders, and long suspensions. What made it even more of a compelling spectacle is that they were good pals who roomed with each other when on Scottish international duty. Friend or foe, Denis refused to concede a penalty area inch to any opponent. A Red Devil, if ever there was one.

Born on 24 February 1940 (in the same week that Jimmy Greaves was having his first kick of life in East London), Denis was the son of an Aberdonian trawlerman, who would have followed his father to sea but for his prodigious talent as a schoolboy footballer.

Scouts working for Huddersfield Town were first to spot him, and it has gone down in football folklore how he arrived in Yorkshire from Aberdeen at the age of fifteen looking like a comic figure out of the *Beano*. He had a squint, wore National Health glasses and weighed no more than eight stone wet through.

Denis was picked up at Huddersfield station by the club's assistant manager, who was another legend in waiting – the one and only Bill Shankly. 'I could not believe my eyes when I first saw him,' Shanks told me years later. 'He looked like a case for Oxfam rather than a young footballer. The first thing we did was get his squint sorted out so that we knew who he was looking at when we talked to him. Then we got some steaks inside him and he started to fill out. Once we let him loose on the football pitch he suddenly became a tiger. It was awesome to be there at the start of one of the great football careers.'

Denis made his League debut with Huddersfield at the age of sixteen, and two years later became Scotland's youngest ever player at the launch of an international career that brought him a record 30 goals in 55 appearances. The first manager to pick him for Scotland was Matt Busby, who never made any secret of his belief that Denis was one of the finest players ever to come south of the border.

His transfer to Manchester City for £55,000 in 1960 was a British record, and his 21 goals in 44 games alerted Italian clubs who were throwing money at British players following the success of the great Welshman John Charles at Juventus. Within a year of Denis arriving at Maine Road, City sold him to Torino for £110,000 in another record deal.

For 21-year-old Denis, the following twelve months were the most miserable of his life. 'I hated my time with Torino,' he told me. 'Perhaps if I had been older I could have handled it, but I suffered terrible home-sickness. They treated their players as if they owned them body and soul, and I felt like a prisoner. There was little satisfaction on the pitch because the Italian game was totally negative, and I used to have two or three defenders marking me every time I went on the pitch. My big bust-up with the club came when they refused to release me to play for Scotland. I knew then that I just had to get back to Britain or go mad.'

He attempted to get rid of his homesick blues by enjoying himself off the pitch in the company of his Torino team-mate Joe Baker, the Englishman from Hibernian who had a thicker Scottish accent than Aberdonian Denis. Their exploration of the Turin nightlife very nearly cost them their lives. Joe was at the wheel of his flash new Alfa Romeo with Denis beside him when they were involved in a high-speed crash. Both were dragged unconscious from the wreckage, but thankfully their injuries were not long term.

It was Matt Busby who came back into Law's life to rescue him from his dismal exile. For a third time, the transfer record was broken as he made the move to Old Trafford in the summer of 1962 for £116,000.

Over the next ten years, Denis ignited the United attack with his fire and flair. He was an FA Cup winner in 1963, European Footballer of the Year in 1964, and a League championship winner in 1965 and 1967. He remains the only Scot to have been elected European Footballer of the Year.

Sadly, he missed the ultimate prize of the European Cup winners' medal in 1968. A knee injury reduced him to the role of hospital-bed observer as he watched the Wembley triumph on television. Brian Kidd took his place, and celebrated his nineteenth birthday with a goal as he fed off the probing passes of another Scot, Pat Crerand, whose skilled support had been an important part of the Lawman's success story at Old Trafford.

He scored 171 League goals for United in 309 matches, and took his FA Cup goals haul to what was then a record 40 goals. This total did not include the six he scored for Manchester City against Luton in a 1961 tie that was abandoned.

A fiercely proud Scot, Denis just could not stomach the prospect of England winning the World Cup in 1966. On the day of the final at

Wembley he took himself off to the golf course rather than watch the game on television. When news filtered through to him that England had beaten West Germany he threw his golf bag to the floor in disgust.

A year later he had the satisfaction of being a goal-scoring member of the Scottish team that beat world champions England 3–2 at Wembley. I always put him in his place by reminding him of a game in which he played at Wembley on 15 April 1961 . . . England 9, Scotland 3.

His Manchester United career ended in rancour in 1973 when Tommy Docherty let him go on a free transfer. 'The first I knew about it was when I saw the news being announced on television,' an aggrieved Law said. 'I thought I would end my career at Old Trafford.'

Shrugging off a recurring knee problem, Denis returned to Manchester City and in the last game of the following season almost reluctantly back-heeled the goal that helped push Manchester United down into the Second Division.

He had the satisfaction of making his World Cup finals debut in the last season of a magnificent career in which he inspired hundreds of youngsters to try to play the Lawman way. They could copy his style but few could get close to imitating his awareness and anticipation that always put him a thought and a deed ahead of the opposition.

A good family man with five sons, he moved out of football to concentrate on several business interests. But he was gradually drawn back to the game he had served so well as a broadcaster on radio and television. He had always described himself as the worst spectator in the world, and it took him several years to discipline himself to watching the game he had played better than almost anybody else in history.

Now a sixty-something, he is a regular meeter and greeter at Manchester United and an amusing after-dinner speaker with scores of stories up those famous sleeves of his (he used to insist on extra-long sleeves so that he could hold the cuffs in the palms of his hands). He has the same cheeky grin and Danny Kaye looks and that little bit of cockiness that marked his game when he was The King of Old Trafford . . . The King who was never dethroned.

It has been quite a voyage of adventure for the trawlerman's son from Aberdeen.

Chapter Twelve

George Graham:
An Unsolicited Tribute

There is a common denominator running through the majority of managers featured up to this point: they came from impoverished backgrounds in the West of Scotland, and in several cases grew up fatherless. George Graham continued the tradition.

I have to weigh my words carefully when writing about my pal, George, otherwise we could be suspected of being consenting adults. In the hands of an unsympathetic writer, he could be presented as having been a bone-idle player and, later, something of a wide-boy of a manager. I will paint a picture that presents him more as a gifted player and as a manager with few equals. Frankly, the truth about George probably lies somewhere in between these two identikits, but I hope to prove to you that he is a man worthy of great respect – despite getting caught with, so to speak, his hand in the till.

He was born in the Lanarkshire pit-village of Bargeddie on St Andrews Day, 30 November 1944, when Winston Churchill was celebrating his 69th birthday and looking forward to victory over Hitler and the Nazis. While George was enjoying his first breath of life his father, Robert, was losing a fight for his life. He died on Christmas Day, 1944, a victim of tuberculosis. George was barely three weeks old. He was the seventh child, and an extra mouth for his suddenly widowed mum, Janet, to feed.

George has horrendous stories to tell about his childhood and how his mother, fighting to survive on just a widow's pension, would literally dig with her bare hands to make ends meet. She worked on a local farm 'tattie howking' – that's potato picking for non–Scots. She was paid something like two shillings for each wire basket that she filled. When things got really desperate she would fill a basket at double speed and then toss the tatties over a hedge into the adjoining field. Later, in the evening, she would take George for a walk in his pram, pick up the pilfered potatoes and hide them beneath George in the pram. Potato soup was a staple diet for the Grahams.

I tell this story just to illustrate how tough George had it in his formative years. He suffered appalling experiences that helped shape the player and the person he was to become after starting his football career as a fifteen-year-old apprentice with Aston Villa. George is something of a football historian, and he was attracted to Villa – even ahead of Rangers – because of their strong Scottish background. He knows all about pioneers at Villa Park like William McGregor and George Ramsay, and he will tell you that the rampant lion on the Villa badge has a Scottish roar.

He had barely established himself in Joe Mercer's Villa first-team when The Doc came calling, and – for what would not be the last time – he was hooked by Tommy Docherty's golden tongue and followed him to Chelsea. George had been given a passport to paradise. He had the time of his life in the King's Road environment, arriving right at the peak of the swinging sixties. I do not expect any argument, particularly from George, when I say that he was one of the most handsome, engaging young sportsmen on the London scene, and mini-skirted dollybirds all but threw themselves in his path. They formed a 'Gorgeous George' fan club, and did their best to distract his attention from the priority of playing football. But George managed not to take his eye completely off the ball. Playing as a striker and with a reputation for heading spectacular goals, he scored 46 goals in 102 games and was leading Chelsea marksman for two successive seasons.

He had a hot and cold running relationship with The Doc, which was stretched to snapping point when he was one of the eight players Docherty sent home from Blackpool for breaking a late-night curfew (creeping down a hotel fire escape to try to escape The Doc's attention).

Docherty decided to break up his often brilliant, occasionally brittle Chelsea team after a second successive FA Cup semi-final defeat in 1966. He sold Terry Venables, George's closest friend, to Tottenham, replacing him with 'Chuckleboots' Charlie Cooke from Dundee. Two months later he allowed George to move to Arsenal for £50,000 plus striker Tommy Baldwin.

From being a loping player at Chelsea, George became a relaxed midfield playmaker and support striker at Arsenal, where he teamed up with fellow Scots Frank McLintock, Ian Ure, Eddie Kelly, English-born Scot Bob Wilson and, later, Peter Marinello. In 227 League games for the Gunners, he scored 59 goals and picked up the nickname 'Stroller' because of his casual, almost swaggering style. He was greatly influenced at Highbury by, first, Dave Sexton, and then Don Howe, who took over as first-team coach when Sexton replaced The Doc as manager at Chelsea.

The casual gait of Graham could be deceptive, and he surprised many defences with sudden acceleration and sharp shooting after exchanging rapid return passes with team-mates. He greatly matured both as a player and as a man at Highbury, and after helping Arsenal win the League and Cup double he won the first of his twelve Scotland caps. The man who selected him was none other than Tommy Docherty.

He was a key midfield influence as Arsenal reached the 1972 Centenary FA Cup final (beaten 1–0 by Leeds), and then he got another call from The Doc, who this time persuaded him to join him in his latest adventure at Old Trafford.

'I have signed Britain's Gunter Netzer,' trumpeted Docherty, making him United captain. But it all turned into a nightmare as United nose-dived into the Second Division, and The Doc unceremoniously moved George on to Portsmouth in exchange for Welsh international centre-forward Ron Davies.

He played 61 games for Pompey before signing for Crystal Palace, where his old buddy Terry Venables was in charge. The end of his playing career was hastened by two horrific injuries, each received while playing in the United States: first of all a broken ankle in 1977 and then a broken leg a year later.

By now, George had the coaching bug. He followed Venables to Queen's Park Rangers as youth team coach and, in 1982, landed his first managerial job in charge of Third Division Millwall. Those of us who had known George the playboy were astonished at his change as he developed into an iron-fisted manager at Millwall, instilling discipline into the club and guiding them to promotion in 1985.

Arsenal watched his progress with interest, and in 1986 invited him back as manager at Highbury as successor to his former mentor Don Howe. It was the start of a sensational revival by Arsenal and leading it was a galvanised George Graham, who demanded perspiration as well as inspiration from his team.

I find that most football teams reflect the image of their managers. In George's case, the opposite was true. He can be a humorous, warm, entertaining companion, yet his Arsenal side tended to play more with a snarl than a smile. The always immaculately dressed man who prides himself on his appearance sent out a team fashioned more for dull defence than enterprising attack (George, by the way, completely refutes this, and insists that his teams were more entertaining than was chronicled by we critics).

They were not always pretty to watch, but the end result was stunning – six trophies in just over eight years: Littlewoods Cup (1986–87), League championship (1988–89 and 1990–91), Coca-Cola Cup and FA Cup winners (1992–93), European Cup Winners' Cup (1993–94).

Then, in the winter of 1995, came an explosion in George Graham's football world that could be measured on the Richter scale. He was investigated for allegedly taking kick-back money from transfer deals. Arsenal sacked him, and he was banished from all football for a year.

I collaborated with George on his inside story of the scandal: *The Glory and the Grief*. He went up rather than down in my estimation as I got close to him during the toughest moments of his life. Lesser men would have crumbled under the pressure, much of it self-inflicted. But George was determined to come through his ordeal a stronger and better person.

He did not try to protest his innocence, but was ready to own up to naivety. 'If I could turn the clock back, there is little that I would do differently in my reign as Arsenal manager,' he told me. 'The only definite change would be that I would say "no, no, no" when Norwegian agent Rune Hauge decided he wanted to thank me for all I'd done to help him open doors for transfer business in England. The fact that he wanted to show his appreciation with two generous cash gifts put a temptation in my way that I was unable to resist. It is no defence, but I am sure that few people could have resisted accepting the money. I have never claimed to be some sort of shining knight, and I am as weak as the next man where it comes to life's temptations. I concede that greed got the better of me, but only temporarily.'

George eventually handed the money – the little matter of £425,000 – to Arsenal. He came out of it all empty-handed, and without a job; his career in ruins. As I write, he remains the only manager to have been caught and punished for what we all know is a common occurrence in football. George Graham, scapegoat.

Guided by legal eagles, George and I went out of our way not to use the word 'bung' to describe the money he had received. We were instructed to call it 'an unsolicited gift'. I passed this message on to the then editor of the *Sun*, Stuart Higgins, another good old friend of mine, who assured George he was in the best possible hands when the *Sun* bought the serialisation to the book.

So you can imagine how George and I felt when, on the first day of the book's serialisation, the *Sun* ran a headline that filled the front page with the words, 'George Graham confesses: "I took £425,000 bung!"'

When I telephoned Stuart to complain on George's behalf, he told me with a tongue buried deep in his cheek: 'Uh, well, you see "unsolicited gift" wouldn't fit into the space we had.'

In his year out of the game George got himself together mentally and physically. He quietly married his second wife, Sue, who had been an incredible source of strength to him; he went on training runs every day, turned his Hampstead garden into a showpiece, and kept close to the game as an excellent radio and Sky television summariser. It was a lesson to anybody on how to come through adversity as a winner.

George bounced back as Leeds manager in 1996, and then surprised everybody – probably even himself – by taking charge of Tottenham in 1998. He lifted the Worthington Cup after just four months in the job, but was never allowed to feel at home at White Hart Lane by a faction of the crowd who saw Arsenal red every time they looked at him. He was just beginning to put the spur back into Spurs when he was dismissed in March 2001 for being too open with the media about his budget restrictions at Tottenham.

Quietly and courageously, he had been battling against what threatened to be crippling rheumatoid arthritis. He took his pain without complaint, and made a welcome return to the media roundabout as an expert summariser with Sky and an occasional columnist with the *Daily Mail*. He still has plenty to give the game if the right challenge comes along.

The boy from Bargeddie has come a long, long way from his dreadful start in life. As somebody who's had a close-up view of much of his journey I would like to pay an unsolicited tribute inspired by his favourite poem by Rudyard Kipling: *George, you ARE a man, my son*!

Chapter Thirteen

Kenny Dalglish:
The Silent Assassin

There have been few more successful footballers and managers in the history of the game than Kenny Dalglish. Yet, as he comes into his middle age, his memories are haunted by three footballing tragedies that throw a dark shadow over all the great things that he achieved on and off the pitch.

This dream of a footballer suffered the nightmare of witnessing three of the worst crowd catastrophes ever: he was at Ibrox during the 1971 'Old Firm' match when stairway thirteen at the decaying stadium collapsed, killing 66 fans; in 1985 he was a member of the Liverpool team against Juventus in the European Cup final when a wall came down as fans rioted, and 39 Italian supporters died; after the horror of Heysel came the heartbreak of Hillsborough, 95 Liverpool fans dying in a crowd crush on the day the Dalglish-managed Reds met Nottingham Forest in the 1989 FA Cup semi-final.

No man should have to be burdened with such grief and tragedy, and the impact of it on Dalglish – particularly the Hillsborough disaster – had us worrying about his health. But he had the strength of character to come through the storm with his head held high and to somehow find the energy and enthusiasm to conjure success at pastures new.

Dalglish has always been a fiercely private man, allowing few people close to him. I was one of the first English reporters to run into the Dalglish wall. He had just scored two goals for the Scotland Under-23 side in a 2–2 draw against England on a disgraceful mudheap of a pitch at Derby's Baseball

Ground in 1972, and I asked him the simple question, 'What was it like playing on that surface, Kenny?'

'Nae comment,' he said, then walking past me as if I was not there, a little like the way he had just treated the English defenders.

It was the sign of things to come. When Liverpool manager Bob Paisley bought him from Celtic as replacement for Kevin Keegan in the summer of 1977 he handled the press with a suspicion that could have been interpreted as contempt. He would answer questions in mumbled monosyllables, and on the occasions when he did decide to utter sentences few English ears could understand his heavy Glaswegian accent.

We had been forewarned of his reticence to give interviews by Ian Archer, a fine Scottish sportswriter who briefly graced the pages of the London *Daily Mail* before returning to Scotland to become a respected reporter on the page, radio and screen.

Ian was once walking through the centre of Glasgow minding his own business when out of nowhere he found himself confronted by the young, blond, red-cheeked Dalglish.

'Wisnae,' said Dalglish to a startled Archer.

'Wisnae what?' Archer responded (understanding that Kenny was saying 'wasn't').

'Wisnae offside,' replied Dalglish before disappearing into the crowd.

Archer was baffled, and it was only after several minutes of excavating his brain that he remembered that a month earlier he had written in a match report that a Dalglish goal for Celtic had looked suspiciously offside.

'This was', said Ian, 'the most piercing, informative and longest interview Dalglish ever gave me.'

Dalglish had come out of the Scott Symon school of communication skills. When Symon was manager of Rangers, a reporter telephoned him at Ibrox from the far side of Glasgow. 'It's foggy here,' said the reporter. 'What's it like at your end?'

'I never comment on the weather,' said Symon before putting down the receiver.

This was the Dalglish way of dealing with most reporters when he was playing, and quite often when he was manager. He seemed to want to guard his thoughts like a Scottish terrier with a bone. Often, all we got were growls. For reporters from my generation, brought up on the quote-boats pushed out by the likes of Bill Shankly and Tommy Docherty, it was difficult to fathom why 'King Kenny' did not want to share his views and opinions with we commoners.

Richard Keys, perceptive anchorman of the Sky football team, is one of the few media people to have got through the Dalglish defences. 'He is a wonderful, warm family man,' he reports. 'He does not suffer fools gladly, but when you get to know him and win his confidence there is no more loyal or trustworthy friend.'

In recent years Dalglish has allowed himself to become much more open with his opinions as a television match summariser whose knowledge of what he is watching makes him worth listening to, even if you have to strain to understand that still-thick accent. Perhaps he has taken lessons from his delightful daughter, Kelly, who as a TV presenter brightens our screens with a smile that has Dalglish written all over it. We used to see that smile a lot as Kenny beamed at his team-mates after banging in goals galore for Celtic, Scotland and Liverpool. But when we tried to get him to talk about his goals after the match the smile was replaced with a near-snarl. 'Nae comment,' he would say. 'Ye saw it. Ye describe it. I'm nae goin' tae do yer job for ye.'

For PR, you would have to give Kenny three or four points out of ten. As a player and, later, as a manager he gets maximum points.

His golden years were at Anfield, yet Bill Shankly always considered him 'the one that got away'.

He had a trial at Liverpool as a fifteen-year-old schoolboy in August 1966, playing for the 'B' team in a 1–0 victory against Southport reserves in the Lancashire League. Shanks had his mind focused on the upcoming season and took no notice when his training staff sent Dalglish home without signing him.

When Shanks saw Dalglish playing for Celtic a few seasons later he nearly blew a gasket as he realised Liverpool could have had him for nothing. It was eleven years after that trial that he finally arrived as a Liverpool player for a fee of £440,000, by which time Shankly had put himself out to grass.

Born in Dalmarnock in the East End of Glasgow on 4 March 1951, Kenneth Mathieson Dalglish was brought up in the docklands area of Govan, a goalkick distance from Ibrox where his favourite team, Rangers, were at home.

Like the great Hughie Gallacher before him, he started out as a goalkeeper, playing between the posts for his Milton Bank primary school team. It gives me the chance to repeat the line: a classic case of a goalkeeper turned poacher. By the time he was capped as a Scottish schoolboy international he had moved forward to right-half, scoring twice on his debut in a 4–3 victory over Northern Ireland Schoolboys.

His ambition was to play for Rangers, but they did not seem to realise he was on their doorstep. After failing to impress Liverpool, he then showed his wares at West Ham. Again, no interest. This was 1966, remember, the year of Moore-Hurst-Peters winning the World Cup for England. Imagine if you could have put a mature Dalglish alongside them. I confess here to having inherited claret-and-blue blood and the pictures I conjure in my mind of all four playing together for West Ham are stunning, but then like my dreams they fade and die.

So it was back to Glasgow for young Kenny, and the Protestant son of an engineer signed as a part-time professional for Jock Stein and the very Catholic Celtic. Assistant manager Sean Fallon clinched the deal, leaving his wife outside in the car while he popped into the Dalglish home. 'Just be a few minutes,' he said to his wife. Three hours later he returned with the Dalglish signature safely on a contract. His wife pointed out the little matter that it was their anniversary and he was supposed to be taking her out.

Between playing for Celtic's nursery side, Cumbernauld United, Dalglish worked as an apprentice joiner, which could explain why he later showed he knew all the angles on a football field.

A year later, with Celtic the newly crowned kings of Europe, he became a full-time professional and played in a Parkhead reserve team that became known as the Quality Street Gang. Just imagine walking casually into a ground to watch a reserve match to see performing in front of you players of the calibre of Dalglish, Lou Macari, Danny McGrain and Davie Hay.

Jock Stein was never one for shooting off his mouth, so we sat up and took notice when he said: 'I've got a couple of forwards who are going to become the talk of the game, Kenny Dalglish and Lou Macari. They're a bit special.'

I was in Aberdeen the night Tommy Docherty sent twenty-year-old Dalglish on for his international debut in a 1–0 European championship victory over Belgium. 'He will develop into one of the all-time greats, take my word for it,' The Doc said later as he celebrated the news that the win at Pittodrie had clinched his appointment as full-time manager of Scotland.

'I've got the job at just the right time,' said The Doc. 'It's years since we have been so rich in young talent. As well as Dalglish, I can call on players like Alan Hansen at Partick, Danny McGrain and Lou Macari at Celtic, and Martin Buchan at Aberdeen. The future's bright.'

What would Berti Vogts give for players of that calibre coming through?

Dalglish went on to win a record 102 caps and scored 30 goals, the same output from Denis Law in 55 matches for Scotland. In truth, Kenny was rarely as impressive for his country as his club. I rate him one of the greatest British club players I have seen in more than fifty years of football watching, but there are many I would put ahead of him on the international stage. Perhaps he needed the familiarity of club team-mates around him, but for whatever reason he struggled to find his club form for Scotland.

Anfield was plunged into mourning when Kevin Keegan decided to take the Deutschmark and transfer his talent to Hamburg in 1977. Little did the Liverpool fans realise that his replacement in the number 7 shirt, the modest, unassuming Dalglish, would prove himself the greatest player in the club's history (he continually comes out top in the polls despite support for the likes of Keegan, Ian St John, Billy Liddell, Roger Hunt, Ian Rush and Graeme Souness).

There is not a British player who can match Kenny's medals collection. Just look at what he achieved on top of his 102 caps for Scotland:

With CELTIC
League Championship: 1972, 1973, 1974, 1977
Scottish Cup Winners: 1972, 1974, 1975, 1977
Scottish League Cup: 1975
Goals output: 167

With LIVERPOOL
European Cup Winners: 1978, 1981, 1984
League Champions: 1979, 1980, 1982, 1983, 1984, 1986
League Cup Winners: 1981, 1982, 1983, 1984
FA Cup Winners: 1986
League goals output: 118

Footballer of the Year: 1979 and 1983
Player's Player award: 1983

Dalglish plundered his goals with the cold professionalism of an assassin gunning down a victim. The only player to have topped a century of goals in both the English and Scottish leagues, he had a great awareness of what was happening on the periphery around him, and I have seen no forward to match him as a shielder of a ball. He would frustrate defenders into committing themselves to a tackle, side-step them and then either dart for goal or bring a team-mate into play with a perfectly weighted pass. Kenny was an unselfish team player who was quite happy to share the goal glory with colleagues. His partnership with Ian Rush was a joy to behold, provided you were not the defenders trying to obstruct their double act. They seemed to have a telepathic understanding, and Kenny made dozens of goals for his Welsh sidekick. 'I knew that if Kenny was in possession and I ran into space, the ball would arrive just where and when I wanted it,' said Rush. 'There was nobody to touch him for making an accurate pass in a packed penalty area.'

Dalglish was appointed player-manager in the wake of the Heysel Stadium tragedy, and put the smile back on Liverpool faces by capturing the League championship and FA Cup double in his first season.

Kenny repeated the championship success in 1988 and 1990, making his final League appearance in May 1989. Bob Paisley reached down into his long memory and said: 'Of all the players I have played with, coached and managed in more than forty years at Anfield I have no hesitation in saying that Kenny is the most talented.'

Following the Hillsborough disaster, Dalglish was magnificent in the way he carried the city's grief on his shoulders. He worked tirelessly to try to ease the pain of survivors and the distressed relatives of those Liverpool fans who lost their lives so senselessly on the terraces of a tired football ground. Dalglish was dignity personified. He attended as many funerals as possible, read lessons, helped out with counselling and dug deep down into his very soul to try to bring solace to the bereaved.

Kenny never made an issue of the stress and strain he was under, but it must have taken its toll. He got his mind back on football and lifted the FA Cup after a 3–2 extra-time victory over Everton at Wembley. Liverpool were beaten to the League championship – and another double – in the last seconds of the 1988–89 season, when Michael Thomas scored an injury-time goal that clinched the title for Arsenal.

Liverpool regained the championship the following season, and were going for another hat-trick – following the treble of the early 1980s – when Dalglish astonished everybody by announcing that he was quitting. He was walking out with the club top of the table and locked in a fifth-round FA Cup saga with Everton that had ended 4–4 the day before Kenny decided to leave.

As we all guessed, Dalglish's health was suffering under the enormous pressure he had been under. He said that he was 'a person pushed to the limit' and admitted that on match days he felt as if his head was exploding.

He took eight months out of the game before making a shock reappearance as manager of Blackburn Rovers. Bankrolled by chairman Jack Walker, he led Rovers to promotion from the old Second Division in his first season, and captured the Premier League championship three years later. Kenny was only the fourth manager to win the championship with two different clubs – Tom Watson (Sunderland and Liverpool), Herbert Chapman (Huddersfield and Arsenal), and Brian Clough (Derby and Forest) were the others.

Dalglish then decided that the pressure at Ewood Park was too great, and took the less demanding role of director of football. In 1997 he followed Kevin Keegan as manager at Newcastle, an unhappy association that lasted only until the summer of the following year. He then returned to his roots at Celtic as director of football, but it was a less than successful comeback that ended with the sack, his disappointment cushioned by a pay-off of more than £600,000. He started the new millennium on the outside looking in at a game to which he had given so much.

Dalglish went through his playing career expressing himself the best way he knew how, with his feet. And the message was loud and clear: Kenny Dalglish was here. Few Scots have had such a deep and lasting influence on the English game. What a pity he did not want to tell us more about it.

Chapter Fourteen

Graeme Souness:
Sweetness and Sourness

When they were making the film *Braveheart*, the producers missed – right on Scotland's doorstep – an ideal person to play a leading warrior. I refer, of course, to Graeme Souness, who could have stepped into any of the gory-glory roles without requiring an acting lesson. He would simply needed to have played it the way he played his football. His tackling would have been enough to frighten the English invaders to death.

Of all the players featured in this book, I promise that Souness is the one you would least have wanted to face in a confrontation for a 50-50 ball. He had such a will to win that he gave the impression he would have kicked his own granny to come out on top.

Graeme, born in the tough Broomhouse district of Edinburgh on 6 May 1953, went to the same Carrickvale school that Dave Mackay had attended a generation earlier. They must have been hewn out of the identical lump of granite, because Souness had all the Mackay motivating mannerisms and liked to boss the pitch in the same intimidating way as his schoolboy idol.

His encyclopedic knowledge of all that Mackay achieved swayed him to join Tottenham at the age of fifteen when any of the Scottish clubs would willingly have opened their doors to him.

I gleaned earlier than most that Souness was not only a star in the making, but also a headstrong boy who knew his own mind. Jim Rodger, the sleuth of a reporter on the *Scottish Daily Express*, was so close to Tottenham manager Bill Nicholson that he knew all the Spurs secrets and kept most of them close to his chest, never sharing them with readers or colleagues. He earned a mutual trust with chairmen, managers and players that got him an ear in boardrooms and dressing-rooms throughout football.

Jim was a legend in Scotland, on nodding terms with prime ministers and princes as well as most of the people who mattered in football. He telephoned me in the Fleet Street office of the *Express* one day in 1970 and whispered, in the conspiratorial tone that he always used, 'Get over to the North London digs of Graeme Souness and talk him out of doing anything silly. Bill Nick thinks he's going to walk out on the club.'

'Graeme who?' I said. 'I wouldn't know what he looks like, let alone where he lives.'

'He's the hottest young prospect in the country,' Jim said in a scolding tone, and proceeded to give me Graeme's address. 'You'll be doing Bill Nick a big favour if you can tell him to just be patient and wait for his chance. He could not be with a better club. If you get him, put him on the phone to me. I'll talk some sense into him.'

That was how 'Rodger the Dodger' operated, working almost as a secret agent on behalf of managers across Britain and then being rewarded with some of the hottest exclusive stories in the game.

In those days I was more concerned with trying to dig out stories on first-team players at all the London clubs, and could not see the point of chasing after a youngster whose career had hardly started. But as I had so much respect for my Glasgow colleague, I drove to Graeme's digs, only to be told by his landlady that he had gone home to Scotland an hour earlier.

'What a waste of time,' I thought. 'As if anybody apart from Jim Rodger is going to be the slightest bit interested in this story.' Wrong!

It got to the point over the next few days when questions were asked in the House of Commons, as the story crossed from the back to the front pages. Graeme, then seventeen, had spent two years at Spurs as an apprentice who considered himself more of a sorcerer. He had gone back to Edinburgh because he said he felt homesick.

Tottenham reacted by suspending him without pay for two weeks. Graeme's local MP took up the case, and questioned in the House what right a football club had to deal with 'a minor' like this when his only 'crime' was to suffer from homesickness. 'Is homesickness something that should be punishable?' demanded the MP, managing to make Souness sound as hard done by as Oliver Twist. The story became the property of columnists with poison pens, and Bill Nicholson, fatherly manager of Tottenham, was unfairly pilloried. Souness, without having kicked a ball in senior football, was suddenly the best-known young player in the land.

The suspicion at Spurs was that their hot young property had been 'got at' and was being tempted away from Tottenham.

'I have never known such an ambitious and impatient young man,' an exasperated Nicholson told me. 'He has a wonderful future in the game, but he wants to run before he can walk. He can't understand why I'm not already considering him for the first-team. He wants to jump ahead of established professionals like Alan Mullery, Martin Peters and Steve Perryman. His chance will come, but he must show patience. If he's ever picked for Scotland I wonder if they will find a cap big enough for his head.'

A suitably repentant Souness returned to Tottenham, but he wore out the carpet to Bill Nicholson's office to the point where the veteran Spurs boss decided, reluctantly, he had no option but to let him go. He had made one brief first-team appearance in a UEFA Cup tie (substituting for Martin Peters in a match in Iceland) before being sold to Middlesbrough in December 1972 for £27,000, which was a hefty fee in those days for a virtually unknown and untried player.

Within five months of signing the young Scot, Middlesbrough manager Stan Anderson was replaced by Jack Charlton, who took an immediate shine to Souness. 'I could see straightaway that the lad had enormous potential, an opinion shared by Graeme!' said Jack, who was making his managerial debut. 'I felt that he was being played out of position as a left-sided midfielder or left-back, so I moved him to a central midfield position, and gave him more responsibility.'

Jack gave a hint that Souness was still hot to handle when he added, 'It took a lot of nagging before he would do what I wanted him to do. He liked to dwell on the ball and tended to be over-elaborate. I had to give him a few rockets before he got the point and started to make the sort of quick, positive passes that were right for the team. He had an arrogant streak in him, but that's no bad thing if you're going to try to dominate the midfield the way that he does.'

It was the Souness power and drive in midfield that played a prominent part in pushing Middlesbrough to the Second Division championship in 1973–74 by an extraordinary record margin of fifteen points.

His cap fitted perfectly when manager Willie Ormond picked him for his international debut against Bulgaria in 1974, and he went on to play 54 matches for Scotland and became an outstanding captain and leader. It was exactly what the supremely self-confident Souness expected of himself.

Kenny Dalglish, one of his regular Scotland team-mates, was impressed by the Souness competitive spirit on which you could warm your hands. He recommended him to Bob Paisley when he moved to Anfield, and within six months Graeme was performing a supporting role in midfield to Dalglish. Perhaps Kenny preferred the thought of playing with rather than against him! The fee of £352,000 was, at the time, a record deal between two English clubs. Liverpool money has rarely been better spent.

Souness had at last found the stage that he felt his talent deserved. He was an instant hit with the Anfield fans – and an instant hit on opponents, who could not believe how fiercely he tackled in Liverpool's cause. At the end of his first season Liverpool retained the European Cup, Dalglish's delicate chip beating Bruges at Wembley, with Souness and Alan Hansen helping to give the team a strong Scottish heartbeat.

With his Pancho Villa moustache and pugilistic nose, Souness looked every inch a gladiator, and he used to put the fear of God into any fancy-Dan opponent who was not prepared to risk life and limb to win the ball. Once he got it, Graeme knew exactly how to use it in the best interests of the side. He could find team-mates with perfectly placed passes, and also knew how to find the net with shots delivered, like his tackles, with vicious intent.

In seven success-soaked seasons at Liverpool, more than half of them as skipper, Souness won everything there was to win. The highlight came in 1984 when he led the Reds to the unique treble of League championship, Football League Cup and the European Cup.

Souness, whose motto could have been 'Go to work on an ego', now needed new challenges, and he spent two seasons with Sampdoria, steering them to the Italian Cup for the first time in their history. Then came a call to return home that he could not resist. He was wanted as player-manager at Rangers. It was a role that suited this born leader down to the Ibrox ground.

It was Souness more than any other person who changed the face of Scottish football for all time. He recognised that if Rangers wanted to be a global rather than just a domestic force, he would need to import players from outside Scotland. He brought in English international stars of the calibre of Mark Hateley, Chris Woods, Terry Butcher, Trevor Francis, Ray Wilkins, Mark Walters, Trevor Steven and Nigel Spackman. For more than a century English clubs had been plundering the cream of the Scottish players. Now the football boot was on the other foot.

He was treading all over tradition, and turned the faces of many Rangers fans green when he paid Nantes £1.5 million to bring in former Celtic striker Mo Johnston. He became the first prominent Catholic player to wear the blue shirt of Rangers in their 116-year history. It was an incredibly defiant – some said daft – thing to do. This proved beyond doubt that Rangers were now in an 'anything goes' period. As new chairman David Murray, who was bankrolling the exceptional enterprise, said: 'Graeme has turned the big ship around single-handed.'

Souness came out all guns blazing from the moment he stepped foot inside Ibrox, and he was so wound up that he managed to get himself sent off in his first game for Rangers. He was leading by example, his actions saying to his players, 'This is the sort of competitive spirit I want.'

The result of the revolution was astonishing. In his first season in charge, the swashbuckling Souness lifted the Scottish championship and the League Cup, beating Celtic 2–1 in the final. Two more championships followed, this time in successive seasons (1988–89 and 1989–90), and two more League Cup finals, with victories over Aberdeen in 1988–89 and Celtic in 1990–91.

Rangers were on the threshold of another championship in 1991 when Souness stunned the Ibrox faithful by agreeing to return to Anfield as successor in the manager's chair to his old team-mate Kenny Dalglish.

This should have been all sweetness for Souness, but it turned into the most sour experience of his career. He just could not get the players to function for him as he had at Rangers, and the Liverpool fans who had once worshipped the ground he tackled on turned on him in an ugly way following a gross misjudgement on his part.

Souness underwent a major heart operation, and the first most people knew of it was when his exclusive story was splashed on the front page of the *Sun*. At that time the *Sun* was poison on the lips of many Anfield supporters because of the way they had covered the Hillsborough tragedy. They would not forgive what they saw as an act of treachery.

He had 'only' the 1992 FA Cup to show for his three years in charge at Liverpool when he had a less than amicable parting with the club in January 1994.

Licking his wounds, Souness went on a whirlwind tour of the football map. He had a year in Turkey as manager of Galatasaray, and brief spells with Torino, Southampton and Benfica before planting his feet firmly at Blackburn Rovers.

He steered Blackburn back to the Premiership in his first season, and as I write he remains a powerful presence at Ewood Park. The sight of him prowling the touchline like a hungry lion, giving referees the angry eye, evokes memories of when he was bossing the pitch for Liverpool, Rangers and Scotland. There has rarely been a more dominant midfield player in the history of the game. Yes, he would have been perfect for that *Braveheart* role.

Chapter Fifteen

Sir Alex Ferguson:
The Guv'nor

It's fitting that we finish the first half of this journey through the history of Anglo-Scottish football with the man who has proved himself 'The Guv'nor' – Sir Alex Ferguson, who has achieved so much in club management either side of the border that I wonder what sort of job he could do running the country.

Mind you, they would have to keep the No. 10 crockery out of reach if there was any sort of crisis. Fergie is infamous for throwing tea-cups at players during half-time team talks, when he can blister walls with his tongue.

Politics held as much appeal as football for the young Ferguson. He was an apprentice toolmaker in the Govan shipyards, and as a firebrand trade union shop steward once led an unofficial walk-out over a pay dispute. Born in the Clydeside area of Glasgow on 31 December 1941, he has never forgotten his working-class roots and socialist principles despite becoming rich beyond his dreams.

A volcano always seems ready to erupt within Ferguson, who is outwardly an unassuming, amiable man with a strong loyalty to his family and to his club, Manchester United. 'Yes, I can and do explode on occasions,' he admits. 'It gets rid of all the enormous strain and tension. I say my piece, make my point and then quickly start to cool down. It's no good bottling things up when you are a manager. That's the quickest way to the cardiac ward.'

Fergie challenges even Bill Shankly as the worst loser football has known. He can rarely bring himself to be gracious in defeat, and his players fear the

'Ferguson Hairdryer' treatment if he feels they have let him and the team down. He stands close to any United player to whom he wants to make a point, and berates them with fire and brimstone that can dry hair from ten paces. David Beckham even got a boot in the eye after a home FA Cup defeat by Arsenal in February 2003. A loose boot kicked in fury by Fergie accidentally cut Becks above the eye. It was an incident that had newspapers turning to psychiatrists to consider if there was something wrong with the United boss. The diagnosis is simple. Ferguson HAS to be a winner. He is out of the Vince Lombardi school of sports psychology. The legendary American Football coach once claimed, 'Winning is not everything. It's the *only* thing.'

It was like this for Fergie from his earliest days as a player when his burning, all-consuming desire to win often dragged him into out-of-control confrontation with opponents and referees. He was like a John McEnroe of the football pitch.

Short-fuse Fergie managed to get himself sent off seven times during an explosive playing career in which he fell just short of international standard. He started playing at senior level with famous amateur side Queen's Park, and over the next fourteen years was a prolific goal-scorer during football travels with St Johnstone, Dunfermline, Rangers, Falkirk and Ayr United.

He was a galloping centre-forward who scored 35 goals in 67 games for Rangers, the club he supported as a boy. Fergie then dramatically quit Ibrox following an argument with the manager as to who was at fault for a Celtic goal in an Auld Firm derby. This was in 1969, when Celtic were the undisputed kings of Scottish football.

After his shock departure from Rangers, Alex had a valuable spell at Falkirk, where he mixed playing with the side of the game that attracted him the most: coaching. He had always had good tactical sense on the pitch, and now started to develop his overall understanding of the nuts and bolts of the game. Outside businesses, including interest in a pub, also started to take his attention as he concentrated on providing for his family.

He wound down his playing career with Ayr United, a single-season stay during which the succession of injuries he had collected with his barnstorming style of play caught up with him and forced his retirement at the age of 32.

Management was now the magnet, and following a debut season in charge at East Stirling in 1974–75, he switched to St Mirren. Showing signs of things to come, he took them into the Premier Division before getting the sack in 1978 following an angry dispute with the directors. The stories coming out of the Paisley club were mixed, one saying he had been fired following a row over players' bonuses (which would tie in with Fergie's past as a militant shop steward), and the other alleging that he had unleashed 'an unpardonable' swearing tirade in the hearing of a lady on the club premises. Alex can put his tongue to the shipyard language of his youth, but is noted for his gentlemanly manners when in the company of women. He lodged a claim for unfair dismissal.

Fergie was quickly snapped up by Aberdeen, who had not won a Scottish championship for more than twenty years. Over the next eight seasons he achieved the remarkable feat of interrupting the domination of Scottish football by Rangers and Celtic. Under his dynamic leadership, Aberdeen won three League championships, four Scottish Cups, one League Cup, and in 1983 – the one that really took the eye – the European Cup Winners' Cup. There was also icing on the cake that year with victory over Hamburg in the European Super Cup challenge match. 'They were unbelievable times,' recalls his skipper at Aberdeen, Gordon Strachan. 'Alex had this almost demonic will to win and managed to instil it into the team. He had us playing out of our skins.'

Aberdeen conquered mighty Real Madrid 2–1 in the Cup Winners' Cup final in Gothenburg, and suddenly Alex Ferguson was the name on the lips of many ambitious and powerful club chairmen looking for their next manager.

A queue of clubs tried to entice him away from Aberdeen, including Rangers, Arsenal, Aston Villa, Tottenham, Wolves and Spanish giants Barcelona. He turned down all approaches until Manchester United came calling in November 1986, just after he had finished a spell as part-time manager of Scotland following the death of Jock Stein.

'United are the only club I would consider leaving Aberdeen to join,' he said. 'I remember the late, great Jock Stein once telling me that the biggest mistake he ever made was turning down Manchester United. I am not about to make the same mistake.'

The United side that Fergie inherited from Ron Atkinson was not just a slumbering giant. It was in a coma. They had won only one of nine League games, and were living in the shadow thrown by ghosts of a great past that seemed to be haunting and taunting them. The League championship trophy had not been in the Old Trafford cabinet since back in the Busby glory days of 1967.

Like a procession of his predecessors, Ferguson struggled to meet the Busby standards. He battled for three years to make any sort of impressive impact at Old Trafford, and it looked to all we media vultures swooping and snooping on the sidelines as if it was going to be too big a job for him. I was ghosting a Jimmy Greaves column for the *Sun* at the time and clearly remember putting the words into Greavsie's mouth: 'How much longer can United afford to have Ferguson wasting their money?' In fact, he came within one match of being shown the door.

'Fergie out!' chanted the Reds fans at Maine Road when United were flattened 5–1 by neighbours Manchester City. The following week they lost at home to Crystal Palace, and you could almost hear the knives being sharpened in the Old Trafford boardroom.

The decisive make-or-break game came in the third round of the FA Cup at Nottingham Forest on 6 January 1990, a day heavy with sadness for Alex because his mother had just died.

United scrambled a 1–0 win at Forest, and it was a victory that turned their season – and Fergie's fortunes – right around. They went on to win the FA Cup and start a sequence of startling success that put even Sir Matt Busby's great achievements in the shade.

As I write, the United trophy haul under Ferguson is eight English Premiership titles, four FA Cups, one League Cup, the European Cup Winners' Cup, and the top prize, the European Cup, that came as the last leg of an extraordinary treble in 1998–99 along with the League championship and FA Cup. In the autumn of 2002 the doom-and-gloom merchants were predicting that United – and Fergie – were past their sell-by date, as they slipped towards the middle of the table miles behind runaway leaders Arsenal. By the end of the season United had captured the Premiership title yet again, and the legend of Alexander the Great was stronger than ever.

What has delighted Fergie most of all was that first championship victory in 1992–93 because the man he so admired, Sir Matt Busby, was still alive to see United win the title after a barren spell of 26 years. 'This is the greatest present we could have given Sir Matt,' Alex said. 'He has been a source of inspiration to me ever since I came into football, and he has continually supported me during some uncomfortable times here at Old Trafford.'

Sir Matt said: 'Alex Ferguson is a great manager now and is going to get even better. Winning the championship will give him the confidence to go on to bigger and better things. The future of Manchester United could not be in better hands.'

Like Sir Matt, he was rewarded for his triumph in Europe with a knighthood. And, like Sir Matt, Ferguson has put his faith at the feet of flair players. Eric Cantona came from Leeds to light the fire of the team that won the inaugural Premiership title in 1992–93. Fergie was one of the few managers who could control the fiery, temperamental Frenchman, perhaps because he saw in him a kindred spirit. When Cantona had the world falling about his ears after he had infamously kung-fu kicked a Crystal Palace fan, Alex supported him all the way through his crisis and talked him into not quitting the game. I know of other managers who, given the same circumstances, would have turned their backs on Cantona.

There is a stubborn and ruthless side to Ferguson. Ask any of the eight players he sacked in just one day at St Mirren. There has also been plenty of evidence at United that he never lets sentiment blind him. For instance, he had no hesitation in moving out two of the players who had served him so well both at Aberdeen and then United, goalkeeper Jim Leighton and Gordon Strachan, when they were showing signs of being past their best. Mark Hughes and Paul Ince, both favourites with the United crowd, were sold when they might have expected several more seasons at Old Trafford. Dutchman Jaap Stam was on his bike within weeks of mildly criticising Fergie in an autobiography. And the silence from Sir Alex was deafening when he stood back and allowed David Beckham's transfer to Real Madrid to go ahead in the summer of 2003.

Bryan Robson, his early captain at Old Trafford, said: 'No matter who you are, your place is not guaranteed at United. There is hardly a player who has not at some time experienced being dropped by Alex. It keeps everybody on their toes. He is The Boss.'

Ferguson is a master at winding up rival managers in what he sees as ongoing psychological warfare. Kevin Keegan and Arsene Wenger are just two who have had unsettling experience of the Fergie mind games. He is a master at manipulating the media to put across his message, and he blatantly used television cameras to force the football authorities to take more care over the timing of matches. The sight of Ferguson standing on the touchline with stopwatch in hand used to be a regular cut-away shot for television directors as he virtually intimidated referees into blowing the final whistle when it suited him. He more than anybody was responsible for the introduction of the sensible and satisfying 'time left' ruling.

There are those who consider Ferguson a bully of a boss, but regardless of what anybody thinks of his methods no one can dispute that he is one of the most successful managers of all time. Critics who say that it is the United chequebook that has made him so all-conquering should remember that he had phenomenal success at Aberdeen on a shoestring budget.

He has bought boldly and brilliantly – Peter Schmeichel, Roy Keane, Ruud van Nistelrooy, Fabien Barthez, Juan Sebastian Veron, Ole Gunnar Solskjaer, Dwight Yorke, Andy Cole, Teddy Sheringham and Laurent Blanc to name just a few. All English football followers (plus Sven Goran Eriksson) should be grateful that he has also insisted on keeping the famous United conveyor belt of youth footballers going, a system that has produced the likes of David Beckham, Ryan Giggs, Paul Scholes, the Neville brothers, Nicky Butt and Wes Brown.

He counts as his biggest blessing – over and above anything he has achieved at Old Trafford – a close-knit family, with his wife, Cathy, as his number one supporter, closely followed by three sons, two of them twins. The values he treasures are loyalty and commitment. He has never given anything less than one hundred per cent to United, and will not tolerate anybody else failing to put in the same effort. His experiences in the Clydeside shipyards fashioned him into a strong-minded, determined and demanding character, and these are the qualities he tries to pass on to his players.

Boyish-looking even in his sixties, wine connoisseur Alex has the red-faced complexion that suggests he has just taken a brisk walk on the Scottish moors. But his youthful looks are misleading. He has always had a head on his shoulders way in advance of his years.

There were genuine fears that Fergie would send his blood pressure through the roof with his touchline tantrums, and he was advised to find something away from football that would help him switch off. He chose to learn to play the piano, and music has gone some way to soothing the savage beast.

I think the nearest the public get to see the real Alex Ferguson is when he is at the races, relaxed and away from the enormous pressures of football management. Part-owner of the fabulous, record-setting racehorse Rock of Gibraltar, he lights up the parade ring and the winners' enclosure with the sunshine of his smile. When he returns to the world of football he is often dour and about as sunny as a wet weekend in Manchester.

But the succession of teams he has assembled have never ever been dour, and each side seems to improve on the previous combination. His teams bring the sunshine streaming down on Manchester, where he has created one of the greatest football clubs in the world on the foundation built by fellow Scot Sir Matt Busby.

When Sir Alex finally abdicates at Old Trafford, he is going to throw an even bigger shadow over his successors than Busby did with his achievements. It is going to take a big man to be able to follow The Guv'nor. Spoken with a strong Glaswegian accent, the phrase 'Follow that, Jimmy!' comes to mind.

PART TWO

The Who's Who
Player Profiles

Here, collated in one volume for the first time, are Who's Who profiles of every post-war Scottish international footballer capped while playing for an English club. I have also slipped in several who did not get the caps that they deserved, and also many who won their international honours while playing in their homeland.

For no other reason than pure entertainment, I have introduced a star-rating system that sums up the impact they made or are making on the English game:

☆	Moderate
☆☆	Average
☆☆☆	Memorable
☆☆☆☆	Inspirational
☆☆☆☆☆	Exceptional

The quotes accompanying many of the entries are from my personal files or taken from archival sources, and I thank the British Library staff at Collindale for their efficiency and cooperation.

I have listed the players in A to Z order, or – more accurately – from Aird to Younger. My apologies if I have missed anybody. Should you know of any omissions, please let me know by sending an e-mail from my website at www.macsoccer.co.uk or by writing to Norman Giller at McFOOTBALL, PO Box 3386, Ferndown, Dorset BH22 8XT.

Or perhaps there is an uncapped Anglo-Scottish player you think merits a mention. Let me know, and I will at least give him the credit he deserves on the website. Thank you. And now, eyes down for a Mcfeast of footballers.

The Pioneers: William McGregor, founder of the Football League (top left) and Lord Kinnaird (top right), an early driving force behind the Football Association and winner of nine FA Cup final medals. The Master: Hughie Gallacher (left), who got everything right on the pitch and many things wrong off-pitch. He was the Cursed Genius.

(© popperfoto.com)

*Alex James (below), the Emperor in Baggy
Shorts. Matt Busby, the player (right) and
Sir Matt Busby, the manager (below right).
In the 1930s he played with distinction for
Manchester City, Liverpool and Scotland.
As manager at Old Trafford from 1946,
he laid the foundations for Manchester
United to become one of the greatest clubs
in the world. Sir Matt, knighted after United's
1968 European Cup victory, survived the
Munich air crash in which eight of his
'Busby Babes' perished in 1958.*

(© popperfoto.com)

Bill Shankly, the player (left) and Shanks, the 'Man of the People' manager (below). He was a driving right-half for Preston and Scotland before starting a memorable managing career that came to its glorious peak at Anfield. Shanks took over as manager of Liverpool in December 1959, guided them up from the Second Division and laid the foundations for the great team, which was led to European Cup triumphs by Bob Paisley.

(© popperfoto.com)

Tommy Docherty (above) was never one to hide his feelings on the touchline. This portrait in passion was taken while he was in charge at Chelsea, where he was rarely out of the headlines. He famously said that he 'had more clubs than Jack Nicklaus' during a roller-coaster career when he was a constant companion of controversy.

(© popperfoto.com)

Jock Stein (opposite) was widely considered by his footballing contemporaries to have been the master manager. He performed miracles in shaping Celtic into the first British club to win the European Cup with a team of players born within a 30-mile radius of Glasgow. His experience as a manager in English football lasted just 44 days at Leeds before he returned to Scotland as manager of the national team. He died of a heart attack after collapsing on the touch line at the climax of a World Cup qualifying tie.

(© popperfoto.com)

Dave 'the Miracle Man' Mackay shows off his Footballer of the Year award in 1969 (right). He came back from twice breaking his leg to lead Derby to the First Division as a central defender after marauding in midfield for Spurs and Scotland.

(© popperfoto.com)

Denis 'the Executioner' Law scores against fellow Scot Bill Brown (below) for Manchester United against the Super Spurs side of the 1960s. He comes onto the pitch with United (opposite) with his sleeve cuffs characteristically down to his palms. This was one of his stylish trademarks.

(© popperfoto.com)

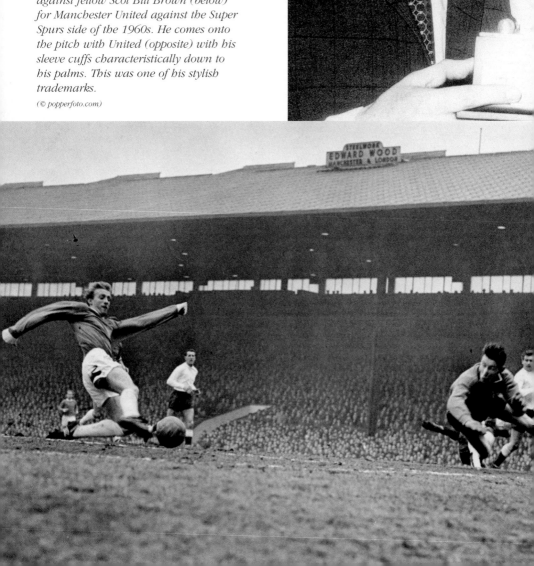

Liverpool started League life
with TEN Scots in the team and
have always had a rich Scottish
tradition. Kenny Dalglish
(below) has been among the
greatest Anglo Scots to wear
the Anfield Red and managed the
club with enormous success.

(© popperfoto.com)

Graeme Souness (left) also managed Liverpool, although with less satisfactory results after returning to Anfield from Rangers.

(© popperfoto.com)

John Wark (opposite) was yet another Scottish force at Anfield, but is best remembered for his wonderful service to Ipswich Town. He had three spells with the East Anglian club and scored more than 200 League and Cup goals, an astonishing contribution from a midfield player.

(© popperfoto.com)

In the early days of Bill Shankly Ian St John (below) was one of the most popular Scottish heroes at Anfield. This is his famous extra-time goal that brought Liverpool the FA Cup in the 1965 final against Leeds. Fellow Scots in that Liverpool squad included skipper Ron Yeats, goalkeeper Tommy Lawrence and anchorman Willie Stevenson.

(© popperfoto.com)

Charlie 'Chuckle Boots' Cooke (above) was the Great Entertainer for Chelsea at Stamford Bridge after moving to London from Dundee in 1966. Here he is trying to find a way through the formidable Leeds defence and barring his way is one of the most competitive Scottish players to come south of the border – Leeds skipper Billy Bremner (opposite). Among the many trophies Billy lifted was the FA Cup after the 1972 Centenary Final against Arsenal at Wembley.

(© popperfoto.com)

Eddie McCreadie (left) was one of Scotland's finest left-backs, who played for Chelsea and then managed them before a fall-out over a new contract after he had guided the club back to the First Division.

(© popperfoto.com)

John 'The Ghost of White Hart Lane' White (left) and 'Slim Jim' Baxter (below left) were two master midfield players who brought their magical skills to the English stage. John, whose passes made the Tottenham double team tick, was tragically killed in 1964 at the age of 27 when hit by a streak of lightning while sheltering under a tree during a lone game of golf. Jim, the Idol of Ibrox, died in April 2002 aged 61 after many years of heavy drinking. Both will live on in the land of footballing legend.

(© popperfoto.com)

The Thinkers: Alex Ferguson (above left) and George Graham brought their Scottish flair for soccer strategy to management in England and between them mopped up all the major domestic and European trophies.

(© popperfoto.com)

Charlie Nicholas (left) was loved by the Arsenal fans, but his reluctance to adapt his individual flair to the team discipline demanded by George Graham signalled a return to the Scottish stage, where he was lauded as one of the most exciting and enterprising of entertainers.

(© popperfoto.com)

Three players who carved out successful careers after retirement from football: Liverpool skipper Alan Hansen (above left) lifts the FA Cup at Wembley in 1986 after victory over Everton in the final. Alan followed Bob Wilson (above right) into the world of television sports broadcasting. Wilson was the first modern English-born player to be capped by Scotland under the family ancestry ruling. He was a magnificent last line of defence for the double-winning Arsenal team of 1970–1. Martin Buchan (opposite) holds aloft the Second Division championship trophy after leading Manchester United back to the top table in 1975. He later became a high-powered sports company representative.

(© popperfoto.com)

Gary McAllister (above left) and
Gordon Strachan (above right) were
the twin engines who drove Leeds
United to the League Championship
in 1991–2. Both have since gone
into management in England. It
was the competitive zeal as well as
the skill that made Scottish players
such a magnet for English clubs, as
illustrated below by Scottish internationals Eddie McCreadie (Chelsea)
and Jimmy Robertson (Tottenham).

(© popperfoto.com)

John (Jock) AIRD ☆☆
Born: Glencraig, Fife, 18 February 1926
English club: Burnley
Position: Full-back
Caps won while in England: 4 (of 4)

Jock Aird joined Burnley from Scottish junior club Jeanfield Swifts in the summer of 1948, and played 132 League games for the Lancashire club. A solid and thoughtful left-back, his tackling was strong and decisive in an era when wingers were in full flight. He was in Scotland's squad for the 1954 World Cup finals, and was unfortunate enough to play in the 7–0 thrashing by world champions Uruguay in Switzerland. It was his fourth and final cap. He later emigrated to New Zealand, where he played in two internationals for the Kiwis against Australia before settling down in Sydney.
QUOTE: 'The game against Uruguay was a total nightmare. The temperature was in the nineties and Uruguay played us off the park. Tommy Docherty said at the final whistle, "This is the first time I've come off a pitch with a sunburned tongue!"'

Charlie AITKEN ☆☆☆
Born: Edinburgh, 1 May 1942
English club: Aston Villa
Position: Defender
No full caps

Signed from Edinburgh Thistle in 1959, Charlie Aitken gave magnificent service to Aston Villa over the next fifteen years, including a Villa record 656 first-team appearances. He was a key man in helping Villa climb from the Third Division back to the First. A sporting and often jovial competitor, he charmed everybody but the Scottish selectors, who rewarded him with just three Under-23 caps. He was a specialist left-back but served Villa in several defensive positions before finishing his career in the United States with New York Cosmos. Later, he ran a jewellery and antiques business in Birmingham.
QUOTE: 'I would have given anything to play for my country, but much of my time was spent outside the First Division and so it was difficult to take the eye. I gave my all for Villa and if you were to cut me open you'd find claret-and-blue blood!'

George AITKEN ☆☆☆
Born: Lochgelly, 28 May 1925
English clubs: Sunderland and Gateshead
Position: Midfield
Caps won while in England: 3 (of 8)

George Aitken was a Roker Park favourite in the 1950s, playing a support role to the Clown Prince Len Shackleton from a midfield base, providing accurate passes after winning the ball with tackles that could be ferocious. He joined Sunderland from Third Lanark, but first made an impact with his local club East Fife, where he gained five of his Scottish caps. At Roker, he linked up with his old East Fife team-mate, Charlie Fleming. His final cap, won while with Sunderland in 1954, was a 4–2 defeat at Hampden in a match in which a top-form Tom Finney ran the Scottish defence into ever-decreasing circles. It was the only time he was on a losing side in his eight internationals. George played 245 League matches for Sunderland before making 58 appearances for Gateshead in their final two seasons in the Football League.

Roy AITKEN ☆☆
Born: Irvine, 24 November 1958
English club: Newcastle United
Position: Midfield
Caps won while in England: 6 (of 57)

Roy Aitken gave blood, sweat and tears for Celtic for fifteen seasons before joining Newcastle when his best was behind him. He was a magnificent midfield marauder for Celtic, skippering the team and driving them on through 483 League games. It turned sour for him in his last season at Celtic, but that should not be allowed to diminish the impact of the service he had given the club since making his first-team debut at the age of seventeen. He played just 54 League games for Newcastle when Jim Smith was in charge, and the discerning Geordie fans must have wondered what might have been had he joined them at his peak. A

six-footer, he used to make his presence felt in midfield with powerful performances that lifted the players around him. He won 50 of his Scottish caps while at Parkhead, and collected his final one during a brief spell with St Mirren. Roy became a respected coach, managed Aberdeen, and then joined the Leeds United staff, where his great knowledge of the game helped shape many of the young Elland Road stars-in-the-making.

Arthur ALBISTON ☆☆☆
Born: Edinburgh, 14 July 1957
English clubs: Man United, West Brom, Chesterfield, Chester
Position: Left-back
Caps won while in England: 14 (of 14)

Few players have made as dramatic an FA Cup debut as Arthur Albiston. It was against Liverpool in the 1977 Final at Wembley, taking over at left-back from injured Stewart Houston. Tommy Docherty's United won the Cup, and when Dave Sexton arrived as the new manager Arthur was retained in defence. He played under five different managers in a time of turmoil at Old Trafford, and after fourteen seasons and 379 League appearances he was allowed by Alex Ferguson to join West Brom on a free transfer. A strong and stylish full-back, Arthur later had a string of clubs including Chesterfield, Chester, Molde in Norway and Ayr United. He did the rounds of non-League clubs and appeared as player-manager of Droylesden. His greatest memories are of playing in four FA Cup finals for United, collecting three winners' medals. He is a frequent coach at United's Under-15s School of Excellence.

QUOTE: 'I could not believe it when United declined to take part in the FA Cup to concentrate on the World Club championship. It was the FA Cup that gave me the biggest buzz of all, particularly the finals at Wembley.'

Graham ALEXANDER ☆☆☆

Born: Coventry, 10 October 1971
English clubs: Scunthorpe, Luton, Preston
Position: Defender
Caps won while in England: 13 (of 13)

English-born Graham Alexander has qualified for Scotland under the heritage rule. He is a utility defender, equally at home in midfield as a ball winner or operating at full-back. He kicked off his career with Scunthorpe, where a team-mate was another future Scotland defender, Matt Elliott. Graham joined Luton and after 153 League games moved on to Preston, where his consistent performances attracted the attention of Berti Vogts. Preston paid just £50,000 for him in 1999, and he has proved a bargain buy for the Deepdale club. He has a steadying influence on the defence, and is a dead-eye marksman from the penalty spot.

John ANDERSON ☆☆

Born: Neilston, 8 December 1929
English club: Leicester City
Position: Goalkeeper
Caps won while in England: 1 (of 1)

John Anderson was the Leicester City goalkeeper who made way for a young Yorkshireman called Gordon Banks. He was capped once by Scotland, a 2–1 victory against Finland in Helsinki in 1954. John joined Leicester from Arthurlie in December 1948, and over the next ten seasons made 261 League appearances. A lack of inches – he stood just over 5ft 9in – prevented him from making more of an impact, but he had quick reflexes and was noted for his shot stopping and courage in an era when goalkeepers were sitting targets for shoulder-charging forwards.

Steve ARCHIBALD ☆☆☆☆

Born: Glasgow, 27 September 1956
English clubs: Tottenham, Blackburn, Reading, Fulham
Position: Striker
Caps won while in England: 22 (of 27)

A former Rolls-Royce mechanic, Steve Archibald started his career with Clyde but it was at Aberdeen that he established himself as a player with a natural instinct for scoring goals. He helped Alex Ferguson's Dons win the Scottish League championship before joining Tottenham in May 1980 for an

£800,000 fee that was then a record between English and Scottish clubs. He immediately formed a prolific goal-scoring partnership with Garth Crooks, who had signed for Spurs the previous month. In his first season at White Hart Lane, he hit a total of 25 League and Cup goals and collected an FA Cup winners' medal in the 3–2 FA Cup final replay victory over Manchester City. Jock Stein gave Archie his international debut in May 1980, a 1–0 win over Northern Ireland at Windsor Park. It was his first of 27 caps. The blond, quicksilver striker helped Spurs win the 1984 UEFA Cup and he finished with 78 goals in 189 appearances before moving to Barcelona following a long-running dispute with manager Keith Burkinshaw. The fee was £1.15 million. He had five productive seasons in Spain before briefly playing with Blackburn, Reading, St Mirren and Fulham. He then went into management with East Fife, and later got himself embroiled in controversy over his attempted owner-ship of Airdrieonians. It turned into a financial disaster and his company came in for heavy criticism from liquidators.

Bertie AULD ☆☆☆

Born: Glasgow, 23 March 1938
English club: Birmingham City
Position: Midfield
Caps won while in England: 0 (of 3)

Bertie Auld kicked off his career with Celtic but got fed up with manager Jimmy McGrory continually chopping and changing the team, and so he agreed to a move to Birmingham City in 1961. He established himself as a winger with the Blues in 126 League games before Jock Stein brought him back to Parkhead to team up with Bobby Murdoch as midfield partners in a 4–2–4 formation. They gave Celtic drive and direction, and the all-conquering team reached its peak with the European Cup victory in Lisbon in 1967. Bertie later played for and managed Hibernian, and also took charge at Partick and Dumbarton. He then became a Glasgow publican.

QUOTE: 'I was all set to go to Everton with Bobby Collins in 1958, but I pulled out at the last minute. I enjoyed my stay with Birmingham, but I wouldn't have missed all that happened to me at Celtic for the world.'

Jim BAXTER ☆☆☆☆☆

Born: Hill O'Beath, 29 September 1939
English clubs: Sunderland,
Nottingham Forest
Position: Midfield
Caps won while in England: 10 (of 34)

Slim Jim Baxter gets a five-star rating not because of what he achieved with English clubs, but because of what he achieved *against* England. Anybody who witnessed his stunning performances in the Home Championship matches of 1963 and 1967 will agree they were watching a genius of a footballer at work. Both games were at

Wembley, the first while the Scots were still in the shadow of a 9–3 defeat by the Auld Enemy, and the second following England's 1966 World Cup triumph that left most Scots totally underwhelmed. In the 1963 match Scotland were reduced to ten men when skipper and left-back Eric Caldow was stretchered off with a broken leg, which made Baxter try that much harder. He cleverly and completely ran the game from his midfield command post, scoring both Scotland's goals in a 2–1 victory and swaggering off at the end with the ball famously stuck up his jersey. He had owned the match, so it was only right that the ball should also belong to him. Four years later he teased and tormented the new World Cup holders, taking the mickey with the full range of his tricks as he steered the Scots to a 3–2 victory that had their supporters claiming they were the true world champions – ignoring the fact that England were reduced to nine fit men! Born in the Fife mining village of Hill O'Beath, Jim combined his early playing career at Raith Rovers with working down the pits. It was when he moved to Rangers in 1960 that the football world sat up and took notice of his mesmerising ball control and passing skills. In the first of two spells at Ibrox he won three championship, three Scottish Cup and four League Cup winners' medals. He suffered a broken leg in a European Cup tie against Rapid Vienna in December 1964, and was never quite the same force again. Jim moved into English football, first with Sunderland and then Nottingham Forest, but he was a shadow of the great player who had dominated the Scottish stage. Sadly, he became more noted for his playboy activity off the pitch rather than his performances on it. Rangers took him back after what were virtually three lost years in England, but the magic had gone and he hung up his 'talking boots' in 1970 after bringing his League appearances total for Rangers to 254 games and 24 goals. What the record book does not show is how many goals he made with passes that were delivered with perfect precision. Jim played his football with a smile on his face, and with an arrogance that could be irritating to the opposition but irresistible for the lucky spectators. He ran a pub at the end of his career, which was the worst possible environment for a man who could never say no to a pint or three. His heavy drinking lifestyle led to two transplants in the 1990s, and he finally succumbed to cancer on Saturday 14 April 2001. It had been April Saturdays when he had made April fools of England in the summertime of his unforgettable career. Of all the players featured in this Who's Who of Anglo-Scots few, if any, could match his skill.

QUOTE: 'I loved every second of playing the game, and liked to think of myself as an entertainer. What pleased me so much about those victories over England at Wembley was that we did it in such style. My mate Jimmy Greaves played in both games, and it gave me great delight to tease and taunt him for years afterwards. It stopped him stuffing that bloody 9–3 result down our throats . . . well, almost!'

Andy BEATTIE ☆☆☆☆
Born: Aberdeen, 11 August 1913
English club: Preston
Position: Full-back
Caps won while in England: 7 (pre-war)

The distinguished playing career of Andy Beattie straddled the Second World War that took away his peak years. He guested for both Nottingham Forest and Notts County during the war, when he showed Midlands supporters that he was a skilful and strong left-back who always used the ball intelligently out of defence. His best years were in the 1930s with Preston when he was a team-mate at both club and country level of Bill Shankly, collecting an FA Cup winners' medal in 1938. Bobby Beattie, his namesake signed from Kilmarnock and an international forward, was also in the Preston team that won the Cup. Like Shanks, Andy Beattie went into management. He travelled the football roundabout with Barrow, Stockport, Huddersfield, Carlisle, Nottingham Forest (notably), Plymouth Argyle, Wolves, Notts County and Sheffield United, before becoming a scout and consultant to a string of clubs. He had two spells in charge of the Scottish international team, famously quitting the job after just two matches in the 1954 World Cup finals after a dispute with the selectors. Andy died in

1983, aged 70, and the football world mourned the loss of a man who had given his life to the game.

Willie BELL ☆☆☆
Born: Johnstone, 3 September 1937
English clubs: Leeds, Leicester, Brighton
Position: Left-back
Caps won while in England: 2 (of 2)

Willie Bell was a Scottish amateur international midfield player when he joined Leeds from Queen's Park in 1960. Manager Don Revie switched him to left-back, and he was a key man in defence at the start of the climb from the depths of the Third Division towards the top of the First. He played 261 games for Leeds before losing his number 3 shirt to England international Terry Cooper. Leicester City and then Brighton took advantage of his hard tackling and neat, left-footed distribution before he switched to coaching at Birmingham City, where his old Leeds team-mate Freddie Goodwin was in charge. He had a two-year spell as manager at St Andrews and then moved into the Lincoln hot seat. A deeply religious man, Bell took the soccer gospel across the Atlantic to the United States, where he became coach at the Baptist Liberty University in Virginia. Willie, a modest and unassuming man, returned at the start of the new millennium to Yorkshire, where he is warmly remembered by Leeds fans for his total commitment to every game.

Paul BERNARD ☆☆

Born: Edinburgh, 30 December 1972
English clubs: Oldham Athletic,
Plymouth
Position: Midfield
Caps won while in England: 2 (of 2)

After starting out at Oldham on the youth training scheme, Paul Bernard established himself in the Oldham midfield to such an extent that he earned himself two full caps to go with his fifteen Under-23 appearances. Aberdeen were so impressed that they paid a club record £1 million to take him to Pittodrie in 1995. His career was threatened in 2000 by a serious Achilles injury, and it was thought he would never play again. But, showing the character that has always shone through in his performances on the pitch, he battled back to prove medical opinion wrong. He failed to convince Barnsley that he was worthy of a first-team place but then got himself a contract with Plymouth Argyle, and started to rebuild his career at Home Park.

Ian BLACK ☆☆☆

Born: Aberdeen, 27 March 1924
English clubs: Southampton, Fulham
Position: Goalkeeper
Caps won while in England: 1 (of 1)

Playing for Southampton in the Second Division, Ian Black was the surprise Scottish selection as goalkeeper for the Home Championship match against England at Hampden Park in 1948. Just his luck that he came up against Tom Finney at his tantalising best. The Preston Plumber beat him with a scorching shot for England's first goal, and then Stan Mortensen silenced the Hampden Roar from the 135,376 spectators as he deftly made it 2–0 to virtually end Black's international career almost before it had started. He was never invited back by the selectors. Two years later, after 97 League games for Southampton, he joined Fulham and even managed to get on the Craven Cottage scoresheet during seven seasons with the London club before losing his first-team place to Tony Macedo.

Adam BLACKLAW ☆☆☆☆

Born: Aberdeen, 2 September 1937
English clubs: Burnley, Blackburn,
Blackpool
Position: Goalkeeper
Caps won while in England: 3 (of 3)

Agile and brave, Adam Blacklaw was the defiant last line of defence in Burnley's brilliant League championship-winning team of 1959–60. He had to play in the shadow of England's exceptional goalkeeper Colin McDonald when he first arrived at Turf Moor as a junior in 1954, but following a serious injury to McDonald he seized his chance and became the regular goalkeeper whose ability deserved many more than the three Scottish caps he was awarded. The son of a ship's carpenter, Adam played for Aberdeen Schools as a centre-forward. This was a case of the poacher turning goalkeeper. Burnley beat a queue of clubs for his signature after he had starred between the posts for Scottish schoolboys against England at Filbert Street. His consistency and commitment was such that he missed just three games over five seasons when Burnley were challenging for everything in sight. To this day, Adam is haunted by a bizarre last-minute incident at Anfield in February 1963 in an FA Cup fourth-round replay against Bill Shankly's Liverpool. With the match deadlocked at 1–1 and seconds away from a second replay, Adam miskicked a clearance against the back of Ian St John, who was moving out of the penalty area. The Saint turned and as he shaped to shoot, Adam brought his fellow Scot down. Ronnie Moran scored from the spot-kick to put Burnley out of the Cup. In the summer of 1967, Adam joined Blackburn, and after three seasons at Ewood Park moved on to Blackpool for a brief spell. He played non-League football for several years and was then appointed Burnley Cricket Club steward in 1980 for the start of a long period in the licensing business. A Burnley Legends bar is named after him at Turf Moor.

QUOTE: 'I had wonderful times at Turf Moor. The best moments were, of course, winning the championship. It was a sheer joy to play behind such wonderful footballers as Jimmy McIlroy and Jimmy Adamson. What a team we

had. The low point was when I gave away the last-minute penalty at Anfield. The final whistle went just moments after I had been beaten by the spot-kick. Even years later, it still hurts!'

James BLAIR ☆

Born: Glasgow, 6 January 1918
English clubs: Blackpool, Bournemouth, Leyton Orient
Position: Inside-forward
Caps won while in England: 1 (of 1)

Starting his career as an amateur with Cardiff City, thoughtful and constructive inside-forward Jim Blair joined Blackpool in the summer of 1935 and it was when he returned to Bloomfield Road after the war that he won his only cap against Wales in 1947. A 2–1 defeat at Hampden meant that he was quickly discarded by the Scottish selectors. He moved to Bournemouth six months after his international experience, and then two years later went on to Leyton Orient, where he scored 26 goals in 104 League matches.

Jim BLYTH ☆☆

Born: Perth, 2 February 1955
English clubs: Preston, Coventry, Hereford, Birmingham
Position: Goalkeeper
Caps won while in England: 2 (of 2)

Brave Jim Blyth had to overcome the handicap of two broken legs before he established himself in the Coventry first-team. He joined the Sky Blues from Preston at the age of seventeen for £22,000 after playing just one League game for the Deepdale club. He took over from Bill Glazier as regular Coventry goalkeeper in 1975, and after winning two Scottish international caps Manchester United came calling. A deal of £440,000 had been agreed in 1978 but Blyth failed a medical on a back problem that plagued him for the rest of his career. He had a loan spell with Hereford and then played fourteen matches for Birmingham City before becoming a respected goalkeeping coach.

Jim BONE ☆

Born: Bridge of Allan, 22 September 1949
English clubs: Norwich City, Sheffield United
Position: Striker
Caps won while in England: 2 (of 2)

Like a light-fingered pickpocket in the penalty area, Jim Bone had the ability of a natural goal-scorer, but it was a lack of consistency that prevented him reaching his full rich potential. He played 39 League games for Norwich after joining the Canaries from Patrick Thistle, and then 30 matches for Sheffield United. He had been a part-timer with Partick while completing his apprenticeship as a coal-mine electrician. But he returned to his homeland as a full-time professional in 1973, playing for Celtic, Hearts and Arbroath before becoming a globe-trotter. His overseas clubs included Toronto Blizzard and Hong Kong Rangers. He had a productive period as skipper of St Mirren, and returned there in 1987 as assistant manager to Alex Smith. Bone had a headline-hitting disagreement with Frank McGarvey, and left the Saints to manage Airdrieonians and Zambian club FC Dynamo. He returned to St Mirren as manager in 1992 but failed in his efforts to steer them to the Premier division.

Tommy BOYD ☆

Born: Glasgow, 24 November 1965
English club: Chelsea
Position: Left-back/central defender
Caps won while in England: 2 (of 72)

Tommy Boyd gets only one star because injuries prevented him making any sort of impact when he joined Chelsea from Motherwell for £800,000 in June 1991 after he had helped the Fir Park club lift the Scottish Cup. He made just 23 appearances for Chelsea in eight months before moving to the number one club in his heart, Celtic, where he gave five-star service over the next eleven years. With 72 appearances, he is Scotland's fifth most capped player. He has always been a credit to the game, and was an inspiring captain of Celtic while giving gritty and determined displays whether at full-back or as a central defender. His distinguished contribution to the game was rewarded with the MBE. Auld Firm rivals Rangers were at the peak of their decade-long domination of the Scottish game and Boyd had to wait until the Scottish Cup final against Airdrieonians in 1995 before picking up a medal at Celtic Park. He was a key member of the side built by Wim Jansen that broke Rangers' stranglehold on the title in 1998, and he was on call for Martin O'Neill when he captured the first two of his League titles as Celtic boss.

Ralph BRAND ☆☆
Born: Edinburgh, 8 December 1936
English clubs: Sunderland, Manchester City
Position: Striker
Caps won while in England: 0 (of 8)

The goals had dried up by the time Ralph Brand crossed the border from Rangers. He was a prolific marksman at Ibrox, plundering 206 goals in 317 games. This puts him third on the Rangers all-time list, behind Ally McCoist and Derek Johnstone. Brand is the only player to have scored in three successive Scottish Cup finals, or four if you include a replay goal. He would have won many more than his eight caps but for the fact that his career coincided with the exploits of a genius called Denis Law. He played in four Championship-winning teams and also in seven cup finals for Rangers, when he was never once on the losing side. There was little left in the tank by the time he signed for Manchester City for £30,000 in 1965. He was beset by

injury problems at Maine Road, and fared little better when he moved to Everton after twenty League appearances. Blue was his lucky colour at Ibrox, but it did not work for him at Maine Road or Goodison, and in 1970 he finished what had been a glorious career in the blue of Raith Rovers.

Alan BRAZIL ☆☆☆☆
Born: Glasgow, 15 June 1959
English clubs: Ipswich, Tottenham, Man United, Coventry, QPR
Position: Striker
Caps won while in England: 13 (of 13)

Amazing Alan Brazil was a lively maker and taker of goals in the old First Division in a short but spectacular career prematurely ended by a recurring back injury. He earned thirteen Scottish international caps while playing for Ipswich, Spurs, Manchester United, Coventry and QPR. He was just 27 and at his peak when he was told that he risked ending up in a wheelchair if he played top-flight football again. It was a devastating blow for a player who was totally committed to the game. Brazil was born in a house overlooking Glasgow's Hampden Park, and left school at fifteen to join Ipswich Town, where he hoped to find the streets paved with goals. He was a buzzing star of Bobby Robson's superb Ipswich team that included fellow Scots George Burley and John Wark. In 1981 they won the UEFA Cup, got to the semi-finals of the FA Cup and were League runners-up to Aston Villa. In 1981–82 Brazil scored 28 goals, including five in one match against Southampton. After he had accepted that his League career was over, he played briefly in Australia with Wollongong City, and in Switzerland with FC Baden. He became director of football at Slough Town, and talks eloquently and enthusiastically about the game he played so well as a radio and television broadcaster.

QUOTE: 'It broke my heart when I was told my career was virtually over, because I felt there was so much more left in me. I now consider myself fortunate to still be involved with the game through my broadcasting work. But there is nothing to match playing the game. Nothing.'

Des BREMNER ☆☆☆

Born: Aberchirder, 7 September 1952
English clubs: Aston Villa, Birmingham, Fulham, Walsall
Position: Midfield
Caps won while in England: 0 (of 1)

A hard-working ball-winner, Des Bremner gave wonderful value to Aston Villa after manager Ron Saunders had paid Hibernian £275,000 for his services in 1979. Saunders later described it as one of the best buys he had ever made. Bremner, a livewire player just like his namesake Billy, was rewarded with just one Scottish cap – and that as a substitute. His most memorable performance came in the European Cup final when his thundering tackles and non-stop running gave Villa monopoly of the midfield against Bayern Munich. Much of his work went unnoticed except by his team-mates, who appreciated that it was his powerhouse play that helped make them the top team in Europe. He was an ever-present in Villa's 1980–81 championship season and played in every one of Villa's European Cup games as well as the World Club Championship and Super Cup ties. He followed Ron Saunders across Birmingham to St Andrews before winding down his career with Fulham and Walsall.

William (Billy) BREMNER ☆☆☆☆☆

Born: Glasgow, 9 December 1942
English clubs: Leeds, Hull, Doncaster
Position: Midfield
Caps won while in England: 54 (of 54)

Leeds legend Billy Bremner was like a sawn-off shotgun, likely to explode at any time as he poured himself into every game as if his life depended on it. There has rarely been a more competitive and committed player at any level of football, and he drove Don Revie's team from midfield as an inspirational skipper who often crossed the boundary of fair play in his desire to win. His Leeds playing career spanned sixteen years, and in that time he led them to two League titles, the League and FA

Cup and two triumphs in what was then the Inter-City Fairs Cup. He was voted Footballer of the Year in 1970, and won 54 caps for Scotland, when his captaincy was an outstanding feature in many games. But he scarred his international record when he was axed for disciplinary reasons following a drink-related incident while on international duty in Denmark. The player who had been rejected by Arsenal and Chelsea as being 'too small' became a giant of the game at Leeds, where he is remembered by a statue raised in his honour. He had ginger hair that contrasted with his chalk-white face, and he used to become whiter the more intensely involved he became in the action. His fiery temperament often outweighed his talent, and he was famously sent off for fighting with Kevin Keegan in the 1974 Charity Shield at Wembley when both superstar players pulled off their shirts and made bare-chested exits. He played out his career with Hull before moving on to Doncaster, where he took them up, down and up again in a see-sawing start to his managerial career. In October 1985, he was called back to Elland Road as manager. But he had only an FA Cup semi-final to show for his efforts before being sacked in September 1988. He died just before his 55th birthday, and Leeds fans mourned the loss of one of their greatest ever players. Certainly, nobody put in more effort in a Leeds United shirt.

QUOTE: 'I would have run through a brick wall for The Boss, Don Revie. He was the greatest manager of all time, and I was proud to be picked as his captain. I saw myself as an extension of him on the pitch, and tried to do everything he asked of me. Skippering my country was very special to me, but playing for Don was even more special.'

Frank BRENNAN ☆☆☆
Born: Airdrie, 23 April 1924
English clubs: Newcastle United
Position: Centre-half
Caps won while in England: 7 (of 7)

Big Francis (Frank) Brennan was a giant in every way – giant in size (6ft 3in and 14 stone), giant in heart and giant in character. There are scores of Frank Brennan stories that still circulate on Tyneside, such as the one about him going on a club tour of South Africa and literally taking only a toothbrush with him. He was a Jekyll and Hyde centre-half, the type who would knock his opposition centre-forward flat and then help him up with a smile and a shrug. Brennan joined Newcastle from his hometown club Airdrieonians for £8,000 in 1946, and collected FA Cup winners' medals in the back-to-back finals of 1951 and 1952. There was public uproar when he decided to leave the club in 1955 because the directors objected to him opening a sports shop. He was only just past his peak, and disappeared into non-League football with South Shields.

Alexander (Sandy) BROWN ☆☆☆
Born: Grangemouth, 24 March 1939
English clubs: Everton, Shrewsbury,
Southport
Position: Left-back
No full caps

Allan BROWN ☆☆☆
Born: Leven, 12 October 1926
English clubs: Blackpool, Luton,
Portsmouth
Position: Inside-forward
Caps won while in England: 11 (of 14)

It seems unjust that Alexander (Sandy) Brown was never recognised for international honours, apart from by the Scottish League selectors when he was with Partick Thistle. He was a gifted full-back for Everton, and would have made a bigger impact but for the arrival at Goodison of England's all-time great number 3, Ray Wilson. Like Frank Brennan, Sandy was always associated with amazing and amusing off-the-pitch stories. On a club trip to New York, he walked into a bar wearing dark glasses and, playing Mr Cool, he told the bartender: 'Scotch on the rocks . . . no ice.' Sadly, because of its frequency in being shown on TV and video, he is best remembered for a spectacular own goal when he dived and headed the ball into his own net against, of all teams, Liverpool. But this great character deserves to be better remembered for his skill and strength on the ball.

QUOTE: 'I'll never be allowed to forget that own goal against Liverpool. I was trying to head the ball clear, and it flew into the net. I wanted the ground to open up and swallow me.'

The football gods were not kind to Allan Brown, for whom Blackpool paid East Fife £25,000 in 1950, then a record between English and Scottish clubs. Brown, a good dribbler with a bullet shot, helped to push Blackpool through to the FA Cup finals of 1951 and 1953, and missed both matches through injury. He moved on to Luton Town, shot them to the 1959 FA Cup final and finished on the losing side against Nottingham Forest. After two seasons with Portsmouth, he became player-manager of non-League Wigan Athletic, and then returned to Luton as manager. He was sacked when the directors discovered he had been interviewed for the job at Leicester City, which he failed to land. Brown was a quiet, intelligent man who had a good tactical brain but little luck as a manager. He later travelled the football roundabout as boss at Torquay, Bury and Nottingham Forest, finally having two spells at Blackpool in between coaching in Kuwait.

Jim BROWN ☆☆
Born: Coatbridge, 11 May 1952
English clubs: Chesterfield, Sheffield
United, Cardiff
Position: Goalkeeper
Caps won while in England: 1 (of 1)

A safe and studious goalkeeper from Albion Rovers, Jim Brown started his English career – like so many great custodians before him (Sam Hardy, Gordon Banks, Bob Wilson) – at Chesterfield. He was transferred to Sheffield United for £80,000 in 1974 and soon after got his one international cap in a 1–1 European championship qualifier draw against Romania. He played 170 League games for the Bramall Lane club and played briefly for Cardiff before moving to the United States, where he played for Chicago Sting. He returned to England, playing for Kettering and then finishing as he had started, at Chesterfield, where he later became the commercial manager.

William (Bill) BROWN ☆☆☆☆
Born: Arbroath, 8 October 1931
English clubs: Tottenham,
Northampton
Position: Goalkeeper
Caps won while in England: 24 (of 28)

Jimmy Greaves did not make jokes about Scottish goalkeepers when Bill Brown was showing a safe pair of hands behind him in the exceptional Tottenham team of the early 1960s. He was continually outstanding in the Spurs side that became the first to clinch the League and FA Cup Double in the twentieth century. He was also the last line of defence for the team that became the first British club to win a major European trophy – the Cup Winners' Cup in 1963. Brown followed his business career as a printer throughout his distinguished stay at Tottenham, and was consistent enough to add 24 caps to the four he won while with Dundee. He played 222 League games for Spurs before making way for Pat Jennings and ending his career with Northampton.
QUOTE: 'It was a sheer joy to play behind that Tottenham defence. There were a couple of years when we got as close as you can to perfection.'

John BROWNLIE ☆☆
Born: Caldercruix, 11 March 1952
English clubs: Newcastle,
Middlesbrough, Hartlepool
Position: Full-back
Caps won while in England: 0 (of 7)

Starting out as an inside-forward with Hibernian, John Brownlie moved to half-back and then found his best position at right-back. He won seven Scottish caps between 1971 and 1977 and attracted Newcastle United, for whom he played 124 League games before moving briefly to Middlesbrough and Hartlepool. John, whose son, Paul, has followed him as a good-quality footballer, embarked on a managerial career that has taken in spells as manager or coach at Cowdenbeath, Clyde, East Stirling, Raith Rovers and Arbroath.

Martin BUCHAN ☆☆☆☆☆
Born: Aberdeen, 6 March 1949
English clubs: Man United, Oldham
Position: Central defender
Caps won while in England: 32 (of 34)

Frank O'Farrell did not have the happiest of times as Manchester United manager, but he made one of the club's most important buys during his brief spell in charge when he persuaded Martin Buchan to move to Old Trafford from Aberdeen for £125,000 in the New Year of 1972. A cultured and confident central defender in the Bobby Moore mould, Buchan immediately stiffened a United defence that had been giving away goals like trading stamps. He was an unflappable skipper through United's ups and downs, leading them back to the First Division in 1974–75 and collecting one winners' medal in three FA Cup final appearances in four years. Buchan was a born leader, and at the age of just twenty skippered the Aberdeen team that, pre-Ferguson, won the Scottish Cup in 1970. He gave magnificent service to United across 455 League and cup games, and then moved on to Oldham in the summer of 1983, where a recurring injury forced his retirement fourteen months later. Buchan tried his hand at management with Burnley, and then successfully went into promotional work for sportswear company Puma. Football is a Buchan family tradition. Both his father and his son played for Aberdeen, and his younger brother, George, followed him from The Dons to Old Trafford. But he was unable to make the same impact as Martin, whose 34 caps for Scotland included World Cup finals action in 1974 and 1978. He remains the only player to have collected both the Scottish Cup and FA Cup as skipper.

QUOTE: 'Lifting the Scottish Cup and FA Cup for Aberdeen and United seven years apart are my favourite memories. It all shot by so quickly, and my advice to any young professionals would be to enjoy every second while you can because it does not last long.'

Peter BUCHANAN ☆
Born: Glasgow, 13 October 1915
English clubs: Chelsea, Fulham, Brentford
Position: Inside-forward
Caps won while in England: 1 (of 1)

A quick, incisive utility forward, Peter Buchanan won his solitary cap while with Chelsea in the 5–0 victory over Czechoslovakia at Hampden in 1937. He played on the right wing and scored one goal. Buchanan had moved to Stamford Bridge from Wishaw Juniors at the age of twenty, and the war came right at the peak of his career. He played on in the immediate post-war years with Fulham and Brentford, for whom he scored seventeen goals in 74 League appearance as an inside-forward.

Craig BURLEY ☆☆☆
Born: Irvine, 24 September 1971
English clubs: Chelsea, Derby County
Position: Midfield
Caps won while in England: 24 (of 46)

Craig Burley followed his Uncle George into English football and into the Scottish team. He joined Chelsea as a youth trainee in 1989 and established himself as one of the most competitive midfield players in the First Division. He became a key man in central midfield for Scotland, playing twenty times for his country while with the London club. Burley moved to Celtic for £2.5 million in 1997, and was elected Scottish Football Writers' Player of the Year for 1997–98, taking the eye with an aggressive attitude that motivated the players around him. His total commitment went a step too far during World Cup '98 and he was ordered off for a foul in the match against Morocco. Derby County brought him back to the English circuit in December 1999, with a club record fee of £3 million. He enjoyed his football under the management of Jim Smith and became a huge favourite with the Derby fans. But knee and Achilles problems put him on the sidelines, and he had a major fall-out with new Derby manager John Gregory. Following Gregory's dismissal in 2003, George Burley took over the managerial reins and Craig had a rethink about

moving back to Scotland while waiting to see how things developed at Pride Park. In May 2003, he announced his retirement from international football.

George BURLEY ☆☆☆☆
Born: Cumnock, 3 June 1956
English clubs: Ipswich Town, Sunderland, Gillingham, Colchester
Position: Right-back
Caps won while in England: 11 (of 11)

'George Burley is a man of honour and integrity, and his many skills will no doubt lead to further opportunities and successes in his managerial career...' So said Ipswich Town chairman David Sheepshanks when announcing in 2002 that he was sacking the man who had been in charge at Portman Road for eight mainly successful years. Not too many managers leave a club with such a glowing testimonial, and it gives an indication of how respected Burley is within the game, both for his tactical knowledge and his 100 per cent dedication. He had his best years as a player with Ipswich, joining them as an apprentice and developing into a thoughtful, footballing full-back in the exciting Bobby Robson era. Burley and teammate John Wark made their international debut together against Wales in May 1979, and became the first Ipswich players capped by Scotland. George played 394 League games for Ipswich, and was an outstanding defender in their triumphant FA Cup and UEFA Cup campaigns. His League debut for Ipswich against Manchester United in December 1973 coincided with George Best's final game for the Reds. He later played for Sunderland, Gillingham and Colchester while studying the coaching side of the game, and he returned to Ipswich as manager in succession to John Lyall in 1994. In 2003 he took charge of Derby County following the suspension and then dismissal of John Gregory.

Francis BURNS ☆☆☆
Born: Glenboig, 17 October 1948
English clubs: Man United,
Southampton, Preston
Position: Left-back
Caps won while in England: 1 (of 1)

Equally comfortable at left-back or in midfield as an anchorman, Francis Burns played a prominent part in Manchester United's memorable 1968 European Cup run and was a squad reserve for the final. He joined the Old Trafford ground staff straight from school, and made his first-team debut at eighteen in a 3–1 win at West Ham in 1967. Burns featured regularly throughout the season at left-back and played in the opening seven games of the European Cup campaign up to and including the first leg of the semi-final, when United beat Real Madrid 1–0 at Old Trafford. The more experienced Shay Brennan was preferred for the final, but Sir Matt Busby made a point of singling out for praise the role Burns had played on the

way to the final. He had established himself as first-choice left-back the following season when he suffered an injury followed by a series of cartilage problems that prevented him cementing his place. His sole international appearance for Scotland was in Vienna in 1969, a World Cup qualifier won 2–0 by Austria. New manager Frank O'Farrell sold him to Southampton for £50,000 in 1972, but he played only twenty League games for the south coast club before joining Preston, where his former United team-mate Bobby Charlton had become player-manager. He played 273 League games for the Deepdale club, and later emigrated to Australia where he set up a cleaning business in Perth.

Kenny BURNS ☆☆☆☆☆
Born: Glasgow, 23 September 1953
English clubs: Birmingham,
Nottingham Forest, Leeds, Derby,
Notts County, Barnsley
Position: Central defender
Caps won while in England: 20 (of 20)

Kenny Burns was the first player Brian Clough and Peter Taylor purchased when they took Nottingham Forest up into the First Division in 1977. It was a deal that astonished many people because he had something of a reputation as a wild man on and off the pitch. But they had a specific role in mind for him, and he answered the challenge of his new job as sweeper with great enthusiasm, mixing strength and a ruthless competitive nature with his considerable skill. His disciplined, dominating displays at the centre of defence were a crucial factor in the run that brought Forest the League championship and also back-to-back European Cup triumphs. Burns played 137 League games for Forest after joining them from Birmingham City in July 1977 for £145,000. He later played for Leeds and had spells with Derby, Notts County and Barnsley in a career that spanned fourteen years. He was a striker for Birmingham, but his game blossomed following the switch to the back of the Forest defence. He was capped twenty times by Scotland and was a member of the 1978 World Cup squad. Footballer of the Year in 1978, he became a pub landlord after hanging up his boots in 1985.

QUOTE: 'Cloughie and Peter Taylor were the motivating forces behind my success at Forest. They had the vision to see how I could slot into the team as a sweeper, and I gave it everything I had to make sure I did not let them or the team down.'

Colin CALDERWOOD ☆☆☆☆
Born: Glasgow, 20 January 1965
English clubs: Mansfield Town, Swindon, Spurs, Aston Villa, Nottingham Forest
Position: Central defender
Caps won while in England: 36 (of 36)

Strong and dependable, Colin Calderwood gave sterling international service alongside Colin Hendry at the heart of Scotland's defence after winning his first cap at the age of thirty. He played a major role in helping Scotland qualify for the 1998 World Cup finals. There was little hint of him developing into such a dominating defender when he left school, and the major clubs did not rush to sign him despite his being capped at Scottish schoolboy level. He had to settle for an apprenticeship at the unfashionable football outpost of Mansfield Town. They did an excellent job grooming him at Field Mill, and Swindon Town were quick to spot his potential. Lou Macari took him to Swindon for £30,000 and he later blossomed under the coaching of Glenn Hoddle and Ossie Ardiles. Calderwood helped Swindon capture the Fourth Division championship with a record-breaking 102 points during the 1985–86 season, and he skippered the side that beat Leicester City 4–3 for a place in the old First Division. He played 330 League games for Swindon before joining Tottenham for £1,250,000 in the summer of 1993. He was a key man in the Spurs defence for six seasons alongside Sol Campbell and then Ramon Vega. He was not first choice when his fellow Scot George Graham took over as Spurs manager, and he moved on to Aston Villa in March 1999 to fill in for Ugo Ehiogu, who was sidelined with a serious eye injury. Calderwood stayed a year at Villa Park before helping Nottingham Forest out of relegation trouble. A recurring back problem forced him to hang up his boots and he quit playing to concentrate on a new career as a coach, starting with the Tottenham reserve team. He was a credit to the game and to himself throughout nearly twenty years as a professional footballer.

Gary CALDWELL ☆
Born: Stirling, 12 April 1982
English club: Newcastle United
Position: Defender
Caps won while in England: 5 (of 5)

Gary Caldwell followed his older brother Stephen from local club Carse Thistle to Newcastle United, and also followed him into the Scottish international team as a central defender. Newcastle had such strength in depth in their squad that they could afford to let Gary go on loan, first to Darlington and then Hibernian, Coventry and Derby with manager Sir Bobby Robson saying, 'The lad is a good prospect and his long-term future is here at St James' Park.' Shorter by two inches than brother Stephen, six-footer Gary still manages to be an impressive player in the air under pressure and is a strong marker and careful with his distribution.

Stephen CALDWELL ☆☆
Born: Stirling, 12 September 1980
English club: Newcastle United
Position: Defender
Caps won while in England: 2 (of 2)

The oldest of the Caldwell brothers, he worked his way through the Newcastle youth ranks to a fringe first-team place and gathered valuable League experience on loan with Blackpool and Bradford City. He was a regular in the Scottish Under-21 team, winning eight caps as a solid central defender. His full international debut came as a substitute in the 1–1 draw in Poland in 2001. By the close of the 2002–03 season, he had laid the foundation to his Newcastle career with 28 League appearances.

Colin CAMERON ☆☆
Born: Kirkcaldy, 23 October 1972
English club: Wolves
Position: Midfield
Caps won while in England: 8 (of 23)

Colin Cameron started his career with Raith Rovers, and was a key midfield force in the team that won two First Division championships and the Coca-Cola Cup in 1994. He had a year on loan with Sligo Rovers in Ireland, and was being closely monitored by Hearts, who signed him in a cash-plus-player deal in 1996. He quickly established himself there in midfield, where he became a driving skipper and a regular in the Scottish international team. In the summer of 2001 he signed for Wolves for £1.75 million, and was prominent in the push that took the Midlands club to the top of the table before they fell away and lost in the play-offs. His second season at Molineux was interrupted by a knee injury followed by a broken toe, but he recovered to play a major part in helping Wolves clinch a place in the Premiership.

Bobby CAMPBELL ☆☆
Born: Glasgow, 28 June 1922
English club: Chelsea
Position: Right winger
Caps won while in England: 5 (of 5)

The record books give Bobby Campbell as having won the first two of his five caps while with Falkirk. In actual fact he was between clubs, having been sold to Chelsea by Falkirk in May 1947, the month and the year that he made his international debut (a 2-1 defeat against Belgium in Brussels). He played at outside-right, but switched to the left wing for his second cap in Luxembourg a week later. Campbell, no relation to the Bobby Campbell who later became manager at Stamford Bridge, scored 36 goals in 188 League games for Chelsea. His one goal for Scotland came in his third match, a home friendly against Switzerland at Hampden that drew a crowd of 123,751. He netted the second goal in a 3–1 victory. Campbell had injury problems, and lost his first-team club place the season before Ted Drake led Chelsea to their first ever League championship. Campbell wound down his career with Reading, and later became a coaching consultant to Bristol City Council.

Willie CARR ☆☆☆☆
Born: Glasgow, 6 January 1950
English clubs: Coventry City, Wolves, Millwall
Position: Midfield
Caps won while in England: 6 (of 6)

Flame-haired Willie Carr was a little ball of fire in midfield for Coventry and then Wolves, giving each team he played for a prickly centre to go with a procession of precise passes. He will always be remembered for the 'donkey kick' goal that he set up for Coventry team-mate Ernie Hunt against Everton at Highfield Road in 1970. He stood over the ball for a free-kick, wedged it between his ankles and then flicked it up for Hunt to volley the ball over the defensive wall and into the net. It was a wonderful piece of invention, but the football authorities were unimpressed and outlawed it. Carr was a formidable force in the Emlyn Hughes-skippered Wolves side that won the Football League Cup in 1980. He played 252 League games for Coventry, and 237 for Wolves before finishing his career with Millwall and then non-League Worcester City. He was always looking for the chance to steal into the penalty area and his support play was rewarded with 55 League goals. When he left football he became a nuts and bolts salesman in Wolverhampton, which was somehow fitting for a player who threw a spanner in the works of many opposition teams.

QUOTE: 'Ernie and I worked on the donkey kick in training, and could not see why it was outlawed. We thought it showed imagination, and should have been encouraged.'

Steve CLARKE ☆☆☆

Born: Saltcoats, 29 August 1963
English club: Chelsea
Position: Defender
Caps won while in England: 6 (of 6)

Chelsea beat Celtic in a battle for Steve Clarke's signature in 1986 after he had established himself as a utility defender with St Mirren. He cost the London club £400,000, and their money had rarely been better invested. Clarke gave Chelsea magnificent service for twelve years as a defender who was at home in any of the back-four positions or as a midfield anchorman. He was at the heart of the defence when Chelsea won the FA Cup in 1997 and captained the team in the European Cup Winners' Cup final victory against Stuttgart. Ruud Gullit encouraged him to switch to Newcastle United as assistant manager, but when this failed to work out Clarke returned to Stamford Bridge where he was employed as a scout and youth team coach.

John COLLINS ☆☆☆

Born: Galashiels, 30 January 1968
English clubs: Everton, Fulham
Position: Midfield
Caps won while in England: 5 (of 58)

John Collins was brought up in the rugby stronghold Borders country and was nearly lost to the fifteen-a-side game, but he was spotted playing the round-ball game for Celtic Boys' Club and Edinburgh's Hutchinson Vale. Hibernian signed him in 1984 and he made his Premier Division debut for Hibs at just seventeen. He won the first of his Scottish caps in 1988, and was then snapped up by Celtic. Collins cemented himself in the Scotland team while at Parkhead, but was unable to do anything to break what was then the Rangers stranglehold on the domestic trophies. He was one of the first players to benefit from the Bosman ruling, and in 1996 he moved on a free transfer to Jean Tigana's Monaco side. He helped Monaco win the French League in his first season, and played a key part in steering them to the European Champions' League the following season with his authoritative passing from a midfield base. Everton beat a queue of clubs to bring him back to the British stage in return for a £2.5 million fee after he had given some eye-catching performances in the 1998 World Cup finals in France. He had been at Goodison for two seasons and had just overcome a recurring toe injury when his good friend Jean Tigana took over as manager of Fulham. Everton accepted a £2.2 million offer and he dropped down a division to help the Cottagers win a Premiership place. Collins had a spell as Fulham captain, and was considering a move into management as he reached the veteran stage as a player. But he ruled himself out of succeeding Tigana when the Frenchman left Fulham in 2003 and he announced he was hanging up his boots.

QUOTE: 'My move to France was educational as well as enjoyable. I learned how to become more of a team player, and I was given the responsibility of playing in central midfield, which suited my game. I was a useful fly-half when I was at school, and I suppose this helped me develop a tactical brain.'

Robert (Bobby) COLLINS
☆☆☆☆☆
Born: Glasgow, 16 February 1931
English clubs: Everton, Leeds, Bury, Oldham
Position: Inside-forward
Caps won while in England: 9 (of 31)

Stocky, sturdy and stealthy, Bobby Collins was a pocket battleship of a player. Standing just 5ft 3in, he was a giant in football boots. He bossed the midfield for Celtic, and won a full house of Scottish medals in ten years before being coaxed to join Everton in 1958–59. Don Revie signed him as his

midfield general for Leeds in 1962 when he was a veteran 31, and he built the team around him. He had his most memorable season in 1964–65 when, at the age of 34, he helped Leeds reach the FA Cup final, was recalled to the Scottish team after six years in the wilderness, and was elected Footballer of the Year. He was ruthlessly competitive, and a master tactician. His career seemed finished in October 1965 when a cruel tackle by a Torino defender broke his thigh bone. Those who had felt the Collins tackle over the years might have muttered out of his hearing, 'He who lives by the sword . . .' It was typical of his battling spirit that he was back in action within seven months. Collins later played for Bury, Oldham and Morton, and during a career that spanned 22 seasons he scored 154 League goals and made hundreds more with his remarkably accurate passing. He had brief spells as a player-coach in Australia and Ireland before managing with little success at Huddersfield, Hull and Barnsley. Bobby coached for a season at Elland Road and then moved out of football into the fashion trade. He later had two years as a chauffeur at Leeds University. There have been few more influential midfield players in post-war British football.

QUOTE: 'I got my best advice in my formative years at Celtic – we were taught that you needed to combine inspiration with perspiration. I followed this throughout my career. Skill counts above all else, but it is no use to a team unless you put in effort to go with the fancy stuff.'

Eddie COLQUHOUN ☆☆☆
Born: Prestonpans, 29 March 1945
English clubs: Bury, West Brom,
Sheffield United
Position: Central defender
Caps won while in England: 9 (of 9)

It was perhaps apt that Edmund (Eddie) Colquhoun should go into the post office business at the end of his playing career because he left his stamp on many opposing forwards. He was a rugged and determined tackler in the era when the big boot often ruled. Spotted while playing for Edinburgh Norton, he joined the junior squad at Gigg Lane before playing for two seasons in the Bury first team. In 1967, he joined First Division West Bromwich Albion, and switched to Sheffield United the following year. It was then that he began to gain his reputation for tough no-nonsense defending at the centre of the defence. He put the muscle into an adventurous Blades side, balancing the silky skill of players of the quality of Tony Currie, Trevor Hockey and Alan Woodward. Colquhoun played 363 League games in eight seasons for United, and as well as all the goals he prevented he also managed to pop up in the opposite area to score 21. He made himself felt for Scotland in nine full internationals, and

became a big favourite at Bramall Lane, where he was an inspirational club captain with his total commitment to every game. His final tackles were made for Detroit Express in the United States.

Alfie CONN ☆☆
Born: Edinburgh, 5 April 1952
English clubs: Tottenham, Blackpool
Position: Midfield
Caps won while in England: 2 (of 2)

Alfie Conn Jnr, as he was known north of the border, became the first player to collect Scottish Cup final medals with both Auld Firm teams, winning with Celtic four years after triumphing with Rangers. In between he became something of a five-minute wonder at Tottenham while playing 38 League games between 1974 and 1976. He was manager Bill Nicholson's final signing for Spurs, and with a succession of brilliant performances almost single-handedly helped save the club from relegation in a dramatic finish to his first season. With his long, flowing hair and clever dribbling, Alfie quickly became a darling of the Tottenham fans. The one man who was not so enraptured was Bill Nicholson, who wanted him to be less of a showman and more of a team player. A succession of injuries restricted his appearances in 1975–76, and he did not hesitate when Jock Stein invited him to sign for Celtic. This caused a sensation because of his background at Rangers, where he had scored 23 goals in 93

League games. He later played at
Hearts, where in the 1950s his father,
Alfie Conn Snr, had been part of the
'Terrible Trio' along with Willie Bauld
and Jimmy Wardhaugh. He briefly
played in the United States with
Pittsburgh, and then with Motherwell
and Blackpool before running a pub in
Glasgow called 'Captain's Rest'.

Eddie CONNACHAN ☆☆
Born: Prestonpans, 27 August 1935
English club: Middlesbrough
Position: Goalkeeper
Caps won while in England: 0 (of 2)

Signed in May 1957 from Dalkeith
Thistle, goalkeeper Eddie Connachan
made 172 first-team appearances for
Dunfermline before transferring to
Middlesbrough in August 1963 for
£5,500. He played in 95 League games
for the Ayresome Park club, and then
went to South Africa, where he
established himself first as a popular
club goalkeeper in East London and
later as an outstanding bowls player.
Connachan was noted for his quick
reflexes, and courage under pressure
from shoulder-charging forwards in the
days when goalkeepers were offered
little protection. Dunfermline fans will
always remember his display against
Celtic when an astonishing sequence of
saves lifted his team to a stunning
victory in the 1961 Scottish Cup final.
He was carried shoulder-high from the
pitch at the end, and Celtic centre-half

Billy McNeill described his display as
'the greatest goalkeeping performance I
have ever seen in my life'.

John CONNOLLY ☆☆
Born: Barrhead, 13 June 1950
English clubs: Everton, Birmingham,
Newcastle, Gateshead
Position: Winger
Caps won while in England: 1 (of 1)

John Connolly has become famous as
the manager who in 2002 steered Queen
of the South to the first trophy triumph
in their 83-year history, when they won
the Bells Challenge Cup. Before his
switch to management, he played as a
winger for three clubs in England
during a career badly affected by
injuries. He starred for Barrhead High
School and Glasgow United before
signing as an amateur for St Johnstone,
turning professional with them in 1968.
Everton paid £75,000 for him in March
1972 and he scored sixteen goals in 116
League matches before moving on to
Birmingham for £70,000 in September
1976. After 57 League games for the
Blues, he was transferred to Newcastle
along with Terry Hibbitt in a swap deal
for Stewart Barraclough. His career was
plagued by injury, including two broken
legs that stopped him building on his
one-cap international career. When
released by Newcastle in 1980 he joined
Hibernian and won a First Division
winners' medal at the end of his first
season at Easter Road. He switched to

Gateshead in January 1982, then on to Blyth Spartans as player-manager before returning to Gateshead twelve months later. He then had a short spell as Whitley Bay boss in 1984. Connolly returned to the Scottish game as manager of Queen of the South, with the Cup triumph proving that he could perform minor miracles.

QUOTE: 'Managers at Queen of the South have been trying to win something since the club was founded in 1919, so being the first to do it has given me my biggest thrill in football.'

Charlie COOKE ☆☆☆☆
Born: St Monance, Fife, 14 October 1942
English clubs: Chelsea, Crystal Palace
Position: Midfield
Caps won while in England: 14 (of 16)

Charlie 'Chuckleboots' Cooke provided more entertainment than almost any other player imported by the English from Scotland. He arrived at Stamford Bridge in the spring of 1966 as replacement for Chelsea's Cockney king Terry Venables, who was moving across London to Tottenham after a fall-out with manager Tommy Docherty. If Terry gave the Blues fans a knees-up, then Charlie was about to provide a Highland fling. He was virtually unknown outside Scotland, but was so popular at Dundee that on the very day he agreed to sign for The Doc he was voted their player of the year. He quickly won over the Chelsea supporters with his dazzling ball skills, running rings round defenders and sometimes looking in danger of disappearing with a flash and a bang up his own exhaust pipe. Whether in midfield or on the wing, Charlie was wonderfully entertaining to watch with his old-style dribbling, yet the feeling among the coaches in the game was that he could have had a bigger influence on matches had he released the ball earlier. It was this hogging of the ball that stopped him winning twice as many international caps, but what fun he gave the spectators. He had a quick mind to go with his quick feet, and became a favourite on the London social scene because he knew there was a world over the moon and beyond the parrot cage. Cooke started his career with Renfrew Juniors and then turned professional with Aberdeen on his way to hero status at Dundee. He had a season at Crystal Palace between two spells at Stamford Bridge during which he played 307 League games, scoring 22 goals and making many more. Charlie tended to decorate rather than decide matches, but those of us lucky to watch him at his best can only have warm memories of his astonishing skill. Married to an American, he later played in the setting sun period of his career with Memphis Rogues and California Surfers before opening a hugely successful soccer school in Cincinnati. I wonder if he teaches his pupils to make an early release of the ball? Somehow, I hope not.

QUOTE: 'They were fantastic days at Chelsea, and I look on them as the summertime of my life. We were what you might call a spirited bunch, and we had a lot of fun along with our football. How bad's that?'

Peter CORMACK ☆☆☆☆
Born: Edinburgh, 17 July 1946
English clubs: Nottingham Forest, Liverpool, Bristol City
Position: Midfield
Caps won while in England: 5 (of 9)

Peter Cormack was Kevin Keegan's best friend in their Anfield days, and there was something about Kevin's all-action game laced into Peter's way of playing. An elegant, high-stepping player, he was signed by Bill Shankly as the last piece of his Double-trophy-winning jigsaw in 1972–73. He cost £110,000 from Nottingham Forest after being recommended by Shankly's brother, Bob, who had witnessed his early performances with Hibernian. Alert in the air and carrying a powerful shot, he made a major contribution to Liverpool's capture of the League Championship and UEFA Cup in his first season. The following year Cormack collected an FA Cup winners' medal after the Wembley defeat of Newcastle, and he earned a second championship medal and another in the UEFA Cup under Bob Paisley's management in 1976. After 67 League games with Bristol City, Cormack moved into management with Partick Thistle, and then coached abroad with Cyprus before becoming Botswana's national coach in 1986. He came back to where his adventure started as assistant manager at Hibs, and was then in charge at Cowdenbeath before concentrating on a lucrative painting and decorating business and hiring out karaoke equipment in the Edinburgh area. His after-dinner speeches are well worth catching for stories of the way it used to be.

Tommy CRAIG ☆☆☆☆
Born: Glasgow, 21 November 1950
English clubs: Sheffield Wednesday, Newcastle, Aston Villa, Swansea, Carlisle
Position: Midfield
Caps won while in England: 1 (of 1)

It was in May 1969 that Tommy Craig created transfer history when, aged just eighteen, Aberdeen made him the first Scottish £100,000 footballer when they sold him to Sheffield Wednesday. He spent the next fifteen years trying to live up to that early potential. The fact that he was capped only once by his country suggests he failed, but his intelligent playmaking made him a key component in each of the teams he played for while travelling the English (okay, and Welsh) football roundabout with Wednesday (214 League games), Newcastle (124), Aston Villa (27), Swansea (47) and Carlisle (114). He mixed industry with flair, and gave shape and tempo to each team while often wearing the captain's armband. Craig first came to the attention of football scouts when playing for Scotland schoolboys alongside a pretty good young striker called Kenny Dalglish. He got an excellent grounding with the youth squad at Aberdeen and he was tipped to win a cupboardful of caps, but niggling knee problems handicapped him, particularly during his time with Aston Villa. In 1984 he took his cultured left foot to Hibernian, where he combined playing with coaching and the role of assistant manager. Three years later he became assistant manager and chief scout at Celtic, and finally 'went home' to Aberdeen in 1995 to help Roy Aitken hold the reins at Pittodrie. His vast experience has been of immense help to the Scottish Under-21 players, who could not have a better tutor.

Pat CRERAND ☆☆☆☆☆
Born: Glasgow, 19 February 1930
English club: Manchester United
Position: Midfield
Caps won while in England: 8 (of 16)

It is always Best-Law-Charlton that come immediately to mind when thinking of the great Manchester United team of the 1960s. The fourth name on the lips of anybody who watched that side in action would almost certainly be Pat Crerand. While Best, Law and Charlton took the eye with their flair and fluency, Crerand quietly went about making the team tick with passing that was right out of the Scottish copybook. He had been a magnificent and sometimes moody midfield playmaker for Celtic, a brittle union during which he was often at loggerheads with the Parkhead hierarchy. The strong-minded former shipyard worker joined Manchester United for £56,000 in February 1963, and three months later collected an FA Cup winners' medal at Wembley. He was a decisive tackler, and when he had won the ball knew exactly how to use it. While Nobby Stiles had the tigerish bite in midfield, Crerand provided the purr. They were both vital cogs in the Manchester United team that lifted the European Cup after two League championship triumphs. Crerand had an equally impressive partnership in Scotland's midfield with the wizard, Slim Jim Baxter. He lacked explosive speed and often walked a tightrope with his tinderbox temper, but when on his game there were few players to match him for dictating the pace and pattern of a game. Anybody who witnessed his performances on the ITV experts panel during the 1970 and 1974 World Cups will confirm that he talked as good a game as he played. Pat (or Paddy, as most of his mates call him) has never been short of an opinion or three. He loved Man United to the extent that when his pal George Best was on his path of self-destruction, it was Paddy who volunteered to become his minder. I felt at the time it was akin to putting an arsonist in charge of a pyromaniac, but for a while at least he managed to get Britain's greatest ever footballer on the right road. Crerand became assistant manager to Tommy Docherty when The Doc took over at United, but they were soon at war with each other and Pat moved on to Northampton Town in 1976 for a brief, unsatisfactory experience of management. Since quitting the game, Crerand has worked as a PR representative for a Manchester engineering company, and remains a popular licensee in Altrincham. He is still regularly involved on the periphery at Old Trafford, and continues to make intelligent and outspoken comments in a part-time media role and as an entertaining after-dinner speaker.

QUOTE: 'There is no question that the outstanding memory for me is of the night we won the European Cup at Wembley. We had pledged to do it for Matt Busby, and I have never known such emotion as when we took the Cup to him after the presentation. It was a priceless moment for all of us.'

Alex CROPLEY ☆☆

Born: Aldershot, 16 January 1951
English clubs: Arsenal, Aston Villa, Newcastle, Portsmouth
Position: Midfield
Caps won while in England: 0 (of 2)

One of the first English-born players to be capped by Scotland under the parentage rule, Alex Cropley was desperately unlucky with injuries. A fractured ankle with Hibernian followed by broken legs with Arsenal and Aston Villa stopped him building on the collection of two caps won while with Hibs. Arsenal manager Bertie Mee was so impressed by his mixture of skill and steel that he paid £150,000 to lure him from Easter Road to Highbury in 1974. He came into the midfield as a balancing partner for king playmaker Alan Ball, but injuries restricted his League appearances to just 34. Cropley then moved to Aston Villa for £135,000, and he was making an enormous impact with his combination of ball winning and scheming when a broken leg put him back on the sidelines. He played briefly on loan with Newcastle, tried his luck in Canada with Toronto Blizzard and made seven League appearances with Portsmouth. He was a complete contradiction in that he did not look strong enough to punch his way out of a paper bag. Yet he used to tackle like a tank and it was his ferocious approach to the game that caused his horrendous injuries. He had a dream of a left foot and could deliver pinpointed passes. His two caps were poor reward for his immense talent. After hanging up his boots at the end of a frustrating career, he became a publican in Edinburgh. He had the talent to have become a five-star player, but never the luck. His breaks were invariably of the painful rather than fortunate kind.

Michael CULLEN ✩✩
Born: Glasgow, 3 July 1931
English clubs: Luton, Grimsby, Derby
Position: Inside-forward
Caps won while in England: 1 (of 1)

Luton Town signed Michael Cullen from Douglasdale Juniors in 1949 after being advised by their scout that the eighteen-year-old Glaswegian could make as well as take goals. He had been a fixture in the Hatters attack for five years when he won his only Scotland cap in the 1–1 draw with Austria at Hampden in 1956. Cullen scored sixteen goals in 112 League matches for Luton, and found the net 35 times in 178 League games for Grimsby. He wound down his career in England with 24 League appearances for Derby County.

George CUMMINGS ✩✩✩✩
Born: Falkirk, 5 June 1913
English club: Aston Villa
Position: Full-back
Caps won while in England: 6 (of 9)

No less a person than Sir Stanley Matthews described George Cummings as his most difficult opponent. He was a prince of left-backs whose greatest years were before the war, first with Partick Thistle and then with Aston Villa. In an era when most full-backs were about thump and clump, he was all style and controlled power. Cummings would win the ball with a crunching tackle and then make intelligent use of it, often taking it on swift downfield runs in the days long before overlapping- or wing-backs were glints in the eyes of coaches. He played 210 League matches for Villa either side of a war that cut into his peak years. It is claimed that grown men cried at Partick when he took the English shilling in 1935, moving to Villa for what was then an enormous fee of £9,350. His three younger brothers followed him to Villa Park, but none of them made the same impact as their big brother. George became club captain, and later a coach at Villa Park before managing various non-League clubs and scouting for Wolves. He passed on in 1987, warmly remembered by those who had seen him play as a defensive master of the game.

Willie CUNNINGHAM ✩✩✩✩
Born: Cowdenbeath, 22 February 1925
English clubs: Preston, Southport
Position: Full-back
Caps won while in England: 8 (of 8)

A tough-tackling, uncompromising right-back, Willie Cunningham was so idolised at Preston that in a supporters' vote on the greatest players of the twentieth century he came second to the legendary Sir Tom Finney. After joining Preston from Aidrieonians for £6,000 in 1949, he made more than 440 League and FA Cup appearances for the Deepdale club that has always had a strong Scottish heartbeat. Willie, who had combined working as a coalminer with his football at Airdrie, won eight Scotland caps and skippered the 1954 World Cup side. He finished his career playing with and then managing Southport when they were a Football League club. Following Willie's death at the age of 75 in 2000, Sir Tom Finney said: 'There have been few harder tacklers in the game, but he always played it fair. The Scottish selectors should have given him many more caps. When we used to walk out on to the pitch I used to think how glad he was on my side rather than against me. He was an extremely tough man.'

Hugh CURRAN ☆☆☆
Born: Glasgow, 25 September 1943
English clubs: Millwall, Norwich, Wolves, Oxford, Bolton
Position: Striker
Caps won while in England: 5 (of 5)

A former Manchester United apprentice, Hugh Curran became a have-boots-will-travel striker who was a consistent goal-scorer with Millwall (26 goals in 57 League games), Norwich City (46/112), Wolves (40/82), Oxford United (39/105) and Bolton (13/47), plus non-League output with Corby. His five Scottish caps came in 1970–71 while he was at Wolves and playing in tandem with Irish international Derek Dougan. They made an odd couple, Curran stocky and determined, the Doog leggy and inspirational. But their

partnership was electric while it lasted. Injury forced his retirement in 1979, and he became a publican.

Christian DAILLY ☆☆☆
Born: Dundee, 23 October 1973
English clubs: Derby, Blackburn, West Ham
Position: Midfield/Defender
Caps won while in England: 49 (of 49)

After more than 150 appearances for his hometown club Dundee United, utility defender Christian Dailly became one of the first British players to take advantage of the Bosman ruling and moved to Derby County in the summer of 1996. He made such an impressive impact in the France 98 World Cup that Blackburn boss Roy Hodgson was encouraged to lure him to Ewood Park for £5.3 million. His stay at Blackburn finished under a cloud when new manager Graeme Souness made it clear that he did not fit into his plans. West Ham beat Everton and Leicester in a three-club chase for his signature, and he moved to Upton Park for £1.75 million in January 2001. While primarily a defensive player, Dailly can also cause problems in the opposition penalty area. Only a desperate late save by David Seaman stopped him heading his way into Scottish folklore in the Euro 2000 play-off at Wembley in November 1999. He dropped down into the First Division with West Ham at the end of the 2002–03 season. His record collection of 34 Under-21 international caps is lasting testimony to the talent he had as a young player.

Kenny DALGLISH ☆☆☆☆☆
Born: Glasgow, 14 March 1951
English club: Liverpool
Position: Striker
Caps won while in England: 55 (of 102)

See Part One for his full career details.

Callum DAVIDSON ☆☆☆
Born: Stirling, 25 June 1976
English clubs: Blackburn, Leicester
Position: Full-back
Caps won while in England: 17 (of 17)

Intelligent on and off the pitch, Callum Davidson abandoned a university degree course to start a football career with St Johnstone. His instincts proved right when Blackburn paid a Saints club record of £1.75 million for him in the spring of 1998. A succession of injuries prevented him showing consistent form at Ewood Park, and he moved on to Leicester two years later for £1.7 million. He made headlines of the wrong sort when his jaw was broken in the infamous incident involving his Leicester City team-mate Dennis Wise, who was sacked in what became one of the most controversial stories of the decade. Davidson recovered from his injury, and his solid performances were a key element in Leicester's successful push for promotion back to the Premiership in the 2002–03 season.

Alex DAWSON ☆☆☆
Born: Aberdeen, 21 February 1940
English clubs: Man United, Preston, Bury, Brighton, Brentford
Position: Centre-forward
No full caps

A rugged centre-forward out of the old school, Alex Dawson was a Busby Babe at Old Trafford, but despite banging in 45 goals in 80 First Division games for Man United he was allowed to move on to Preston in 1961. He continued to regularly find the net for the Deepdale club – 114 goals in 197 League games – and played a prominent part in driving the Second Division team to the 1964 FA Cup final at Wembley, where they lost a thriller to West Ham. Despite all his goals he could not attract the attention of the Scottish selectors, and all he had to show for powerhouse performances at the end of his career was a bagful of goals and a Scottish schoolboy cap. How Berti Vogts would like a marksman of his quality today!

Alistair DAWSON ☆☆☆
Born: Govan, 25 February 1958
English club: Blackburn Rovers
Position: Full-back
Caps won while in England: 0 (of 5)

Right-back Alistair (Ally) Dawson had his best playing years with Rangers, winning his five Scottish caps while a strong and skilful defender at Ibrox. He had a brief 40-match association with Blackburn before moving back to Scotland with Airdrieonians. Dawson is a keen student of tactics, and he started a coaching career with Ayr United. Then he performed minor miracles as manager at Hamilton Academicals, keeping the club in a competitive mood despite crippling financial problems. They lost only 36 of 125 games under his command. His next stop was Stranraer as assistant manager.

year playing career he had a unique collection of English, Scottish, Northern Ireland and Republic of Ireland Cup medals that were won with Celtic (1937), Man United (1948) and Derry City (1954). At the grand old age of 44, he won a runners-up medal with Cork (1956). He also played for Aberdeen and Falkirk, and will always be affectionately remembered as 'Old Bones' Delaney. But for the war, he would have at least trebled his caps collection.

Jimmy DELANEY ☆☆☆☆
Born: Stoneyburn, 3 September 1914
English club: Manchester United
Position: Winger
Caps won while in England: 4 (of 13)

Matt Busby paid Celtic £4,000 for 32-year-old winger Jimmy Delaney in his first year in charge at Old Trafford, and more than thirty years later still rated him one of his greatest ever buys. It was an enormous gamble by Busby because the spindly looking Delaney was considered past his best and nursing a suspect damaged shoulder. He rewarded Busby's faith in him by inspiring the first of the great Busby sides, helping them win a League championship and the FA Cup at Wembley in 1948. Delaney looked as if a strong wind would knock him over, but he was full of tricks and could deceive defenders with clever changes of pace and brilliant ball control. He later moved on to Ireland to add to his legend. At the close of a 25-

Paul DEVLIN ☆☆☆
Born: Birmingham, 14 April 1972.
English clubs: Notts County,
Birmingham City, Sheffield United,
Watford
Position: Midfield
Caps won while in England: 10 (of 10)

A winger disguised as a right-sided midfield player, Paul Devlin came late on to the international scene when his Scottish ancestry was discovered. He kicked off his career with Stafford Rangers before Notts County gave him a League platform. His enthusiastic and competitive performances attracted his hometown club Birmingham City, and he had two spells at St Andrews. In between there was service at Sheffield United during which he was voted Supporters' Player of the Year. His move to Watford in September 2003 was funded by an anonymous backer, believed by many to be pop star Elton John. He has certainly been something of a Rocket Man for

Watford, and in a short period of time he took his Scottish caps collection into double figures.

John DICK ☆☆☆
Born: Glasgow, 19 March 1930
English clubs: West Ham, Brentford
Position: Inside-left
Caps won while in England: 1 (of 1)

'Long John' Dick had a left foot that could have blown open safe doors, but his right was strictly for standing on. Tall and leggy, he first came to prominence with Scottish junior side Maryhill and moved to Upton Park from Crittals Athletic. He formed a prolific left-wing partnership with the flying Malcolm Musgrove, and also dovetailed neatly with clever centre-forward Vic Keeble. Together, they powered West Ham to the First Division in 1958. The end of his reign at the Hammers coincided with the emergence of a young left-half whom manager Ron Greenwood decided would fit in better in the number 10 shirt. His name was Geoff Hurst. Dick, disgruntled over the terms offered him, decided to move on and after notching 153 goals in 326 League games joined Brentford. The trusty left foot was still in good working order, and he scored 45 goals in 72 League matches for the Bees. He got his one Scotland call-up for the 1959 match against England at Wembley in which Billy Wright became the first footballer in the world to win 100 caps. John, who joined the West Ham coaching staff, died in Chigwell in 2000.

Paul DICKOV ☆☆☆
Born: Livingston, 1 November 1972
English clubs: Arsenal, Luton, Brighton, Manchester City, Leicester
Position: Striker
Caps won while in England: 4 (of 4)

Paul Dickov had just forced himself into the Scottish squad with Machester City as a determined and energetic striker when a serious Achilles injury put him out of action. Following his recovery he was allowed to move on to Leicester City for a nominal fee in February 2002, but too late to stop them dropping into the First Division. He forged a prolific partnership with Brian Deane, and they helped shoot the Foxes straight back up to the Premiership. So, at the age of thirty, Dickov was realising the potential George Graham had spotted when he signed him as a trainee with Arsenal twelve years earlier. He had loan spells with Luton and Brighton while learning his trade, and was a fringe player in Arsenal's successful 1993–94 European Cup Winner's Cup squad.

Scott DOBIE ☆☆
Born: Workington, 10 October 1978
English clubs: Carlisle, West Brom
Position: Striker
Caps won while in England: 6 (of 6)

Qualifying for Scotland on account of his granny being born in Campbeltown,

Scott Dobie played a prominent part in shooting West Brom into the Premiership soon after joining the Baggies from Carlisle. He impressed Scotland manager Berti Vogts with his pace and dribbling ability, and the way he can play wide or at the head of the forward line. Gary Megson recognised these qualities when watching him play for Carlisle, and had no hesitation in snapping him up for a bargain £150,000 in the summer of 2001. He came to the Hawthorns as a cover for the first-choice strikers, but quickly seized his chance to establish himself after the players preferred ahead of him suffered injuries. Vogts liked his spirit and made him a regular in the Scotland squad despite an in-and-out 2002–03 season with West Brom when he was often relegated to substitute as the Baggies slipped back into the First Division.

Tommy DOCHERTY ✰✰✰✰
Born: Glasgow, 24 August 1928
English clubs: Preston, Arsenal, Chelsea
Position: Midfield
Caps won while in England: 25 (of 25)

See Part One for his full career details.

Willie DONACHIE ✰✰✰✰
Born: Glasgow, 5 October 1951
English clubs: Manchester City, Norwich, Burnley, Oldham
Position: Left-back
Caps won while in England: 35 (of 35)

The thinking man's full-back, Willie Donachie was a beautifully composed and cultured defender who had his peak years in more than 400 League and Cup appearances for Manchester City. Then, on top of skilled service for Norwich, Burnley and Oldham, he had two spells in the United States at Portland Timbers. Interested in the philosophy as well as the physical side of football, he later became a deep-thinking coach first at the right hand of Joe Royle and then in tandem with Kevin Keegan at Maine Road. He has also coached in Stoke and Sheffield. His 35 Scotland caps included duty in the 1978 World Cup. The following quote is taken from an interview he gave in the United States, and the words ring true for today's young Scots.

QUOTE: 'The important thing for young Americans learning to play soccer is to have a ball at their feet. Good ball control is the first step, and then tactical awareness can gradually be introduced into their game. It is a relatively simple game that becomes complicated if players cannot grasp the team tactics.'

Cornelius DOUGALL ☆☆☆
Born: Falkirk, 7 November 1921
English clubs: Burnley, Birmingham City, Plymouth
Position: Inside-forward
Caps won while in England: 1 (of 1)

Cornelius (Neil) Dougall started his career with Burnley Juniors just as the Second World War broke out, and immediately on his demob from the RAF he signed for Birmingham City after guesting for Coventry and Walsall. He won his only Scotland cap in the same 1947–48 season that he helped to shoot Blues to the Second Division championship. Dougall later became a great favourite at Plymouth Argyle, where he played in nine different positions for the club over a stretch of more than 300 League and Cup matches. He also served Plymouth in coaching and scouting roles as well as briefly occupying the manager's chair.

Dally DUNCAN ☆☆☆☆
Born: Aberdeen, 14 October 1909
English clubs: Hull, Derby, Luton
Position: Winger
Caps won while in England: 14 (all pre-war)

After averaging more than a goal every three games for Hull City, Douglas (Dally) Duncan became a target for a queue of clubs, and it was Derby County who won the race for his signature with a £2,000 offer in 1932. He took over from George Mee (brother of Arsenal's Bertie) on the Derby left wing, and was soon acknowledged by the Scottish selectors as the natural successor to the legendary Alan Morton. Called Dally from his schoolboy days, when he used to 'dally' on his way home while kicking stones in the streets of his native Aberdeen, he was a popular fixture at the Baseball Ground either side of the war and was a member of the 1946 FA Cup-winning team. He joined Luton in October 1946, and after a season playing for them switched to manager. In 1955 he guided Luton to the First Division for the first time in their history, and later became manager at Blackburn. He steered them to the FA Cup final in 1960.

John DUNCAN ☆☆☆
Born: Dundee, 22 February 1949
English clubs: Tottenham, Derby, Scunthorpe
Position: Striker
No full caps

Scotland were so rich in forwards in the 1970s that they could afford to overlook a player of the quality of John Duncan, who was a quick and incisive striker with his hometown club Dundee before moving south to Tottenham. He scored 53 goals in 103 League games with Spurs, and added another twelve at Derby. In 1981 he joined Scunthorpe at the start of a managerial career that took in assignments at Hartlepool United, Chesterfield (two spells) and Ipswich Town. He later worked as a pundit for Eurosport and became a member of the FA's expert video-review panel.

Gordon DURIE ☆☆☆☆

Born: Paisley, 6 December 1965
English clubs: Chelsea, Tottenham
Position: Striker
Caps won while in England: 25 (of 43)

Gordon 'Jukebox' Durie was not the most elegant of players, but his biff-bang style of forward play brought him goals for a succession of clubs. He was popular with the fans wherever he played because they identified with his 100 per cent commitment, and he gave the same total effort every time he pulled on a Scotland jersey. After starring with Hibernian, Durie regularly found the net with Chelsea and Tottenham before returning to Scotland as a major strike-force for Rangers. His most memorable season at Ibrox was 1995–96 when he was Rangers leading marksmen, topping it all off with a hat-trick in the Scottish Cup final against Hearts, the club he later joined after a spell at East Fife. In 2003 he was winding down his career playing indoor Masters football.

Matthew ELLIOTT ☆☆☆

Born: Wandsworth, 1 November 1968
English clubs: Charlton, Torquay, Scunthorpe, Oxford, Leicester
Position: Central defender
Caps won while in England: 18 (of 18)

London-born Matt Elliott became eligible for Scotland because of ancestral ties. A powerful, right-footed central defender, he travelled the football roundabout with Charlton, Torquay, Scunthorpe and Oxford before entering the international arena while playing for Leicester City. He was the first captain to lift a domestic trophy for Leicester at Wembley when he collected the 2000 Coca-Cola Cup after scoring the two goals that beat Tranmere Rovers in the final. Elliott joined the Foxes from Oxford United for £1.6 million in January 1997. Much of the appeal that encouraged the then Leicester manager Martin O'Neill to buy him is that he can double as a striker. His domination in the air makes him a formidable force in both penalty areas. O'Neill tried to take him to Celtic, but Leicester did not want to let their skipper go. Leicester were forced to offer him a free transfer in 2003 because of their financial situation, but he stayed on to play an inspiring part in their promotion push back to the Premiership.

Allan EVANS ☆☆☆☆
Born: Dunfermline, 12 October 1956
English clubs: Aston Villa, Leicester, Derby
Position: Central defender
Caps won while in England: 4 (of 4)

Signed from his local club Dunfermline Athletic for £37,400 in May 1977, Allan Evans became a kingpin in the Aston Villa defence for a stretch of eleven years. He started out as a forward with Dunfermline, but his game took on a new authority and discipline when he switched to defensive duties. He and fellow Scot Ken McNaught were magnificent together at the heart of the defence when Villa won the League championship in 1980–81 and the European Cup the following season. Evans played briefly at Leicester after more than 450 League and Cup games for Villa, and then had a sight-seeing sojourn Down Under with Brisbane United. He returned to Leicester as coach alongside his old Villa team-mate Brian Little, and after a short spell managing at Morton followed Little to Villa and then Stoke in an assistant manager/coaching role.

Bobby EVANS ☆
Born: Glasgow, 16 July 1927
English club: Chelsea
Position: Centre-half
Caps won while in England: 3 (of 48)

Bobby Evans was way past his best by the time he arrived at Stamford Bridge in 1960 after a glittering sixteen-year career with Celtic. Famous for his flaming red hair and tireless running from deep defensive positions, he played more than 500 games for Celtic during which he became one of the most popular footballers of his generation. It is part of his legend how he led Celtic to a 7–1 League Cup final victory over Rangers a year after becoming the first Celtic captain to lift the League Cup against Partick Thistle at Hampden. Evans captained club and country and led by example, standing steadfast in the middle of the defence and matching centre-forwards for muscle and skill in an era when the game was very much about physical contact. He held his passing-out parade with a season at Chelsea and then at Newport. One of the all-time great Scottish defenders, he died in 2001 at the age of 74. 'Few greater players have ever worn the green and white hoops,' said Celtic chief executive Ian McLeod. We saw only a shadow of the great man in England, but he was still good enough to draw this memory from Jimmy Greaves, who was into the early days of his career when Evans arrived at Chelsea: 'Bobby was larger than life and lit up the dressing-room with his personality. He oozed class on the pitch, even though he was into his mid-thirties. He must have been amazing at his peak.'

George FARM ☆☆☆☆
Born: Edinburgh, 13 July 1924
English club: Blackpool
Position: Goalkeeper
Caps won while in England: 10 (of 10)

Goalkeeper George Farm was in the reserves at Hibernian when Blackpool manager Joe Smith brought him to Bloomfield Road in 1948, soon after the Seasiders had been beaten 4–2 by Manchester United in a classic final at Wembley. He gave magnificent service over a span of more than 500 League and cup matches for Blackpool, and was the last line of defence in the unforgettable 1953 'Matthews final', when Blackpool came from behind to beat Bolton 4–3. Often suspect with his positioning, Farm used to get himself out of trouble with superb handling, and his intelligent throwing – particularly to playmaker Ernie Taylor – launched many a counter-attack. He had an unusual method of catching the ball, with his right hand below it and his left on top. George is still warmly remembered at Armadale Thistle, the Scottish junior club where he started out on his great footballing adventure. As a manager he led Raith Rovers to the First Division and Dunfermline to the Scottish Cup in 1968. In a peculiar switch of career, Farm later became a lighthouse keeper.

Barry FERGUSON ☆☆☆
Born: Glasgow, 2 February 1978
English club: Blackburn Rovers
Position: Midfield
Caps won while in England: 2 (of 18)

Central midfielder Barry Ferguson followed older brother Derek to Ibrox and quickly established himself in the first-team squad, eventually skippering Rangers as they battled head to head with Celtic for Scottish supremacy. Rangers vowed to hang on to him when former Ibrox boss Graeme Souness came hunting his signature, and it was only after he had handed in a transfer request that he was reluctantly allowed to move to Blackburn in the summer of 2003 for a hefty £7.5 million fee. Souness, who know just a little about central midfielders, said: 'I have signed a player who I am confident will become one of Europe's most dominant midfield players for the next six or seven years.'

Duncan FERGUSON ☆☆☆
Born: Stirling, 27 December 1971
English clubs: Everton, Newcastle
Position: Centre-forward
Caps won while in England: 3 (of 7)

Sadly, this giant 6ft 4in, 15-stone striker has become more famous for his companionship with controversy rather than his undoubted talent as a striker. While playing for Rangers in 1994 he got involved in a head-butting incident with Raith Rovers opponent John McStay. Rarely, if ever, has anybody suffered so much for a loss of control on a football pitch. It led to Ferguson being sent to jail for three months (he actually served six weeks), and brought into the public arena his wild behaviour on and off the pitch that earned him the cruel yet apt nickname 'Duncan Disorderly'. But just about everybody who gets to know the real 'Big Dunc' loves him, and wherever he plays fans turn him into a cult hero. He mixes shuddering power with delicate skill, and would have won dozens more Scottish caps but for asking not to be considered for any more international games at the peak of his personal troubles. Ferguson first started making a name for himself with Carse Thistle, and then continued to thunder in goals for Dundee United before a £4 million move to Rangers in 1994. As the controversy over his head-butting raged, he moved to Everton on loan. It was the start of a love affair with the Merseyside club (and with the sister of Liverpool's world snooker star John Parrott, whom he married). His move to Everton became permanent, or so he thought, but he was then astonished to find the club had agreed to sell him to Newcastle for £7 million in 1998 to ease their financial troubles. For a short time his partnership with Alan Shearer looked the most dangerous double act since Bonnie and Clyde, but then Ferguson was sidelined by a succession of injuries. He and Everton fans were delighted to be reunited again in 2000 when he returned to Goodison in a £3.5 million transfer, but to his eternal frustration he spent more time in the medical room than on the pitch. He managed to keep in the headlines by tackling burglars in his house, not once but twice. It could only happen to Big Dunc, the most incident-prone footballer of his generation. The exciting prospect of Ferguson and teenage prodigy Wayne Rooney playing together at peak power was kept on the back burner because of Duncan's recurring injuries.

QUOTE: 'I was devastated when Everton manager Walter Smith told me the club had agreed to sell me to Newcastle. As far as I am concerned, I want to spend the rest of my career with Everton and it was great to get the chance to come back to what I think is the greatest club in the world. If only I can regain my full fitness . . .'

Robert (Bobby) FERGUSON ☆☆
Born: Kilwinning, 1 March 1945
English clubs: West Ham, Sheffield Wednesday
Position: Goalkeeper
Caps won while in England: 0 (of 7)

The tag of 'Britain's most expensive goalkeeper' weighed on Bobby Ferguson like a sack of coal when he joined West Ham from Kilmarnock for £65,000 in the summer of 1967. The player who had been so safe and sure with the Killie (with whom he won all his seven caps) suddenly lost his confidence behind a West Ham defence that continually suffered nervous breakdowns. For a while he was replaced in the West Ham goal by Peter Grotier, but once he had recovered his composure he returned to play 240 First Division games for the Hammers. He also had a short spell on loan with Sheffield Wednesday. He later emigrated to Australia, becoming player-coach of Adelaide City. Ferguson then became part-owner of a scuba-diving school, but sold his interest when one of his employees was eaten by a shark. He then switched successfully to running a flooring business.

Willie FERNIE ☆☆
Born: Kinglassie, 22 November 1928
English club: Middlesbrough
Position: Inside-forward
Caps won while in England: 0 (of 12)

A dribbling inside-forward out of the old school, Willie Fernie played 65 League games for Middlesbrough in the late 1950s after giving his best years to St Mirren and Celtic. He returned to Parkhead as a coach, and moved on to Kilmarnock, where he became the first manager to take the Killie into the Premier League. He created his Killie team in his own image, with the

emphasis on all-out attack, which is how he liked to play the game. But this meant the defence was often left wide open, and a disillusioned Willie quit the game in 1977 after a series of heavy defeats and took to the road as a Glasgow taxi driver.

Malcolm FINLAYSON ☆☆☆☆
Born: Bowhill, 14 June 1930
English clubs: Millwall, Wolves
Position: Goalkeeper
No full caps

It speaks volumes for the ability of Malcolm Finlayson that he was able to take over in the Wolves goal from the celebrated Bert Williams without any-body seeing the join. Wolves continued to be just as successful, just as solid and just as safe with Malcolm on the goal-line as when 'The Cat' Williams was the legendary last line of defence. It beggars belief that the Scottish selectors declined to pick him when he was clearly one of the outstanding goalkeepers in the land. He won League championship medals in 1957–58 and 1958–59 and was in the Wolves goal for the winning 1960 FA Cup final against Blackburn at Wembley. Signed by Millwall in 1948 from Renfrew Juniors, Malcolm modelled his game on his idol Frank Swift. He was wor-shipped at The Den, where he played 230 League games before moving to Molineux in 1956. After 179 First Division appearances for Wolves, he retired to concentrate on developing a stunningly successful steel business in the West Midlands, where he will always be remembered and revered as a goalkeeper in the Bert Williams class. There can be no higher praise.

Robert FLECK ☆☆

Born: Glasgow, 11 August 1965
English clubs: Norwich, Chelsea, Bolton, Bristol City, Reading
Position: Striker
Caps won while in England: 4 (of 4)

Unable to hold down a regular first-team place with Rangers, Robert Fleck moved to Norwich in 1987 and gained an immediate rapport with the East Anglian fans. His playing career at Carrow Road was punctuated by four knee operations and a series of headline-hitting disputes, when he was the continual source of transfer speculation. Fleck's 66 goals in 181 League and Cup appearances for the Canaries encouraged Chelsea to pay £2.1 million for him in August 1992, but it was a Stamford Bridge too far. During what was a personal nightmare, he scored just three goals in 40 League games, which worked out at £700,000 a goal. He was released on loan to Bolton and then Bristol City until returning to Norwich in 1995 for £750,000. Playing a deeper role, he scored another sixteen goals in 101 League games before a fall-out with manager Mike Walker led to him moving to Reading. He had played only five games for the Royals when a back injury forced his retirement from top-flight football. Fleck became player-manager of non-League Gorleston and in 2002 he took over as manager of Diss in his adopted county of Norfolk. He combines managing with running youth football schools.

Charlie FLEMING ☆☆☆

Born: Culros, 12 July 1927
English club: Sunderland
Position: Centre-forward
Caps won while in England: 0 (of 1)

Even more than forty years after his retirement, Sunderland fans who witnessed his performances at Roker Park still talk in awe about Charlie Fleming's shooting power. He was nicknamed Cannonball, and there was a procession of goalkeepers who found out why as they waved to the ball on its way into the net after he had unleashed his famed and feared shot. He gained his only Scotland cap while playing for East Fife, where one of his goals has gone into footballing folklore. It was a League Cup semi-final against Rangers at Hampden Park in 1949 and the dead-locked match was into its second period of extra-time. Charlie beat three defenders in a mazy run before crashing the ball into the net from 15 yards to lift the Fifers to their first ever victory over Rangers. The excitement was all too much for the East Fife chairman, who collapsed and died of a heart attack moments after the ball had hit the net.

In his 107 League games for Sunderland, Fleming scored no fewer than 62 goals and most of them were of the spectacular variety.

Darren FLETCHER ☆☆
Born: Edinburgh, 1 February 1984
English clubs: Manchester United
Position: Midfield
Caps won while in England: 2 (of 2)

Darren Fletcher is shouldering not one but two heavy loads as he gets his richly promising career under way. At Old Trafford he is being hailed as 'the next David Beckham' and at home in Scotland he is lauded as the new saviour of Scottish football. As this book goes to press he has played barely half a dozen games for Manchester United, but his performances at youth level have had spectators drooling over his potential. He has Irish roots and United skipper Roy Keane tried to talk him into electing to play for the Republic of Ireland, but true-Blue Darren preferred to wait for a call from Scotland. Coming on as a substitute in only his second international match, he scored a coolly taken goal after four minutes to lift the Scots to a Euro qualifying match victory over Lithuania in October 2003. It brought expectations to the boil, and if he can live up to just half the predictios he could lead Scotland into a new golden era. Fingers crossed.

Alex FORBES ☆☆☆☆
Born: Dundee, 21 January 1925
English clubs: Sheffield United, Arsenal, Leyton Orient, Fulham
Position: Wing-half
Caps won while in England: 14 (of 14)

There cannot be any other player who, like Alex Forbes, was signed while lying on his back in a hospital bed. The red-haired wing-half was recovering from an emergency appendix operation in a Yorkshire hospital in February 1948 when Arsenal manager Tom Whittaker persuaded him to move from Sheffield United to the Gunners for a fee of £12,000. He followed Archie Macaulay, another red-haired Scot, into the Arsenal midfield engine room and formed a great tandem partnership with skipper Joe Mercer. Just five years earlier Forbes had almost been lost to football. He elected to play ice hockey for a local club and briefly turned his back on soccer until talked into playing for Dundee North End. Sheffield United brought him south in 1946, and he started to add skill to his rugged, all-action style. He won FA Cup medals in 1950 and 1952 with Arsenal and then a League championship medal in 1953. A damaged knee virtually ended his career and he played a handful of games for Orient and Fulham before returning to Highbury as a coach. Forbes also coached in Israel before opening a café by Blackfriars Bridge in London. He received some damaging publicity when accused of child abuse, and he later emigrated to South Africa, where he became chairman of the Springbok division of the Arsenal Supporters' Club.

Duncan FORBES ☆☆☆☆
Born: Edinburgh, 19 June 1941
English clubs: Colchester, Norwich, Torquay
Position: Central defender
No full caps

Duncan Forbes gave 33 years' service to Norwich City, first as a player (357 appearances), and later as a coach, on the commercial staff and as a chief scout. He impressed everybody with his drive and leadership powers . . . everybody, that is, except the Scottish selectors, who ignored his consistent fine form in the centre of the Norwich defence. He had joined Colchester from Musselburgh in 1961, and moved to Norwich after 270 League games for the Essex club. Forbes had a short spell on loan to Torquay, and coached at Great Yarmouth and Diss before resuming his loyal service to Norwich.

Alex FORSYTH ☆☆☆
Born: Swinton, Merse, 5 February 1952
English club: Manchester United
Position: Full-back
Caps won while in England: 4 (of 10)

Alex Forsyth came to Manchester United in the whirlwind of transfer business when new manager Tommy

Docherty appeared to be trying to turn Man United into Mac United. He had won four caps at right-back while at Partick, and The Doc was the man who had selected him each time as Scotland boss. Forsyth was a strong and stylish defender, equally comfortable at right or left-back. He began his career as a forward with Arsenal, but was released on a free transfer before making a first-team appearance. Alex moved to midfield and then to full-back, and his early experience as a goal-hunter meant that he was always on the lookout for the chance to be adventurous. His star started to fade after Man United's stunning defeat by Southampton in the 1976 FA Cup final, and by the time Docherty took the team back the following year for a victory over Liverpool, Jimmy Nicholl and Arthur Albiston had taken over as the first-choice full-backs. Forsyth later played with distinction for Rangers and Motherwell.

Campbell FORSYTH ☆☆
Born: Plean, 5 May 1934
English club: Southampton
Position: Goalkeeper
Caps won while in England: 0 (of 4)

Kilmarnock were so well off for goalkeepers in the mid-1960s that they could afford to let their then Scotland international Campbell Forsyth move to Southampton for £10,000. His place in the Killie goal was taken by the next Scotland goalkeeper, Bobby

Ferguson. Forsyth was 31 when he arrived at The Dell, and spent three seasons and 68 League games as Southampton's last line of defence. Unfortunately for him, he is best remembered for being 'the other goalkeeper' when Peter Shilton scored with an 80-yard drop-kick clearance for Leicester against the Saints at The Dell in a 1967 League game.

Doug FRASER ☆☆☆☆

Born: Busby, 8 December 1942
English clubs: West Bromwich Albion, Nottingham Forest, Walsall
Position: Defender
Caps won while in England: 2 (of 2)

'Dependable Doug' Fraser started out as a centre-forward with Blantyre Celtic, but he developed into a tenacious half-back with Aberdeen. He had made 65 Scottish League appearances for the Dons when West Bromwich paid £25,000 for his services in September 1963. Doug became a fixture as an anchorman in the West Brom midfield, and collected an FA Cup winners' medal against Everton at Wembley in 1968. He won his two caps against Holland and Cyprus in 1968–69 when competition for the Scottish midfield shirts was red hot. He later played for Nottingham Forest and Walsall, but it is with the Baggies that he will always be associated after a career at the Hawthorns stretching across more than 350 League and Cup games.

William FRASER ☆☆

Born: Australia, 24 February 1929
English clubs: Sunderland, Nottingham Forest
Position: Goalkeeper
Caps won while in England: 2 (of 2)

William (Willie) Fraser was the first Australian-born player to win a Scottish cap. Brought up in Scotland, he joined Sunderland from Airdrieonians for a £5,000 fee in March 1954 and the following season played against Wales and Northern Ireland in the Home Championship. A steady rather than spectacular goalkeeper, he played 127 League games for Sunderland before a spell at Nottingham Forest that lasted just two matches.

Dougie FREEDMAN ☆☆☆

Born: Glasgow, 21 January 1974
English clubs: Barnet, Crystal Palace, Wolves, Nottingham Forest
Position: Striker
Caps won while in England: 2 (of 2)

Douglas (Dougie) Freedman has had two spells at Crystal Palace, winning the Selhurst Park fans over with his grit, graft and goals. In between he failed to make a lasting impression during stays at Wolves and Nottingham Forest. He started his career as a trainee with Queen's Park Rangers, but had to move to Barnet before he could get regular first-team football. It was his performances at Underhill that attracted Palace interest, and his first move to Selhurst Park was in 1995. Freedman was at the veteran stage of his career when called up by Berti Vogts to try to put some pace, punch and passion into the Scottish attack. Despite a goal in his debut, he could not convince Vogts that he was the answer to his prayers, and he played in only 45 minutes of his second international match. He won lasting hero worship from the Palace supporters by scoring the goal that kept Palace alive in the First Division with an 87th-minute goal, and in the following 2002–03 season earned a place in the Division One team of the year voted for by his contemporaries.

Jimmy GABRIEL ☆☆☆☆
Born: Dundee, 16 October 1940
English clubs: Everton, Southampton, Bournemouth, Swindon, Brentford
Position: Wing-half
Caps won while in England: 2 (of 2)

It is an indication of the abundance of exceptional Scottish midfield players in the 1960s that a wonderfully accomplished player such as Jimmy Gabriel was able to win only two caps. He built the foundation to his eventful career at Dundee before giving the seven best years of his playing life to Everton, where he was a midfield powerhouse and, when necessary, just as dominant in the back line. He helped Everton win the League championship in 1962–63 and the FA Cup in 1966, and later played with authority for Southampton before stopping off at Bournemouth, Swindon and Brentford on his way to a distinguished career in the United States. After playing for and coaching Seattle Sounders and then San Jose Earthquakes, Gabriel returned to Bournemouth as assistant manager and then 'went home' to Goodison as a coach. He also had two brief spells as acting Everton manager, in emergency. In 1995 he made the long trip back to the United States, where he has become an influential voice in the mushrooming worlds of youth soccer and women's soccer. Jimmy has also been heavily involved in the coaching of the superbly organised Husky Soccer division of Washington State University. He is a lovely, larger-than-life character, and an ideal man to spread the soccer gospel across the Atlantic because he will talk football until he is Everton-blue in the face.

QUOTE: 'I'll always have a soft spot for Everton and those wonderful supporters at Goodison. I missed only two matches in the 1962–63 season Everton won the championship, and I considered myself privileged to be on the same pitch as players of the quality of Brian Labone, Roy Vernon and, of course, the Golden Vision Alex Young.'

Kevin GALLACHER ☆☆☆☆
Born: Clydebank, 23 November 1966
English clubs: Coventry City,
Blackburn Rovers, Newcastle, Preston,
Sheffield Wednesday, Huddersfield
Position: Utility forward
Caps won while in England: 49 (of 53)

Recovering from two broken legs early in his career, Kevin Gallacher developed into one of the liveliest and most versatile forwards in the English Premier League. He gave excellent service to Scotland during difficult times, and he rewarded manager Craig Brown's faith in him with a procession of impressive performances. Gallacher was already an international with his first club Dundee United when he joined Coventry City in 1990, but it was in partnerships with Alan Shearer and Chris Sutton at Blackburn that he emerged as a player of true class and quality. A broken arm put him on the sidelines, and his career at Ewood Park seemed to be drifting when Bobby Robson made him his first signing as new manager at Newcastle United. He was reunited with Alan Shearer and became a great favourite on Tyneside with his willingness to work for the team in any position in which he was selected. In his mid-thirties he was still performing with style and pace in travels with Preston, Sheffield Wednesday and Huddersfield.

Tommy GEMMELL ☆
Born: Glasgow, 16 October 1943
English club: Nottingham Forest
Position: Full-back
Caps won while in England: 0 (of 18)

Celtic legend Tommy Gemmell came to Nottingham Forest as the sun was setting on his marvellous career, and he played only 39 games for the Midlands club. He then returned to Scotland for a last hurrah, leading Dundee to a remarkable 1974 League Cup victory over, of all teams, Celtic. Nicknamed Danny Kaye because he looked so much like the entertainer, he was an adventurous and aggressive full-back for Celtic, and will always be remembered in football folklore for the stunning goal he scored against Inter Milan in the 1967 European Cup final. Gemmell has recently been involved in the game by training the players at Stirling Albion, where his son is on the coaching staff.

Archie GEMMILL ☆☆☆☆☆
Born: Paisley, 24 March 1947
English clubs: Preston, Derby,
Nottingham Forest, Birmingham City,
Wigan
Position: Midfield
Caps won while in England: 43 (of 43)

'Atomic Archie' took a magic carpet ride from Preston when signed for Derby by Brian Clough and Peter Taylor. He collected two Championship medals with Derby, and then a third with Nottingham Forest after following Clough and Taylor to the City Ground. Gemmill was a buzzsaw of a midfield player whose intelligent positional play and smart passing gave shape and purpose to every team for which he played. He provided Scotland's one memorable moment of the 1978 World Cup finals, fashioning the goal of the tournament after a now-you-see-me-now-you-don't solo run through the Dutch defence. In 1979–80 he captained the Birmingham City team that won promotion to the First Division, and then took his passing prowess to Wigan, on to Jacksonville in the United States and, finally, back to Derby. No less a judge than Bill Shankly once described him as 'the best British midfield player in the game'. He passed his football gifts on to his son, Scot, while coaching at Forest and later linked up with his old team-mate John McGovern in joint management at Rotherham. Then it was another return to his beloved Derby, this time as the club's European scout.

QUOTE: 'I would have to pick my goal against Holland as the highlight of my international career. It was one of those goals you dream about. It often pops up on television all these years later and it looks better every time I see it! What a pity we had made a mess of the previous matches in the finals.'

Scot GEMMILL ☆☆☆

Born: Paisley, 2 January 1971
English clubs: Nottingham Forest, Everton
Position: Midfield
Caps won while in England: 27 (of 27)

Scot Gemmill followed his father, Archie, into the Nottingham Forest team, and then did something that his dad famously refused to do – he signed for Everton, a move that Archie turned down at the peak of his career. Scot has inherited his father's competitive instincts, and has taken after him with his all-action style, although not having quite the same ball-playing ability. He joined Everton after failing to agree a new contract at Nottingham Forest following his return from France 98. Forest placed him on a week-to-week contract, eventually agreeing to sell him to Everton just minutes before the transfer deadline in 1999 for a nominal £250,000 fee. His bedding-in weeks at Goodison were spent helping the Blues avoid relegation, which ironically had been one of the main reasons why he had wanted to leave troubled Forest. In his first full season on Merseyside he was handicapped by a succession of injuries, and he was struggling with form and fitness when fellow Scot David Moyes took over as manager. He became a willing fetch-and-carry player in central midfield as Moyes recharged his batteries by giving him vital team responsibilities.

David GIBSON ☆☆☆

Born: Winchburgh, 23 September 1938
English clubs: Leicester City, Aston Villa, Exeter City
Position: Inside-forward
Caps won while in England: 7 (of 7)

A small, beautifully balanced midfield playmaker, Davie Gibson was the man who in the 1960s made the superb Leicester City team tick. This was a Leicester with a strong Scottish heartbeat, from manager Matt Gillies through to such quality players as 'Honest John' Sjoberg, Ian King, Frank McLintock, Jimmy Walsh, Hugh McIlmoyle and Andy Lochhead. Gibson was bought from Hibernian for £25,000 while still doing his National Service, and over the next eight years played 280 League games and scored 41 goals. He was always composed on the ball and had immaculate distribution that served Scotland well in seven international appearances. After injury problems, he joined Aston Villa on a free transfer in 1970 and after just nineteen League appearances played at Exeter for two seasons. He opened a pet food and garden shop in Devon before moving back to the Leicester area where he had a postman's round, combined with co-running a residential home.
QUOTE: 'The only time I am shown on television is in the 1963 FA Cup final against Man United. I am seen failing to control a ball thrown to me by Gordon Banks. Pat Crerand takes it off me and passes it to Denis Law, who bangs it into the net. My children tell me, "After 30 years, Dad, you would think you would have learned to trap that ball by now, but you still make a mess of it!"'

Gary GILLESPIE ☆☆☆

Born: Bonnybridge, 5 July 1960
English clubs: Coventry City, Liverpool
Position: Central defender
Caps won while in England: 13 (of 13)

Gary Gillespie made an early entry into the record books when, aged seventeen, Falkirk made him the youngest ever captain of a professional football team. This brought him to the attention of English clubs, and Coventry City won a race to sign him for £75,000 before his eighteenth birthday in 1978. When Joe Fagan took over from Bob Paisley as Liverpool manager in 1983, he made Gillespie his first signing for £325,000. He was bought as cover for Twin Towers Alan Hansen and Mark Lawrenson, and he had to overcome a run of niggling injuries before he could challenge for a first-team place. A cultured central defender with a tough edge to his game, he eventually established himself in the Kenny Dalglish-managed Liverpool team that monopolised the 1980s. He played 156 League games before – on the arrival of Graeme Souness as manager – moving home to Scotland to play for Celtic, the team he had supported as a youngster. The fee was £925,000. He finished his career south of the border where he had started, with Coventry. Good enough to be a professional golfer, he later returned to Merseyside to work for Golf Network.

Alan GILZEAN ☆☆☆☆☆
Born: Coupar Angus, 22 October 1938
English club: Tottenham
Position: Striker
Caps won while in England: 17 (of 22)

The absolute master of the gliding, glancing header, Alan Gilzean had a prolific partnership with Jimmy Greaves at Tottenham. The 'G-men' gunned down defences between them, and then used to down the pints together at the White Hart pub after their home matches. The author knows, because he paid for a lot of them in what were staggeringly enjoyable pre-breathalyser days. Gillie arrived at White Hart Lane from Dundee in 1964 in a £72,500 transfer that manager Bill Nicholson later described as one of the best of the many deals he negotiated. He remains a legend at Dens Park, where his club record haul of 165 goals is going to take some beating. Included in his collection were four goals in a 5–1 destruction of Rangers at Ibrox. Not too many players have managed that on a visit to Fortress Ibrox! In his final season with Dundee he scored a record 52 League goals, and he continued to find the net for Spurs – 93 in 343 League games. A little bit of trivia for you: Gillie played for Aldershot reserves while doing his National Service

in the late 1950s. Not a lot of people know that. At Tottenham, he was happy to play second fiddle to Greavsie, laying on the goals for his sidekick with instant passes and clever flick-headers. His honours at Spurs included an FA Cup winners' medal in 1967, two League Cup final triumphs and a UEFA Cup final victory. Gillie was all grace and style, the epitome of how great Scottish forwards play the game. He went hunting goals in South Africa and then managed non-League Stevenage in the mid-1970s, and after working as a transport manager in Enfield was rumoured to be still sinking those pints. His son, Ian, was a Spurs apprentice who went on to play for Northampton and then had a full career in Scotland. He was always handicapped by being compared with his dad, a genius at the game.

QUOTE: 'I used to play in fifteen-a-side games when I was a kid growing up in Scotland, so if you ever managed to get the ball you would hold on to it as long as possible. This is how I learned my ball control.'

Stephen GLASS ☆☆
Born: Dundee, 23 May 1976
English clubs: Newcastle United, Watford
Position: Midfield
Caps won while in England: 1 (of 1)

He has a left foot like a magic wand, but Stephen Glass was unable to wave it to the satisfaction of Newcastle manager

Sir Bobby Robson. Glass arrived at Newcastle with a huge reputation during the dying embers of Kenny Dalglish's brief reign as boss at St James' Park. His fee was set by a transfer tribunal at £650,000, while Aberdeen valued him as worth twice that. He started to live up to his billing when Ruud Gullit took over as Newcastle boss, and won his first Scotland cap as a substitute against the Faroe Islands. His left foot was put into cold storage by Robson, and disgruntled Glass put in a transfer request. He moved to Watford under the Bosman ruling in June 2001 and quickly became an influential force on the left side of the Watford midfield. Then, in the summer of 2003, he elected to move back home to Scotland with Hibernian.

Andy GORAM ☆☆☆
Born: Bury, 13 April 1964
English clubs: Oldham, Notts County, Sheffield United, Man United, Coventry
Position: Goalkeeper
Caps won while in England: 4 (of 44)

It is testimony to Andy Goram's talent as a goalkeeper that he was voted the greatest custodian in the history of Glasgow Rangers in a worldwide poll to find the club's best ever players. With a mix of his rapid reflexes, excellent positioning, safe handling and dare-devil saves, he more than anybody was responsible for Rangers enjoying a remarkable 44 games without defeat over a stretch of seven months in the 1992–93 season.

Amazingly, he kept 107 clean sheets in his 258 games for Rangers and was the last line of defence for the last six of their nine-in-a-row championships. Born in Lancashire of Scottish heritage, he served his apprenticeship with West Brom and then started his career with Oldham Athletic. He spent seven years at Boundary Park and performed well enough to earn the first of his 43 caps. In 1987 he moved to Hibernian, playing 138 League games and achieving the distinction of becoming a double international when he represented Scotland at cricket. Walter Smith made him one of his first targets when he took over as manager at Ibrox in 1991, and the £1 million fee turned out to be a bargain as Goram took over in goal from Chris Woods. A personality goalkeeper who rarely keeps his feelings to himself, fun-loving, sometimes overweight Andy has prolonged his career with have-gloves-will-save service for Notts County, Sheffield United, Motherwell, Man United, Coventry, briefly back to Oldham and then a return to Scotland with Queen of the South.

Richard GOUGH ☆☆☆☆
Born: Stockholm, Sweden, 5 April 1962
English clubs: Tottenham, Nottingham Forest, Everton
Position: Central defender
Caps won while in England: 8 (of 61)

Like his old team-mate Andy Goram, Richard Gough had his best years at

Ibrox where – also like Goram – he entered the land of Rangers legend. Captain of Rangers from 1990 to 1996, he was the only player to win a medal in each of the record nine successive championships, which speaks volumes for his consistency and his powers of leadership. A strong and decisive central defender, he was commanding in the air, timed his tackles to perfection and then looked to pass the ball out of defence with precision. One of the most popular players ever to pull on the Scotland jersey, he won 61 caps, including those earned in the World Cup campaigns of 1986 and 1990. He was born in his mother's homeland of Sweden, and then moved to South Africa where his Scottish father, Charlie, a former Charlton and Army wing-half, continued his football career. Gough started playing professionally with Dundee United, and had two years with Tottenham before beginning his romance with Rangers. He followed a splendid partnership with Gary Mabbutt at Spurs with an even more memorable double act with Terry Butcher at Rangers, the English and Scottish captains side by side. He was brave beyond measure, and earned the nickname Captain Blood because of the bloody injuries he collected in the cause of his club and country. In the autumn of his career he played briefly with Nottingham Forest, made an impressive impact in the United States with San Jose Clash and Kansas City Wizards, and enjoyed a final fling with Everton, when back in harness with his old Rangers boss Walter Smith. On top of his ability as a player, Gough was also an articulate and dignified sportsman, who was an ideal role model for young players coming into the game. He now spreads the gospel in California, where he coaches San Jose Clash.

QUOTE: 'My strong advice to any young professionals would be to ensure they maintain a high level of fitness. I have always prided myself on being as fit as possible, and this means leading the right lifestyle away from football and eating the right things. I remember playing with Walter Smith as a seventeen-year-old reserve at Dundee United, and he set the standards of sportsmanship and commitment that I have tried to maintain ever since.'

Arthur GRAHAM ☆☆☆
Born: Glasgow, 26 October 1952
English clubs: Leeds United, Manchester City, Bradford City
Position: Winger/midfield
Caps won while in England: 10 (of 10)

Arthur Graham came south from Aberdeen to Leeds for £125,000 in 1977 when Jimmy Armfield was in charge at Elland Road. Jimmy, an all-time great England right-back, knows a thing or three about left wingers and he saw Arthur as a natural successor to the maestro, Eddie Gray. He started out as an orthodox outside-left with Leeds, but then dropped back into midfield from where his creative runs often caused chaos in opposition defences. Graham was more a maker than taker of goals, but also knew how to get the ball into the net, and included three hat-tricks in his haul of 47 goals in 260 League and Cup games. Ron Atkinson took him across the Pennines to Old Trafford in the summer of 1983 for a basement price £50,000. He performed reasonably well for Man United before making way for the dashing Dane Jesper Olsen. After playing 31 games for Bradford, he coached the reserves and had a short period as caretaker manager before finishing his career as a part-time player with Halifax. He then became a youth coach, working for the Eddie Gray schools. Youngsters could not have had a better teacher. He always played the game in the right spirit and with a high level of skill and commitment.

George GRAHAM ☆☆☆☆
Born: Bargeddie, 30 November 1944
English clubs: Aston Villa, Chelsea, Arsenal, Man United, Portsmouth, Crystal Palace
Position: Midfield
Caps won while in England: 12 (of 12)

See Part One for his full career details.

Andy GRAY ☆☆☆☆☆
Born: Glasgow, 30 November 1955
English clubs: Aston Villa, Wolves, Everton, Notts County, West Brom
Position: Striker
Caps won while in England: 20 (of 20)

Anybody who tunes into Sky TV's excellent coverage of the football scene will know that Andy Gray talks an even better game than he played. And that's saying something, because Gray was an exceptional centre-forward. He played in the old-style way, with bash, crash and dash to go with his not inconsiderable ball skills. Gray laid the foundation to his career at Dundee United, scoring 36 League goals in 62 games before moving to Aston Villa for £110,000 in September 1975. This proved a steal by manager Ron Saunders. Just four years later he sold him to Wolves for what was then a British record transfer fee of £1,469,000 after he had become the only player to scoop the PFA Player of the Year and Young Player of the Year awards in the same season. A troublesome knee handicapped Gray at Wolves, but he still managed to bang in 38 goals in 133 League games. This encouraged Howard Kendall to spend £250,000 bringing him to Everton in November 1983 when most good judges thought his best was behind him. Kendall's gamble paid off as Gray's bubbling personality and driving, direct play helped lift Everton morale on the pitch and in the dressing-room. He forged a winning partnership with fellow Scot Graeme Sharp, both of them finding the net in the 2–0 1984 FA Cup final victory over Watford. Injuries interrupted Gray's career again, but he came back to help push Everton through their winning crusades for the League championship and European Cup Winners' Cup. When Gary Lineker arrived from Leicester City, Gray decided he would prefer to continue his goal hunt back at Aston Villa despite a petition from fans pleading for him to stay at Goodison. He had poured so much into the game with his courageous physical approach and aerial bombardments that his body was giving up, while his spirit was still willing. He played briefly for Notts County, Rangers (in the first of the nine-in-a-row championship seasons) and West Brom, and then became an enthusiastic coach and assistant manager at Villa Park until the call of television proved too strong.

QUOTE: 'I get a completely different view of the game now that I work in television, and I have to say in all honesty that I think the overall standard of the Premiership is just sensational. I cannot believe the quality has ever been better than it is now, and I feel privileged to get such a close-up look at it all.'

Eddie GRAY ☆☆☆☆☆

Born: Glasgow, 17 January 1948
English club: Leeds United
Position: Winger
Caps won while in England: 12 (of 12)

A Nureyev on grass, Edwin (Eddie) Gray rivalled even George Best for close ball control. Anybody who doubts that statement did not witness his goal for Leeds against Burnley in April 1970 when, with subtle changes of pace and deceiving dips of the shoulder, he beat six defenders in the space of a hallway carpet on the way to walking the ball into the net. It was one of those goals where you didn't ask the time but the date. In the same match, he scored with a precision-placed 30-yard shot. When he came to Elland Road for a trial match as a teenager Jack Charlton watched him, and told manager Don Revie: 'Don't let that kid out of here without his name on a contract. I don't want some other club signing him and us having to play against him twice a season!' He scored 52 goals in his 455 League games for Leeds, and was a creative member of the famed-and-feared team that won two League championships, and was runner-up four times. Gray overcame a succession of injuries to play in three FA Cup finals, a League Cup final, two UEFA Cup finals, a European Cup Winners' Cup final and, in 1975, a European Cup final. His injuries cost him at least another twenty caps. He had coaching experience at Hull City and Middlesbrough, managed Rochdale and Leeds, started a successful schools coaching business and returned to Elland Road as assistant manager to David O'Leary. Talk to any top pro from the 1960s and 1970s and they will confirm that Eddie deserves to be bracketed with the all-time great Anglo-Scottish players.

QUOTE: 'They were incredible days at Leeds under Don Revie when we were challenging for every trophy there was. The secret of our success was a mixture of having brilliant players in a well-organised team, and a competitive team spirit that meant we had our minds on winning. It was the one-for-all-and-all-for-one attitude that Don instilled in us.'

Frank GRAY ☆☆☆☆
Born: Glasgow, 27 October 1954
English clubs: Leeds, Nottingham Forest, Sunderland, Darlington
Position: Left-back
Caps won while in England: 32 (of 32)

Like brother Eddie, Francis (Frank) Gray started his professional career at Leeds. He was a specialist left-back and occasional midfielder, and – in contrast to his brother – was functional rather than magical with his left foot. He played 332 League games in two periods with the Yorkshire club and was a member of the 1973–74 championship-winning team. Along with Eddie, he suffered the disappointment of defeat in the 1975 European Cup final, but was compensated by collecting a European Cup winners' medal in 1980 with Brian Clough's Nottingham Forest. This was at the end of his first season with Forest following a £500,000 move in 1979. He returned to Elland Road in March 1981 and played for a short while under his brother's management. Remarkably, he stacked up twenty more Scottish caps than the dozen won by his more naturally gifted brother. Frank later served Sunderland in 146 League games, helping them gain promotion as Third Division champions in 1988. A period as player and then manager at Darlington was followed by scouting assignments for Blackburn and Sheffield Wednesday, management at Harrogate and then a sunshine move to Bahrain in a coaching capacity.

Tony GREEN ☆☆☆
Born: Glasgow, 13 October 1946
English clubs: Blackpool, Newcastle United
Position: Midfield
Caps won while in England: 6 (of 6)

Tony Green's career was cruelly cut short right in its summertime when he was basking in the glory of having made thousands of new fans and friends on Tyneside. He had alerted major clubs to his potential with a procession of outstanding performances for Blackpool after joining them from Albion Rovers in 1967. A serious tendon injury sidelined him just as clubs were lining up to look at 'the new Alan Ball'. Newcastle manager Joe Harvey kept his eye on the situation and when he had recovered nipped in quick to take him from the North-West to the North-East where, in just 33 League games, he won cult-hero status with the Geordie fans. They were in raptures over his left-footed wizardry in midfield, and it came as a terrible shock when he was forced to quit the game at 27 because of a knee injury. 'This is one of the saddest days of my life,' Joe Harvey said, when breaking the news that Green would never play again. 'I rate him the best buy I have ever made, and he had so much to give. It's a tragedy.' Tony had the character to shrug off the disappointment and get on with his life. He became a schoolteacher in Blackpool, sat regularly on the pools panel and became involved in media work.

Bryan GUNN ☆☆☆☆
Born: Thurso, 22 December 1963
English club: Norwich City
Position: Goalkeeper
Caps won while in England: 6 (of 6)

Goalkeeping in the shadows of Jim Leighton at Aberdeen, Bryan Gunn elected to come south to Norwich in 1986 to start a rapport with Carrow Road fans that transcended football. He was bought as a replacement for England international Chris Woods, who made the journey o'er the border to Rangers.

Over the next ten years Gunn was a reliable last line of defence for the Canaries in 477 first-team games, and was twice elected Norwich Player of the Year. He captured the hearts of people everywhere when his two-year-old daughter Francesca died of leukaemia. With the help of the *Eastern Daily Press* and its sister paper, the *Evening News*, he set up an appeal and he and his wife worked tirelessly to raise a significant amount of money to help fight leukaemia. In 1998 he returned to Scotland to play for Hibernian, an assignment that ended the following year in the nightmare of a broken leg. He went back to his beloved Norwich City to work in the commercial department, and in 2002 the City Council came up with the imaginative and popular idea of making Bryan the Sheriff of Norwich.

QUOTE: 'As well as my six Scottish caps, I remember with pride becoming the first goalkeeper since Gordon Banks to keep three successive clean sheets at Anfield.'

Alan HANSEN ☆☆☆☆☆
Born: Alloa, 13 June 1955
English club: Liverpool
Position: Central defender
Caps won while in England: 26 (of 26)

The author has worked as a scriptwriter with Alan Hansen and can vouch for the fact that he epitomises professionalism and perfectionism. He has become a master of the broadcasting medium by putting in the same 100 per cent attention to detail and delivery that he used to when standing proud and immovable alongside Mark Lawrenson at the heart of the Liverpool defence. Hansen was all style and beautiful Scottish skills in more than 500 League and Cup appearances for a Liverpool team that was dominant throughout the 1980s. He was one of the most successful British footballers of all time until a knee injury forced his retirement in 1991, winning all the honours available at club level at least twice. Along with his talent as a player came natural leadership qualities and he captained Liverpool to their double in 1986. It was beyond belief when acting Scottish manager Alex Ferguson decided not to take him to the World Cup finals in Mexico. The author would rate him just a step behind Bobby Moore as the most assured and authoritative central defender he has seen in British club football. He started his career with Partick Thistle, following his older brother John, who was capped twice by Scotland. The trademark scar on Alan's forehead was caused when he walked into a plate-glass door at the age of seventeen, at a time when he was tossing up whether to follow golf or football as a career. He was then playing off two, and his game has deteriorated to the point where he is now off three! Alan Hansen, a class act. What sort of manager would he have made?

QUOTE: 'Management never appealed to me. I prefer the power without responsibility that you have as a so-called expert. I always try to call it as I see it and tell the truth. It seems to work because the camera quickly picks up insincerity and dishonesty. I loved my life as a footballer and am equally content in my role in television. The one disappointment is that I never played in an Open championship, my dream as a boy growing up in Alloa.'

Joe HARPER ☆☆
Born: Greenock, 11 January 1948
English clubs: Huddersfield, Everton
Position: Striker
Caps won while in England: 0 (of 4)

'King Joey' Harper – that's what they still call him at Aberdeen, where his haul of 205 goals is a club record that will take a lot of beating. He collected his goals in two stays at Pittodrie, and he also had two spells at his local club Morton either side of a 28-match stay at Huddersfield. Harper joined the Dons for the first time in 1969 as a winger, but it was when he switched to a central striking position that he became a deadly marksman. A move to Everton in December 1973 brought him twelve goals in 43 League appearances but little satisfaction. He returned to Scotland with Hibernian in 1974, and was back at Aberdeen two years later. His career was effectively finished by a knee injury in 1979, and his international caps collection was curtailed at four after he had become involved in the infamous Copenhagen nightclub scandal that led to five players being suspended. When he retired his club record stood at 199 goals, but six goals were added in 2002 when it was agreed by the Scottish authorities to allow Dryborough Cup goals to be included. He stayed involved in the game as a manager of Highland League clubs, and became a columnist for the Aberdeen *Evening Express*.

Asa HARTFORD ☆☆☆☆
Born: Clydebank, 24 October 1950
English clubs: West Brom, Man City, Nottingham Forest, Everton, Norwich, Bolton, Stockport, Oldham, Southport
Position: Midfield
Caps won while in England: 50 (of 50)

Lined up for a transfer from West Bromwich Albion to Leeds in 1971, Richard (Asa) Hartford failed a medical test when he was told he had a hole in his heart. Leeds pulled out of the deal and the strong rumour was that Asa's career was finished. Wrong! Over the next seventeen years he became one of the few players to join the 700 League games club, featuring with nine English clubs and Fort Lauderdale in the United States. He was also a member of the Scottish international 50-cap club, which won him an automatic place in the Scottish Football Association's Hall of Fame. Asa – named by parents who loved singer Al (Asa Yoelson) Jolson –

played 260 of his League matches in two periods with Manchester City, the club he later rejoined as coach and then assistant manager after coaching at a string of clubs including Stoke and Blackburn. Thirty-six of his Scotland caps were won while with City, for whom he was a constructive orchestrator of attacks with his driving, disciplined play from a midfield command post. As David Coleman once famously said on TV: 'He is a wholehearted player.' In a career full of incidents he had an incredible encounter with Brian Clough, who bought him for £420,000 and after just three games decided he was not the player he thought he was and sold him on to Everton. Only Cloughie would have done that, and it could only have happened to Asa.

QUOTE: 'It was devastating when I got the medical report at Leeds, but I felt fine in myself and was determined to prove that I was as fit as the next man. I was proud to join the 700 club, and also to captain Scotland on the way to my 50 caps. Not bad for somebody who was written off as finished!'

David HARVEY ☆☆☆
Born: Leeds, 7 February 1948
English clubs: Leeds, Bradford City
Position: Goalkeeper
Caps won while in England: 16 (of 16)

Born in Yorkshire of a Scottish father, David Harvey was remarkably patient while waiting for his first-team chance at

Leeds. He played more than 200 games in goal for the Central League reserve side as understudy to Gary Sprake before breaking into the first-team. A strong, decisive goalkeeper with huge hands, he was the last line of defence in 349 League matches and appeared in three FA Cup finals, keeping a clean sheet against Arsenal in the Centenary 1972 final. Many rated him the best goalkeeper in the 1974 World Cup finals, but his career was interrupted at its peak by injuries received in a car smash. This cost him a place in the 1975 European Cup final. He had spells in the early 1980s with Vancouver Whitecaps and Drogheda, then a second stay at Elland Road before making his final League saves with Bradford City. He took on a pub, delivered fruit and veg to hotels, was player-manager at Whitby, worked as a postman, and then took off for the Orkney Islands, where he has become self-sufficient on an old farm. The man who continues to deliver the post made a little bit of history when, in a Charity Shield match, he became the first goalkeeper to take (and miss) a penalty at Wembley.

David HAY ☆☆☆

Born: Paisley, 29 January 1948
English club: Chelsea
Position: Defensive midfield
Caps won while in England: 0 (of 27)

Stylish and composed whether operating in midfield or at full-back, Davie Hay was at his peak playing for Celtic. Chelsea bought him for £225,000 when he impressed in the 1974 World Cup, but his career at Stamford Bridge was prematurely cut short by injury in 1979 after he had made 120 appearances for the Blues. Hay joined Ally McLeod at Motherwell, eventually taking over as manager and guiding them to the First Division title. Celtic invited him back as their boss, but it was not the happiest of reunions and he moved abroad to Norway where he steered Lillestrom to the Norwegian championship. He then returned home to his roots at Paisley, managing St Mirren and then, after a break in Florida, scouting for Celtic. Hay was building a successful career as a respected players' agent when he accepted an offer to join Jim Leishman in revolutionising Livingston.

Jackie HENDERSON ☆☆☆

Born: Glasgow, 17 January 1932
English clubs: Portsmouth, Wolves, Arsenal, Fulham
Position: Utility forward
Caps won while in England: 7 (of 7)

A spitfire of a forward with Portsmouth, John (Jackie) Henderson scored 70 goals in 217 League games before being persuaded to join Wolves. He felt uncomfortable with what he described as their 'kick-and-rush' style and quickly moved on to Arsenal after just nine appearances for the Midlands club. Henderson became a victim of his own versatility at Arsenal, and was moved across the forward line without managing to establish himself in one place. Chunky and muscular, he was at his most lethal on the left wing, cutting in and scoring with scorching shots or brave diving headers. After scoring 29 goals in 111 games for the Gunners, he moved across London to Fulham for 45 appearances before closing his playing career with Poole Town in Dorset, where he worked outside football for a builders' merchant.

Willie HENDERSON ☆☆

Born: Baillieston, 24 January 1944
English club: Sheffield Wednesday
Position: Winger
Caps won while in England: 0 (of 29)

English fans saw only flashes of the genius of Willie Henderson, who spent a year at Sheffield Wednesday after he had given his best for Rangers during a marvellous career in which he was a wizard of a winger. He had a tongue as biting as his feet, and could needle opponents with caustic comments at the same time as taking them apart with his speed and skill. All his caps came while he was with Rangers, and he later added to his international experience when he captained the Hong Kong national team! He could be effective in midfield, but it was his blistering runs down the left wing that stay etched in the memory.

Colin HENDRY ☆☆☆☆☆

Born: Keith, 7 December 1965
English clubs: Blackburn Rovers, Manchester City, Coventry, Bolton, Preston, Blackpool
Position: Central defender
Caps won while in England: 35 (of 51)

Easy to spot on a football field because of his thatch of near-white hair, Colin Hendry was a magnificent warrior of a central defender for Dundee, Blackburn Rovers, Manchester City, Rangers and Scotland. He was the heart of the Kenny Dalglish-managed Blackburn team that won the Premiership in 1994–95. Hendry dominated the airways, and tackled with a determination that frightened the opposition and inspired his team-mates. He became an equally powerful influence with Rangers at Ibrox. His 51-cap international career finished ignominiously. He was banned for six matches for elbowing a San Marino opponent while skippering Scotland in a World Cup qualifying match in which he scored two goals. The violent conduct was out of character for a defender who was always competitive but rarely unsporting. The Hendry flame was just a flicker when he came back south to play for Coventry, Bolton and, on loan, at Preston and Blackpool.

David HERD ☆☆☆☆
Born: Hamilton, 15 April 1934
English clubs: Stockport, Arsenal, Man United, Stoke
Position: Centre-forward
Caps won while in England: 5 (of 5)

Football was in David Herd's blood. He started his career playing alongside his dad, Alex, in the 1951 Stockport County team, and he later followed his father as a Scottish international. Arsenal signed him for £8,000 in the summer of 1954 when he was still doing his National Service. Playing as a target man centre-forward, he netted 107 goals in 180 games for the Gunners, yet was never totally accepted by manager George Swindin, who used him as bait in trying to sign a string of players including Denis Law and George Eastham. Undemonstrative and easy-going in an era when centre-forwards were of the hit-and-hurt variety, he almost reluctantly agreed to join Manchester United for £35,000 in 1961. His exploits coincided with the rise of the holy trinity of Best, Law and Charlton, yet he still managed to shoot himself into United legend with an extraordinary output of 144 goals in 262 matches. Herd's five caps came while he was at Arsenal, and it seems astonishing that the Scottish selectors did not pick him to play with his United sidekick Denis Law. They were devastating together in the 1963 FA Cup final, putting three goals between them – two to Herd – past Leicester's goalkeeper Gordon Banks. A broken leg in 1967 (against Leicester) knocked a lot of the confidence out of him after he had helped United to two League championships, and he hung up his shooting boots following a season with Stoke. He tried his hand at management at Lincoln, making way in 1972 for young Graham Taylor. Herd now runs a garage in Urmston, a ten-minute drive from Old Trafford, where he is a frequent and popular visitor.

QUOTE: 'I would have been quite happy to stay at Arsenal, but there was always a sense that they were never 100 per cent satisfied with me. I had the best years of my career with United, and never regretted for one second making the move. The highlight has to be my two goals in the FA Cup final at Wembley. Magical memories!'

George HERD ☆☆☆
Born: Gartcosh, 6 May 1936
English clubs: Sunderland, Hartlepool
Position: Inside-forward
Caps won while in England: 0 (of 5)

One of the first players to celebrate goal scoring with a somersault, George Herd was in a constant spin of delight at Sunderland, where he had a prolific partnership with a fairly confident player called Brian Clough. Herd won his five caps with Clyde, first as a right winger and then as a central marksman, where his deft ball control meant he could make as well as take goals. He moved to Roker for £40,000 in 1961 and scored 47 goals in 278 League games. He played briefly at Hartlepool, and after retiring became a respected coach specialising in bringing on youth players at his old Sunderland hunting ground.

Jim HERRIOT ☆☆☆

Born: Airdrie, 20 December 1939
English clubs: Birmingham City,
Mansfield Town
Position: Goalkeeper
Caps won while in England: 8 (of 8)

The name and the fame of James Herriot spread beyond football when an author called Alf Wright happened to catch him playing in goal for Birmingham City in a televised 1970 match. At that moment Alf was sitting at a typewriter trying to think of a pen name for himself. James Herriot sat warmly in his imagination, and it became the pseudonym for a procession of books about a Yorkshire vet. The 'real' Jim Herriot was a saviour of St Andrews, with safe hands that saved shots rather than the lives of animals. He played 181 League games for the Blues after moving to the Midlands from Dunfermline Athletic, where he had hero status. Herriot had loan spells with Mansfield before returning home to Scotland to play briefly with Partick Thistle. He later became a bricklayer on Strathclyde, no doubt thinking about building defensive walls.

John HEWIE ☆☆☆

Born: South Africa, 13 December 1927
English club: Charlton Athletic
Position: Defender
Caps won while in England: 19 (of 19)

One of the most versatile players ever to step foot on a soccer pitch, John Hewie played in ten positions for Charlton Athletic – including four times in goal in an emergency. He was at his most effective at left-back, the position in which he won sixteen of his nineteen Scottish caps. Tall and elegant, he was a footballing defender who learned his craft on the playing fields of South Africa, to where his Scottish father had emigrated. Charlton manager Jimmy Seed netted him by accident during a trip to South Africa to try to sign Bill Perry, who elected instead to join Blackpool. Hewie proved a wonderful consolation prize, playing 495 games for Charlton. An excellent cricketer, he was also a fine baseball player who once represented England in an international match. Here's a little fact to add to any trivia collection – John once played football *against* Scotland for South Africa in 1956. He returned home to South Africa at the end of his playing career before coming back to England to settle in the Midlands.

Gary HOLT ☆☆
Born: Irvine, 3 September 1973
English club: Norwich City
Position: Defensive midfield
Caps won while in England: 2 (of 4)

After a stop-start-stop launch to his professional career, Gary Holt settled down at Kilmarnock, where his combative style in midfield attracted Norwich. He became a permanent fixture in the Norwich engine room after joining them for £100,000 in the spring of 2001. Holt had been recommended to Celtic while serving as a soldier in Germany in 1993, but he failed to make an impact at Parkhead and moved on to Stoke, who released him without giving him a first-team game. His uncomplicated driving and determined play earned him two caps while with Killie, and he added two more caps following his move to Carrow Road, where his positive performances have earned him a close rapport with the Norwich supporters.

Jim HOLTON ☆☆☆
Born: Lesmahagow, 11 April 1951
English clubs: Shrewsbury,
Manchester United, Sunderland,
Coventry, Sheffield Wednesday
Position: Central defender
Caps won while in England: 15 (of 15)

In an all-too-short life, Jim Holton managed to force himself into the land of footballing legend. 'Six foot two,

Eyes of Blue, Big Jim Holton's after you . . .' was a threatening crowd chant that accompanied his agricultural scything tackles when at the heart of the Manchester United defence. His take-no-prisoners approach was in stark contrast to the smoothness and style of Martin Buchan, playing alongside him in the Tommy Docherty era at Old Trafford. Signed by The Doc from Shrewsbury in January 1973, he was right at the peak of his popularity with the United fans when a twice-broken leg robbed him of much of his shuddering power. He made token appearances with Sunderland, Coventry and Sheffield Wednesday, and continued his career in Miami and Detroit before accepting that he would never recover the old force first developed as an apprentice with West Bromwich Albion. A likeable gentle giant away from the football field, he ran the Old Stag pub in Coventry until his sudden death in 1993 at the age of 42.

Bobby HOPE ☆☆☆
Born: Bridge of Allan, 28 September 1943
English clubs: West Brom,
Birmingham City, Sheffield
Wednesday
Position: Midfield
Caps won while in England: 2 (of 2)

A composed and authoritative midfield player, Bobby Hope will always be associated with West Bromwich Albion, despite late-career action with Birmingham City and Sheffield Wednesday. He was a pass master for West Brom across more than 400 League and Cup matches, occasionally introducing venom to go with his skill. Stocky and well balanced, he was a vital link in the Albion team that won the FA Cup in 1968 with a wonder goal by Jeff Astle. While Astle was the hammer of the attack, Hope was the architect and they had a long-running partnership that caused problems for even the tightest defences. After retiring, Hope ran a sub-post office and then a sandwich bar. He managed non-League clubs Bromsgrove Rovers and Burton Albion, and used his expert judgement for West Brom as their chief scout.

David HOPKIN ☆☆☆

Born: Greenock, 21 August 1970
English clubs: Chelsea, Crystal Palace, Leeds United, Bradford City
Position: Midfield
Caps won while in England: 7 (of 7)

David Hopkin completed a full circle in 2002 when he returned to the Morton club where he had started his professional career in 1989 after being spotted playing for Port Glasgow Boys' Club. He had fetched fees totalling £8.4 million during travels on the football roundabout with Chelsea, Crystal Palace (twice), Leeds and Bradford City. Injuries at key times in his career in England stopped him making as big an impact as he might have done, but when at peak fitness this powerfully built, ginger-haired six-footer made his presence felt in midfield. David's most dominating displays were with Crystal Palace, for whom he scored 25 goals to go with the ball winning and tidy distribution that were the main features of his game. His return to Morton was on a free transfer. It had been quite an adventure, including seven appearances for his country.

Stewart HOUSTON ☆☆☆

Born: Dunoon, 20 August 1949
English clubs: Chelsea, Brentford, Man United, Sheffield United, Colchester
Position: Defender
Caps won while in England: 1 (of 1)

The one cap awarded to Stewart Houston does not do justice to his talent as a left-back of exceptional ability and great strength. He made a quiet start to his career with Chelsea and Brentford, and then established himself as a class act at Manchester United, taken there by the manager who brought him to England in the first place, Tommy Docherty. In his first season at Old Trafford, he played under the captaincy of George Graham, to whom he later became trusted assistant manager at both Arsenal and Tottenham. Houston did not have the best of luck with his playing career, for instance missing the 1979 FA Cup final because of a ligaments injury received just two weeks before what promised to be the game of his life. As well as providing diligent defence, he also delivered thirteen goals in 205 League appearances for Man United. In a short stay at Bramall Lane he helped Sheffield United win the Fourth Division title in 1982. He then became player-coach at Colchester, and later moved on to coach at Plymouth and Walsall. Always a deep thinker about the game, he was the ideal number two to George Graham and played a vital background part in shaping the all-conquering Gunners team. He became manager at Queen's Park Rangers after Graham's ignoble departure from Highbury, and joined up with him again at Tottenham following a spell as assistant at Ipswich.

John HUGHES ☆
Born: Coatbridge, 3 April 1943
English clubs: Crystal Palace,
Sunderland
Position: Striker
Caps won while in England: 0 (of 8)

John 'Yogi Bear' Hughes was virtually a spent force by the time he arrived in England as a Crystal Palace player. He had given his all to Celtic in 416 games during which he had a haul of 189 goals. The 1966–67 season in which Celtic became European Cup winners was at one and the same time the best and most frustrating of Big John's career. He played in five of the ties on the way to

the final in Lisbon, but was the unlucky one to be left out by manager Jock Stein. He moved to Palace in a double transfer along with Lisbon Lion Willie Wallace in 1971. It looked great on paper but did not work on the pitch. They scored just eight goals between them before injury-prone Hughes switched to Sunderland, where a broken leg in his debut ended his career. Palace fans still talk about a spectacular goal that he scored against Sheffield United, just a brief glimpse of the raw power he used to regularly show for Celtic, where he was more noted for his vigour than his skill. He later managed at junior level and became a coach of the Scottish Junior Football Association team. Hughes also ran a pub in his native Coatbridge.

William (Billy) HUGHES ☆☆☆
Born: Coatbridge, 30 December 1948
English clubs: Sunderland, Derby,
Leicester, Carlisle
Position: Striker
Caps won while in England: 1 (of 1)

The younger brother of 'Yogi' Hughes, Billy had his most memorable moments in England at Wembley in 1973 when his powerful performance helped Second Division Sunderland cause one of the shocks of the century with a victory over mighty Leeds United in the FA Cup final. A skilful dribbler in the best traditions of old-style Scottish forwards, he packed a wicked shot and scored 74 goals in 287 League games for

Sunderland. He won his only cap as a substitute against Sweden in 1975. Hughes came through the Sunderland junior ranks and served the club for ten years until failing to impress new boss Jimmy Adamson. He continued his career at Derby, Leicester and Carlisle, without managing to recapture the form that made him a favourite at Roker.

Don HUTCHISON ☆☆☆
Born: Gateshead, 9 May 1971
English clubs: Hartlepool, Liverpool, West Ham, Sheffield United, Everton
Position: Midfield
Caps won while in England: 24 (of 24)

Capped under the heritage ruling, Don Hutchison has been a constant companion of controversy and incident during a see-sawing career since joining Liverpool from his original club Hartlepool in 1991. He had established a stunning midfield partnership at Anfield with Jamie Redknapp when, in 1994, he was involved in a well-publicised stripping incident in a city centre bar. Soon after, the then manager Roy Evans sold him to West Ham for £1.5 million. He struggled to settle at Upton Park, despite scoring eleven goals in 30 first-team appearances, and he quickly moved on to Sheffield United. Hutchison regained his old authority with the Blades, and Everton were encouraged to take him back to Merseyside in February 1998 in return for a £1 million fee. He got himself involved in a bitter contract dispute at Goodison, and in the summer of 2000 he was on his travels again, this time back to his native North-East with Sunderland in return for £2.5 million. Hutch became a major power in midfield for the Black Cats, but then – amid denied rumours that his wife was unsettled – he returned to West Ham in 2001 for a whacking fee of £5 million. A serious injury sidelined him for much of the 2002–03 season when under-pressure Hammers desperately needed the midfield drive that is his trademark. Had he been fully fit, it is unlikely that West Ham would have been relegated from the Premiership. They lost only one of the ten matches in which he played at the back end of the season.

Tommy HUTCHISON ☆☆☆☆
Born: Cardenden, 22 September 1947
English clubs: Blackpool, Coventry, Man City, Burnley, Swansea
Position: Winger/midfield
Caps won while in England: 17 (of 17)

What an adventure Tommy Hutchison has had since leaving Alloa for Blackpool in February 1968. He played more Football League matches than any other Anglo-Scot in history. This was his games catalogue – Blackpool (165), Coventry (314), Manchester City (46), Burnley (92), Swansea (178), for a grand total of 795 matches, fourth on the all-time list behind Peter Shilton (1,005), Tony Ford (931) and Terry Paine (824).

He also played 68 Scottish League matches with Alloa, and had a spell in Hong Kong with Bulova. A tall, high-stepping player who liked to operate on the wing or in a wide midfield position, Hutchison added to his legend by scoring in both the opposition goal and his own during the 1981 FA Cup final against Tottenham. Fans everywhere identified with his attractive, attacking style of playing. He closed his long-running career as player-manager with Swansea, and then worked with special-needs school children and the unemployed. He was a special foot-baller, and is a special man; a great ambassador for Scotland.

QUOTE: 'The game it seems everybody remembers is the FA Cup final in which I scored for City and for Spurs. My accidental goal from a Glenn Hoddle shot that gave Spurs their equaliser was as good a header as I ever made – what a pity it was into the wrong net!'

power. His peak years were with Nottingham Forest between 1955 and 1960. He rattled in 43 goals for them in 184 League matches, and was a telling force in their 1959 FA Cup final triumph against Luton. Imlach had a clone on the right in the stocky shape of Roy Dwight, who was like a rocket man with his electric pace. The rocket man reference is a deliberate link with Elton John, real name Reg Dwight, who was at Wembley in 1959 to see his cousin score for Forest before being stretchered off with a broken leg. Dwight and Imlach were the twin engines of Forest in the days when wingers were still the vogue. When making his international debut in the 1–1 draw against Hungary at Hampden in 1958, Imlach became the first Forest player capped by Scotland. All four of his Scottish appearances were on his preferred left wing. Imlach, first spotted while playing for his local club Lossiemouth, died in October 2001, aged 69.

Stuart IMLACH ☆☆☆
Born: Lossiemouth, 6 January 1932
English clubs: Bury, Derby,
Nottingham Forest, Luton, Coventry,
Crystal Palace
Position: Winger
Caps won while in England: 4 (of 4)

Standing just 5ft 5in, Stuart Imlach was a winger out of the old school. He was equally effective on either wing and had pace, skill and two-footed shooting

Eoin JESS ☆☆
Born: Aberdeen, 13 December 1970
English clubs: Coventry City, Bradford City, Nottingham Forest
Position: Support striker
Caps won while in England: 3 (of 18)

A support striker who likes to drive through from the centre of midfield, Eoin Jess has had a hot-and-cold association with the English football scene. He established himself as a regular in Scotland's team while playing for his hometown club Aberdeen, but a £2 million transfer to Coventry in 1996 saw him struggling to adapt to his new challenge. He was back with the Dons after only 28 League appearances, this time for a bargain basement £700,000. His return to Aberdeen was less than satisfying, and he was persuaded by Bradford City manager Jim Jefferies to join the Bantams on loan and then, in 2001, a free transfer. Jess was producing peak performances when Bradford ran into financial problems. They were forced by the administrators to let Jess go, and in the summer of 2002 he joined Nottingham Forest. He scored in his debut as a substitute, and quickly bedded into the Forest team with midfield passes that provided direction and drive.

Allan JOHNSTON ☆☆
Born: Glasgow, 14 December 1973
English clubs: Sunderland,
Birmingham City, Bolton,
Middlesbrough, Sheffield Wednesday
Position: Winger/midfield
Caps won while in England: 17 (of 17)

From his earliest days at Hearts, Allan Johnston was picked out as a major star in the making, but for baffling reasons has never fully lived up to the expectations. A queue of British clubs wanted to take him from Tynecastle, yet he elected to join French club Rennes. In April 1997, Peter Reid paid £550,000 to take him to Sunderland and played

him as a wide midfielder whose thrusting runs down the wing caused problems to defences. He was dropped into the reserves after a contract dispute, and to get first-team action went on loan to Birmingham City and then Bolton. Rangers brought him home to Scotland in the summer of 2000, but he was unable to force himself into the Gers League team on a permanent basis. A year after his arrival at Ibrox he was back in the North-East, this time with Middlesbrough after Rangers had accepted a £600,000 fee. Once again it was a case of a lot of promise but little end product, and after an injury and just a handful of League appearances he was allowed go on loan to Sheffield Wednesday.

Mo JOHNSTON ☆☆☆
Born: Glasgow, 30 April 1963
English clubs: Watford, Everton
Position: Striker
Caps won while in England: 4 (of 38)

Loved and loathed in his native Scotland in equal measure, Maurice (Mo) Johnston has had a remarkable career during which he has rarely been out of the headlines. He first made a name for himself at Partick Thistle when he found the net 41 times in just 85 games. Watford manager Graham Taylor had his ear to the ground, and realised he was just the piece he was looking for to finish his Elton John-financed jigsaw. Johnston maintained his remarkable striking rate with Watford, scoring 23 goals in only 38 games and helping fire them to the 1984 FA Cup final, in which they went down 2–0 to Everton after he had a headed goal disallowed. A sparky, tigerish striker with incredibly quick reflexes, he joined the Celtic club he had supported as a boy for £400,000 in October 1984. Goals continued to pour from his golden boot, 55 in 99 games before he got the wanderlust and moved to France with Nantes in 1987. Then came the £1.2 million transfer that split Scotland, and had Celtic fans raging and calling him a Judas. He signed for their deadly enemies Rangers, the first Catholic to play for the Ibrox club. The explosion of disbelief could have been measured on the Richter scale. 'Mighty Mo' scored 36 goals in 76 games for Rangers, but his life in Glasgow was made hell by Celtic supporters who refused to forgive what they saw as his treachery. To escape the pressure, Johnston moved back to England with Everton in 1991. Manager Howard Kendall later called it the worst transfer deal he had ever done. Mo finished his British goal hunting with Hearts and Falkirk before a final flourish in the United States with Kansas City Wizards, where he earned hero status with a return to his old goal-scoring form and then, at 39, he switched to coaching in the American League. Mo scored thirteen goals in his 37 matches for Scotland, and would have won many more caps but for a drink-related incident during a tour of Australia.

QUOTE: 'One reason for joining Rangers was that the prospect of doing something that went against tradition appealed to me. I also fancied working with manager Graeme Souness, who I reckoned was different class. I won medals with both Celtic and Rangers, so I have happy memories of both clubs.'

Willie JOHNSTON ☆☆☆

Born: Glasgow, 19 December 1946
English clubs: West Brom,
Birmingham City
Position: Left wing
Caps won while in England: 0 (of 22)

How sad that Willie Johnston is best remembered for being the player sent home in disgrace from the 1978 World Cup finals for taking a banned, performance-enhancing drug. He deserves better than that, because Johnston was an exceptional player who needed no artificial stimulants to worry the best defences in the world with his speed and skill out on the left wing. Willie had a tinderbox temper and was often ordered off for retaliating against defenders, who used brute force to try to stop him humiliating them. In between two memorable spells with Rangers he played with distinction for West Bromwich Albion and, briefly, Birmingham City. He became worshipped in Vancouver where, at the back end of his career, he performed minor miracles on the wing for the Whitecaps. The high spot for 'Wild

Willie' was a two-goal performance for Rangers that helped them overcome Moscow Dynamo in the European Cup Winners' Cup final in Barcelona in 1972. He hung up his twinkling boots in 1985 after providing fleeting glimpses of his old magic with Hearts and Falkirk. Willie, with a million memories for his customers, became a pub owner in Kirkaldy. He was so highly thought of in Vancouver that when they launched a new club strip in 2001 it was Willie who was invited back as guest of honour for the occasion. That's a better memory than the drug incident.

Derek JOHNSTONE ☆

Born: Dundee, 4 November 1953
English club: Chelsea
Position: Centre-forward/centre-half
Caps won while in England: 0 (of 14)

In Derek Johnstone, Scotland found the nearest anybody could come to Welsh legend John Charles in that he was equally effective at centre-forward or centre-half. He had a *Roy of the Rovers* start to his career. He was just 16 years 355 days old when Rangers manager Willie Waddell selected him to lead the attack against Celtic in the 1970 League Cup final. It has entered the land of footballing folklore about how the 'Ibrox Kid' headed the only goal of the match to end a five-year run of Celtic League Cup triumphs. He showed his versatility in the Rangers run to the European Cup Winners' Cup in 1972, playing at centre-forward in the quarter- and semi-finals and then at centre-half in the unforgettable 3–2 victory over Moscow Dynamo in the final. In the first of two spells at Ibrox, he played in two treble-winning sides, collected three Championship medals, five Scottish Cups, five League Cups and the European Cup Winners' Cup medal. He was also club captain for three years. In 1983 he swapped the blue of Rangers for the blue of Chelsea, but after a brief and miserable injury-hit stay at the Bridge he returned to Ibrox, where he was idolised as the king of the airways. It will always be a mystery why he won only fourteen caps, and why manager Ally MacLeod took him to Argentina for the 1978 World Cup without giving him a kick. In 564 games for Rangers he scored 210 goals – 132 of them in the League. He prevented hundreds more in his defensive role. Johnstone was briefly manager of Partick Thistle in 1986, and became a football pundit for Radio Clyde during a time when what appeared a complicated domestic life kept him in the headlines. Here's another for the trivia collection: Derek once scored a goal before the match should have started. He banged the ball into the net after 45 seconds in the 1976 Scottish Cup final with all but the referee's watch showing a minute still to go to the three o'clock kick-off! A week earlier he had the ball in the Dundee United net in 22 seconds.

Jimmy JOHNSTONE ☆
Born: Uddingston, 30 September 1944
English club: Sheffield United
Position: Winger
Caps won while in England: 0 (of 23)

'Jinky' Jimmy Johnstone was one of the greatest wingers ever to lace a pair of football boots, almost up there with Meredith, Matthews, Finney, Garrincha and Best. He could have been uttered in the same breath as them had he not been so moody and unpredictable. Like so many of his generation, he learned his skills with a small tennis ball – a tanner ball player who would be worth £20 million-plus in today's transfer market. When in the right frame of mind he was one of the Great Untouchables, but his temperament turned him into a Jekyll and Hyde player. Managers were never quite sure which one would turn up, and there were some headline-hitting occasions when neither turned up! Yet another of the short, fiery red-headed Scots that seemed to roll off a conveyor belt, Johnstone was never far from controversy throughout a career in which he gave his best years to Celtic. The flame had gone out by the time he got to Sheffield United for eleven League appearances after playing a mesmerising part in Celtic's nine successive League championships from 1966 to 1974. He later ran a wine bar and was always in demand for media and personal appearance work. It was nothing unusual for him to beat six or seven defenders in a twisting, turning run that thrilled the spectators but aggravated team-mates waiting for a pass. The wonder is he did not disappear in a maze of his own making. They don't make them like Jinking Jimmy anymore.

QUOTE: 'Our European Cup win in Lisbon was the greatest performance ever! We showed the other British clubs like Manchester United and Liverpool that it could be done. It was Celtic who led the way, and I loved being part of it.'

Robert (Bobby) JOHNSTONE
☆☆☆☆
Born: Selkirk, 7 September 1939
English clubs: Manchester City,
Oldham Athletic
Position: Wing-half
Caps won while in England: 5 (of 17)

The youngest of the 'Famous Five' who made Hibernian the flavour of the fifties, Bobby Johnstone had full and rewarding careers both sides of the border. In the first of two spells with Hibs, he was one of the generals of the team that won three Scottish championships and finished runners-up three times. In 1955 he moved to Manchester City for what was then a whopping £22,000. It was a change of Roads from Easter to Maine, but he still knew the right direction to goal and he became the first player to score in back-to-back FA Cup finals when City lost to Newcastle in 1955 and beat Birmingham in 1956. Johnstone had traditional Scottish ball skills, and always knew where to be to make the most of any situation with deftly delivered, defence-piercing passes or clever dribbling runs. After returning to Hibs for an encore, he played out his career at Oldham and pulled the strings for the team that won promotion from the Third Division in 1962–63. Johnstone, a far better player than his seventeen-cap collection suggests, was so well thought of that he was selected to represent Great Britain against the Rest of Europe in 1955. He grew up in the heartland of Scottish rugby and had to choose between the two sports. It was soccer's gain that he chose the round ball. He also represented South Scotland at cricket. After a final wind-down period with Witton Albion, he became a controller in the building industry, and an exceptional bowls player. 'Bobby Dazzler' Johnstone passed away in August 2001.

QUOTE: 'I could have achieved so much more but for the fact that I had a crocked knee for the last ten years of my career. I was always having to have pain-killing injections to keep me going.'

Joe JORDAN ☆☆☆☆☆
Born: Carluke, 15 December 1951
English clubs: Leeds, Man United, Southampton, Bristol City
Position: Striker
Caps won while in England: 52 (of 52)

Gap-toothed Joe Jordan became a have-boots-will-travel goal-hunter after leaving Morton for Leeds in 1970. His adventures took him on to Old Trafford, AC Milan, Verona, Southampton and Bristol City. It cannot be claimed that he was a gentleman of Verona because he used to knock the hell out of rival centre-halves in the crash-and-bash style of old-time centre-forwards. He was not pretty to watch but he was mightily effective on his way to collecting an aggregate of more than 100 goals for his various English employers and eleven goals in 52 appearances for Scotland. Joltin' Joe lost his front teeth in a collision while playing for Leeds reserves early in his stay at Elland Road, and the gap became a profitable trademark when the advertising gurus presented him as the face of Scottish football. He scored in each of the World Cup finals of 1974, 1978 and 1982. Jordan retired at 39 after service for Terry Cooper's Bristol City, a club he later twice managed as well as taking charge at Hearts and Stoke. He also had a spell as coach of Northern Ireland under the management of Lawrie McMenemy. Lou Macari then took him to Huddersfield as assistant manager, and he later had to fight for unfair dismissal after being sacked while on holiday in Spain in May 2002. Ten months later he was awarded a £31,000 pay-off by an employment tribunal.

QUOTE: 'The toothless tiger image didn't do me any harm because it raised my profile. I loved playing the game and just wish I could go through it all again.'

Hugh KELLY ☆☆☆☆
Born: Culross, 23 July 1923
English club: Blackpool
Position: Wing-half
Caps won while in England: 1 (of 1)

Hugh Kelly was known as 'the one who missed out' at Blackpool. He played in the two FA Cup finals of 1948 and 1951 when Blackpool were beaten, but missed the famous 'Matthews final' of 1953. A disciplined and determined midfield player, he joined the Seasiders from Jeanfield Swifts at the age of 21 and played wartime football before establishing himself as a regular in the Blackpool side across a stretch of thirteen years and 429 League games. His one cap was gained against the United States in the 6–0 victory at Hampden in 1952. For many years, he ran a café in the North Shore area of Blackpool.

John KELLY ☆☆
Born: Paisley, 21 February 1921
English clubs: Barnsley, Halifax
Position: Winger
Caps won while in England: 2 (of 2)

John Kelly was a fast, direct outside-left who was unlucky to be around at the same time as Liverpool's exceptional Scottish left winger Billy Liddell. He began and ended his career with Morton, and in between played 217 League games for Barnsley and 38 for Halifax.

Losing the best years of his career to the war, he was good enough to win two Scotland caps in 1948 when he was on the winning side against Wales and Northern Ireland. Lawrie Reilly and then Liddell were preferred in the number 11 shirts in subsequent matches. Kelly had good close ball control, and fine finishing instinct that brought him 25 League goals for Barnsley.

Andy KERR ☆☆
Born: Lugar, 29 June 1931
English clubs: Manchester City, Sunderland
Position: Utility player
Caps won while in England: 0 (of 2)

All-rounder Andy Kerr joined Partick Thistle as a defender and left them as a centre-forward when Manchester City paid £11,000 for him in 1959. He struggled to settle at Maine Road and was back in Scotland within five months, this time with Kilmarnock. A beautifully composed player who was comfortable in any defensive position or leading the attack, he shot the Killie into a championship-challenging position with more than 80 League goals in less than three years. Sunderland were next to be attracted by his performances and they paid £25,000 to take him to Roker Park in April 1963. He scored five goals in eighteen League games for Sunderland, playing a supporting role in getting them promoted before a return home to Scotland for a brief stop at Aberdeen, then on to Glentoran and, finally, to Inverness Caledonian.

Brian KERR ☆

Born: Motherwell, 12 October 1981
English clubs: Newcastle United
Position: Midfield
Caps won while in England 1 (of 1)

It was from the springboard of the Newcastle United reserves that Brian Kerr won his first Scottish international cap, coming on as a substitute in the 1–1 draw with New Zealand. This gave Scottish fans a glimpse of a player who was coveted by Rangers and Hibernian as a schoolboy, but he chose to start his career at Newcastle, where his first-team opportunities have been restricted. Sir Bobby Robson has gone on record as saying that he is impressed by Brian's tenacious and inspiring work in midfield, and he awarded him the captaincy of the United reserve side. A dislocated-shoulder injury slowed his progress at St James' Park, and he had a brief loan spell with Coventry City and then Livingston.

Robert (Bobby) KERR ☆☆☆☆

Born: Alexandria, Strathclyde, 16 November 1947
English clubs: Sunderland, Blackpool, Hartlepool
Position: Midfield
No full caps

At 5ft 4in, Bobby Kerr was the smallest ever FA Cup-winning captain when he led Second Division Sunderland to their sensational 1973 victory over mighty Leeds. It seems extraordinary that the Scottish selectors ignored a player who was both a polished and competitive midfield player, but this was an era when the Scots were overloaded with talent (eat your heart out Berti Vogts!). He gave magnificent service to Sunderland, having the character to overcome two broken legs early in his career – the first in a reserve match, and the second a year later in a challenge with Norman Hunter in a 1966 FA Cup tie. He recovered to lead Bob Stokoe's Sunderland to the Second Division championship in 1976 and, in all, played 368 League games and scored 56 goals for the North-East club. Kerr spent fifteen years at Roker Park from his apprenticeship days, and then followed Bob Stokoe to Blackpool before playing out his career back in the North-East at Hartlepool. He later ran a pub in Houghton-le-Spring.

Kevin KYLE ☆☆

Born: Stranraer, 7 June 1981
English club: Sunderland
Position: Striker
Caps won while in England: 7 (of 7)

A raw, lanky, 6ft 3in striker, Kevin Kyle had trials with Chelsea, Blackpool and Oldham before signing for Sunderland in 2000 from his local Stranraer club. He was loaned out to help him gain first-team experience with Huddersfield, Darlington and Rochdale. It is a sign of the times that even while he was only on the periphery of the Sunderland first-team, Scottish boss Berti Vogts came looking for him and awarded him seven caps in a short period of time. He struggled to make an impressive impact in the Sunderland team relegated from the Premiership in 2002–03, but was recalled to the Scottish squad by a desperate Berti Vogts. At the start of the 2003–04 season he began to find his true goal-blasting form at Sunderland, and he had Stadium of Light fans wondering if they had discovered a 'new' Niall Quinn.

Denis LAW ☆☆☆☆☆

Born: Aberdeen, 24 February 1940
English clubs: Huddersfield, Manchester United, Manchester City
Position: Striker
Caps won while in England: 52 (of 55)

See Part One for his full career details.

Tommy LAWRENCE ☆☆☆☆

Born: Dailly, 14 May 1940
English clubs: Liverpool, Tranmere Rovers
Position: Goalkeeper
Caps won while in England: 3 (of 3)

It was out of affection rather than animosity that the Kop fans at Anfield called Tommy Lawrence 'The Flying Pig'. Tommy was, let's say, a little portly and the sight of him hurling himself across the goal was beautifully captured in that nickname. Born, like manager Bill Shankly, in Ayrshire, he was already on Liverpool's books when Shanks arrived at Anfield in 1959. He had moved to the north-west of England with his parents as a schoolboy, and signed first as an amateur and then as a professional with Liverpool. He understudied Jim 'Fingers' Furnell until making his breakthrough into the first-team in October 1962. His reliability, super fitness and consistency is revealed by the astonishing fact that over the next eight years he missed only four games. Joe Mercer, one of football's most respected elder statesmen, once described him as a 'sweeper keeper' because he specialised in coming out of the penalty area to control the ball with his feet like an extra defender. His outstanding season was 1968–69 when he let in just 24 goals in 42 games, a First Division record until his successor Ray Clemence lowered it to sixteen goals in 1978–79. Lawrence, who won League championship medals in 1964 and 1966 sandwiching an FA Cup triumph in 1965, retired after 80 games for Tranmere Rovers, and later worked at a wire factory in Warrington.

Jimmy LEADBETTER ☆☆☆☆
Born: Edinburgh, 15 July 1928
English clubs: Chelsea, Brighton, Ipswich
Position: Winger/midfield
No full caps

See Part One for his full career details.

Graham LEGGAT ☆☆☆☆
Born: Aberdeen, 20 June 1934
English clubs: Fulham, Birmingham City, Rotherham
Position: Winger/inside-forward
Caps won while in England: 11 (of 18)

The author has had to dig hard in the archives for most of his facts and figures in this Who's Who section, but Graham Leggat made it easy for him. He has his own excellent fact-filled website at www.grahamleggatsoccer.com. Leggat, who was the personification of the properly skilled and schooled Scottish forward, has fashioned two outstanding careers. First of all there was Leggat the player, giving magnificent service to Aberdeen and Fulham, plus taking just passing interest at Birmingham City and Rotherham. Along the way he collected eighteen caps and eight goals for Scotland. Primarily a right winger, Leggat had the ability to adapt to any forward position and often played as a central striker, or old-fashioned inside-forward. His 127 goals in 254 League games for Fulham included four in the 10–1 massacre of Ipswich on Boxing Day 1963, the first three coming in a four-minute burst. Ipswich Town's larger-than-life chairman, John Cobbold, said that only their goalkeeper was sober. Here's a piece of trivia for you: the very next day, at Portman Road, Ipswich beat Fulham 4–2! Back problems prevented Leggat making more of an impact during moves to Birmingham and to Tommy Docherty's Rotherham, and he switched to coaching Aston Villa's youth players. In 1971, he started part two of his eventful life. He emigrated with his wife and two children to Canada to take up the job of player-coach to Toronto Metros. This was the launching pad to him becoming the most famous personality in Canadian soccer. He started a broadcasting career with CBC in 1972, and in 1986 was promoted to the prestigious role of host and commentator for The Sports Network (TSN), following which he became the highly respected voice and face of soccer in Canada.

QUOTE: 'My life has been like a football match – a game of two halves. The footballing side was wonderful, and I particularly recall playing alongside all-time greats like Denis Law and Johnny Haynes. My move to Canada has been a fantastic adventure, and I've been overwhelmed by the warmth of the Canadian people. Working in television has helped me keep closely involved with the game that I love. I feel a very lucky man to have experienced so much on both sides of the Atlantic.'

Jim LEIGHTON ☆☆☆☆
Born: Johnstone, 24 July 1958
English clubs: Manchester United, Reading
Position: Goalkeeper
Caps won while in England: 16 (of 91)

Scotland had no braver nor more committed servant than Jim Leighton, who was a defiant last line of defence across 91 international matches during which he went beyond the call of duty with his courage and daring. His career is unavoidably interwoven with that of Alex Ferguson, who helped make him and almost break him. It was in Fergie's brilliant Aberdeen team that Leighton first emerged as a goalkeeper of world class. When Ferguson moved to Old Trafford Leighton followed him in 1988 in what was then a goalkeeper-record £750,000 deal. He produced a procession of performances that would have satisfied most managers. But Fergie's standards are higher than most and in 1990 he publicly humiliated the man who had served him so well by dropping him for the FA Cup final replay against Crystal Palace after he had made some glaring mistakes in the first match. He had loan spells with

Arsenal, Reading and Sheffield United, and returned to Scotland to play for Dundee and Hibs before, at the age of 41, ending his wonderful career where it had started, with Aberdeen. Leighton had the character to shrug off brutal criticism of some of his performances by critics harbouring in the safety of commentary and press boxes. He tried hard to explode the Jimmy Greaves-inspired myth that Scottish goalkeepers should not be trusted with the crockery, he always played with dignity and was never frightened to dive in where it hurts. Not bad for somebody who started out as an obscure clerk in the Renfrewshire Employment Office.
QUOTE: 'I am proud to have been a member of the Scottish squad for four World Cup finals, and it's nice to recall that I did not concede a goal in the seven matches of the Euro '96 qualifying campaign. The MBE in 1998 was recognition that I must have been doing something right!'

Lawrie LESLIE ☆☆☆
Born: Edinburgh, 17 March 1935
English clubs: West Ham, Stoke, Millwall, Southend
Position: Goalkeeper
Caps won while in England: 0 (of 5)

It is fitting that Lawrie Leslie should follow immediately after Jim Leighton in this Who's Who section. He matched Jim in the bravery department, and might have won many more caps but for breaking a leg right at the peak of his career. Leslie first made his reputation as a fearless and agile goalkeeper with Hibs, won his five Scotland caps while playing for Airdrieonians and then made a £15,000 move to West Ham in 1961. It was the following year that he broke his leg and this cost him his first-team place. He played 78 League games for Stoke, and then made his final saves for Millwall and Southend. He later became a highly respected goalkeeping coach.

Billy LIDDELL ☆☆☆☆☆
Born: Dunfermline, 10 January 1922
English club: Liverpool
Position: All-round forward
Caps won while in England: 28 (of 28)

It is not often that a club is named after a player, but this happened when Billy Liddell was making his thrilling runs at Anfield. Liverpool became known as 'Liddellpool' as the 'Flying Scot' appeared to play defences on his own. Those of a certain age will swear that he rivals Kenny Dalglish and Kevin Keegan as the greatest player ever to pull on the red shirt of Liverpool. He was not only a strong, competitive player, but also a model sportsman who won the respect of all his opponents. Matt Busby, a Liverpool hero of the 1930s, was instrumental in bringing him to Anfield. Billy turned down an approach from Hamilton Academicals to sign for Liverpool in 1939, scoring in a 7–1 debut match against Crewe and netting a hat-trick in his second appearance against Manchester City's mighty goalkeeper Frank Swift. The war knocked five years off his League career, but after distinguished RAF service he still managed to make 495 League appearances, during which he scored the little matter of 216 goals. He could play in every one of the forward positions, and was equally dangerous whether coming in from the left wing or bursting through the middle. He was the key player in the Liverpool side that captured the League championship in 1946–47, and he collected an FA Cup runners-up medal in 1950 – scant reward for one of the greatest players ever to come out of Scotland. He and Stanley Matthews shared the honour of being the only players selected to represent the Great Britain sides of 1947 and 1955. But for the war, he would have doubled his caps collection. An intelligent and extremely dignified man, Liddell later became bursar at Liverpool University and a Justice of the Peace. When he passed on in 2001, football mourned one of its finest ambassadors.
QUOTE: 'There were not great financial rewards in football when I was playing, but I would willingly have played for my club and country for nothing. We had a different outlook on the game then, and we could not have played any harder or with more commitment had a bag of gold been put on the table. I will always have Liverpool red blood, mixed with the blue of Scotland!'

Jimmy LOGIE ☆☆☆☆
Born: Edinburgh, 23 November 1919
English club: Arsenal
Position: Inside-forward
Caps won while in England: 1 (of 1)

People of a certain age will weep when they think of the modern Scots winning caps galore when a footballing genius like Jimmy Logie was restricted to just one international appearance. Logie – a bricklayer in Edinburgh – signed for Arsenal from Lochore Welfare in the summer of 1939, two months before war was declared. Adept at making or taking goals, he had to wait until 1946 to properly start his Highbury career and quickly made up for lost time. He was a little dynamo, making the forward line tick with his clever passes and stealing unseen into areas where he could do most damage to the defence. Logie helped Arsenal win the League championship in 1947–48 and again in 1952–53 while scoring 76 goals in 326 appearances. A player in the mould of 1930s Arsenal hero Alex James, he was majestic for the Gunners in the 1950 FA Cup final when they flattened Liverpool 2–0. The Scottish selectors were reluctant to give caps to Anglos during Logie's peak years, and he was 33 before he played his one international match in the 3–1 defeat of Northern Ireland in Belfast in 1953. He had his passing-out parade in the Southern League with Gravesend and Northfleet. Jimmy, a footballing master, died in 1984.

Peter LORIMER ☆☆☆☆☆
Born: Dundee, 14 December 1946
English clubs: Leeds, York City
Position: Winger/midfield
Caps won while in England: 21 (of 21)

Few, if any, players have struck the ball harder than Peter 'Hot Shot' Lorimer. From the moment of making his Leeds debut at the age of just 15 years 289 days in 1962, Lorimer became famed and feared for the power of his shooting. He had two memorable spells with Leeds, scoring a club record 168 League goals in 526 games. In Don Revie's great Leeds side of the 1960s–1970s, Lorimer provided the power on the right to balance the silken skills of fellow Scot Eddie Gray on the left. Time and again, Lorimer would cut in from the right wing and crash thunderbolt shots into the net with a right foot that was worth its weight in goals. He also created dozens more for predators such as Allan Clarke and Mick Jones with careful crosses that were often struck low and swerving, needing only a deft touch to turn them into the net. In between his service to Leeds he fitted in net-bulging action for Toronto Blizzard, Vancouver Whitecaps and York City. Lorimer stretched his association with Leeds to 25 years when playing a cultured midfield role in the 1980s under Eddie Gray's management, and then unleashed his final shots with Whitby and Hapoel Haifa in Israel. His pub close to Elland Road, the Commercial, has become a regular meeting place for Leeds fans, and they always find Peter willing to talk about the 'good old days'. He helps run the Leeds ex-professional team, and is a regular broadcaster with intelligent things to say about the game he served so memorably.

QUOTE: 'My shot was once measured at 90 miles per hour. But to be honest I didn't care if the ball just rolled across the line. The only thing that mattered was that it counted as a goal.'

Brian McALLISTER ☆
Born: Glasgow, 30 November 1970
English clubs: Wimbledon, Plymouth, Crewe
Position: Central defender
Caps won while in England: 3 (of 3)

Central defender Brian McAllister played just 85 League matches in more than ten years at Wimbledon, punctuated with loan assignments at Plymouth and Crewe. Eleven of his appearances were as a substitute as he battled to win a regular place in the first-team. Yet he managed to win three Scottish international caps in 1997, the first two against Wales and Malta, and the last as a late substitute against Belarus. McAllister started his career with the Dons when they were still at Plough Lane, and was there when the Crazy Gang spirit was ablaze. Commanding in the air and possessing a powerful left foot, he was a solid rather than spectacular player. He would have

made a much bigger impact on the game in England but for a cruel run of injuries.

Gary McALLISTER ☆☆☆☆☆
Born: Motherwell, 25 December 1964
English clubs: Leicester City, Leeds, Coventry, Liverpool
Position: Midfield
Caps won while in England: 57 (of 57)

Starting out at his hometown club Motherwell in 1981, Gary McAllister has had a twenty-year adventure that now continues in the minefield of management in his role as player-boss of Coventry City. McAllister is one of those players who always seems to have time and space in which to operate even while all around him is bedlam. It has led to criticism that he is too casual and laid-back, but it is a style that has suited him and the teams that he has served with such distinction. Since leaving Motherwell in 1985 he has passed with honours for Leicester City, Leeds, Coventry and Liverpool, and he is in the Scottish Hall of Fame for winning 57 caps. At Elland Road, he linked up in midfield with fellow Scot Gordon Strachan and they – along with Monsieur Eric Cantona – were the main motivators of the Leeds team that won the League championship in 1991–92. McAllister was into veteran territory at the age of 36 when he had his most memorable season on joining Liverpool from Coventry under the Bosman ruling. He was the field marshal who gave design and direction to the Liverpool team that completed the unique FA Cup-League Cup-UEFA Cup treble in 2000–01, and rounded it all off by being voted man of the match in the UEFA Cup final. The following year he returned to Coventry, this time as player-manager and with plans for a slow wind down to a marathon playing career that has been both eventful and exemplary.

QUOTE: 'My legs will tell me when to pack in playing. But while I am still enjoying it and managing to give something to the team I will continue to select myself.'

Lou MACARI ☆☆☆☆
Born: Edinburgh, 7 June 1949
English clubs: Manchester United, Swindon Town
Position: Striker/midfield
Caps won while in England: 18 (of 24)

After a high-flying playing career in which he was a spitfire of a striker and then a smooth glider of a midfield player, Luigi (Lou) Macari continually crash-landed as a manager. The aircraft metaphors are deliberate, because Macari the manager reminds me of a pilot who believes that after crashing he must get straight back into a plane or always have a fear of flying. He was a small (5ft 5in) but stunning striker for Celtic, particularly when working in harness with young partner Kenny Dalglish. Bill Shankly was desperate to take him to Anfield, but Macari elected instead to join the Tommy Docherty revolution at Old Trafford. Shanks, spitting Liverpool-red blood, said, 'The boy's a fool. He will live to regret it.' It looked as if £200,000 Macari had got it wrong when he struggled to bed himself into the United attack, but he turned things around after switching to a midfield supporting role. Famously teetotal and a non-smoker, he was one of the fittest players in the land and it was his energy and enterprise that played a big part in pushing United to promotion as Second Division champions in 1974–75 and to three FA Cup finals in four years. His switch to management, first as a player-boss with Swindon, brought him painful experiences that would have persuaded most people to walk away from the game. He had a fall-out with assistant manager Harry Gregg over the way Swindon should play, and the club sacked them both. Macari was reinstated, and he led Swindon through some of the best seasons in their history before becoming involved in, first of all, a betting scandal and then a tax fraud investigation (he was found not guilty, while others from Swindon were jailed). He took charge at West Ham, but had to resign in the backwash of the match-gambling inquiry that cost him a £1,000 fine. Macari spent just four months in charge at Birmingham City, and then had two stays at Stoke City, sandwiching a nightmare reunion with his old club Celtic. His players objected to what they saw as his heavy-handed style of management and his criticism of them in public. Celtic felt they could not have their manager warring with his players and sacked him after eight months. He returned to Stoke but was unable to prevent them being relegated. Soon after, he had to come to terms with an appalling family tragedy. His nineteen-year-old son, Jonathan, was found hanged after a promising football career had come to nothing. Macari poured himself back into football, but it had another kick for him when, in the summer of 2002, he and his assistant Joe Jordan were sacked by Huddersfield while they were both away on holiday. Cash-strapped Huddersfield had to settle Lou's contract with a series of set payments. You can bet that the indefatigable Macari will pick himself up and try to fly again.

Archie MACAULAY ☆☆☆
Born: Falkirk, 30 July 1915
English clubs: West Ham, Brentford, Arsenal, Fulham
Position: Inside-forward/wing-half
Caps won while in England: 7 (of 7)

Archie Macaulay joined West Ham from Rangers as an inside-forward with all the Scottish passing and dribbling skills in 1937, and continued his Upton Park career after the war as a commanding wing-half. He moved across London to First Division Brentford in October 1946, and won his first cap six months later in the 1–1 draw against England at Wembley. By the time of his second cap he was a member of Arsenal's 1947–48 championship-winning squad, playing right-half in tandem with Joe Mercer on the left. He was honoured with a prestigious place in the Great Britain team against the Rest of Europe, and won another five caps for Scotland. He wound down his League playing career with Fulham, and then went into the self-catering business. But the football bug was still biting and he became player-manager of Guildford City in the Southern League before going home to Scotland as number two at Dundee. Then he accepted an invitation to take charge at Third Division Norwich City, and created a side good enough to reach the FA Cup semi-finals in 1959. He led them into the Second Division the following season, and later managed West Brom and Brighton.

Frank McAVENNIE ☆☆☆
Born: Glasgow, 22 November 1959
English clubs: West Ham, Aston Villa, Swindon
Position: Striker
Caps won while in England: 4 (of 5)

Sadly for Frank McAvennie, his un-disciplined off-the-pitch activities over-shadowed much of what he achieved in his football career. This one-time road sweeper got caught up in drug scandals, and was often in the headlines for extra-marital affairs. Let's stick to his playing performances. He started in senior football with St Mirren after being discovered playing for local Junior side Johnstone Burgh. He hit the celebrity circuit when he moved to West Ham, where he did the business on the pitch to the tune of 33 goals in 85 League games. Celtic took him back to Scotland for £750,000 in 1987, and he continued to bang in the goals – 34 in 66 matches, including two in the 1988 Scottish Cup final against Dundee United to give Celtic the double in their centenary year. He was missing the London nightlife, though, and returned to West Ham for £1.25 million in March 1989. At his peak he was quick, had good ball control and was powerful in the air, but the edge had gone off his game by the time of his second spell at Upton Park. It was later revealed that he had been taking heavy drugs while leading a champagne lifestyle. He played in Hong Kong, and made three substitute appearances in an abortive transfer to Aston Villa before returning briefly to Celtic and playing on loan at Swindon. McAvennie's off-pitch lifestyle had caught up with him and he was just a shadow of the player who had represented Scotland seven times. Early in the new millennium he was living in distressed circumstances in a flat in Gateshead, and football friends rallied round and staged a testimonial match featuring St Mirren against Celtic. He swore that the drugs scene was behind him.

QUOTE: 'It was the biggest mistake of my life when I started taking cocaine. Now I want to help any youngsters avoid making the same mistake. Look at the mess it made of my life.'

Neil McBAIN ☆

Born: Campbeltown, 15 November 1895
English clubs: Manchester United, Everton, Liverpool, Watford, New Brighton
Position: Wing-half/goalkeeper
Caps won while in England: 3 (of 3)

Neil McBain played only one post-war match, but it got him into the record books as the oldest player ever to appear in a League game. He was 51 years 120 days old and manager of New Brighton when he turned out in goal in an emergency at Hartlepool on 15 March 1947. Before the war, McBain had been a top-quality wing-half with Ayr United, Manchester United, Everton, St Johnstone and Liverpool. He was later player-manager for Watford and had two spells in charge at his original club, Ayr United.

Jim McCALLIOG ☆☆☆☆

Born: Glasgow, 23 September 1946
English clubs: Chelsea, Sheffield Wednesday, Wolves, Manchester United, Southampton, Lincoln City
Position: Midfield
Caps won while in England: 5 (of 5)

Smooth and stylish, Jim McCalliog played in two FA Cup finals ten years apart – collecting a winners' medal with Southampton in 1976 to go with the runners-up medal he pocketed with Sheffield Wednesday in 1966. Few schoolboy players have been in such demand as McCalliog. Leeds signed him as an amateur but it was with Tommy Docherty's Chelsea that he started his career. The Doc could not keep him happy on the periphery of the first-team at Stamford Bridge, and he moved to Hillsborough in October 1965. He scored nineteen goals in 150 League appearances for Wednesday, and then moved on to Wolves, where he netted 34 goals in 163 League games. Then The Doc called again and he followed him to Old Trafford, where he fitted in 38 matches before joining Lawrie McMenemy's 'All Stars' at Southampton (72 League games, 8 goals). McCalliog liked to attack from deep positions, combining skilled scheming with intelligent support striking. He had a spell as player-coach at Lincoln, played in Norway and with Chicago Springs, managed Halifax and Runcorn, and later ran the County Hotel in Harrogate and worked in the media. McCalliog had a decent career but without quite managing to live up to his reputation as a teenager, at which time The Doc told the author: 'He will develop into the greatest midfield player ever to come out of Scotland.'

Neil McCANN ☆☆

Born: Greenock, 11 August 1974
English club: Southampton
Position: Forward
Caps while in England: 2 (of 18)

Manager Gordon Strachan went hunting in his homeland of Scotland when he was given the money to strengthen his Premiership squad, and in the summer of 2003 he parted with £1.5 million for Rangers stalwart Neil McCann. It was the second time of asking for Strachan, who tried to sign him three years earlier when in charge at Coventry. McCann was handed the number 10 Kevin Davies shirt, and started to establish himself in the Saints side with his driving runs on the left flank of the midfield. He laid the foundation to his career with Dundee and Hearts before becoming a regular in the Rangers squad, alternating between midfield and the left wing. McCann won the first of his eighteen Scottish caps while with Hearts.

Brian McCLAIR ☆☆☆☆☆

Born: Airdrie, 8 December 1963
English club: Manchester United
Position: Striker/midfield
Caps won while in England: 26 (of 30)

After a spluttering start to his footballing life, Brian McClair emerged as a sparkling player in a two-pronged career that saw him win hero status at both Celtic Park and Old Trafford. He set out as an apprentice at Aston Villa and before making any impression at Villa Park was allowed to move on a free transfer to Motherwell. He combined his early football with studying at Glasgow University, where he obtained a degree in mathematics. McClair proved he knew all the angles on the football pitch when he joined Celtic in 1983 for £75,000. He won a Scottish Cup and League championship medal, and in 1987 was voted Scotland's Player of the Year. His 99 goals in 145 League games inspired Man United manager Alex Ferguson to shell out £850,000 in the summer of 1987. McClair gave wonderful service to United over the next eleven years, scoring 126 goals in 449 appearances, 61 of them as substitute. He collected winners' medals in the FA Cup (2), League championship (4), the European Cup Winners' Cup and the League Cup, netting the only goal in the final to sink Nottingham Forest. Equally effective as a midfield schemer or support striker, McClair concentrated on a passing role for Scotland and scored just two goals in his 30 international appearances. A sign of his popularity is that 47,743 spectators paid to watch United play Celtic in his testimonial match. In 1998, he returned briefly to Motherwell before becoming Brian Kidd's coach at Blackburn. When Rovers were relegated, McClair was invited back to Old Trafford to coach the United reserves and then to take over as coach of the youth academy. The youngsters could not have a better teacher, and they rewarded him in April 2003 with a record ninth FA Youth Cup triumph.

QUOTE: 'I combined my early career with my studies, and it took a lot of discipline to give total concentration to both my football and my degree course. But I have never regretted it, and would advise any youngster that it is worth the effort. I consider myself fortunate to have played for two of the greatest clubs in the world in United and Celtic, and it was one of my proudest moments when so many people turned out to see the two teams play in my testimonial. I felt enormously honoured.'

Ally McCOIST ☆
Born: Glasgow, 24 September 1962
English club: Sunderland
Position: Striker
Caps won while in England: 0 (of 59)

Now television's Mr Bubbly Man, Ally McCoist was far from buoyant when attempting to establish himself in the English League. He had a miserable time with Sunderland when joining them from St Johnstone at the age of nineteen in 1981. It is now history how he returned north of the border after a fruitless year at Roker Park (eight goals in 56 games) and went on to become one of the greatest goal-scorers in Scottish football history. His extraordinary haul of 355 goals for Rangers is a record that may never be beaten . . . by a Scot!

Eddie McCREADIE ☆☆☆☆
Born: Glasgow, 15 April 1940
English club: Chelsea
Position: Left-back
Caps won while in England: 23 (of 23)

It is with some justification that Eddie McCreadie feels he was badly rewarded by Chelsea for dedicated service as a player and later manager. A footballing left-back with a shuddering tackle and quick recovery powers, McCreadie joined Tommy Docherty's Chelsea from East Stirling and over the next eleven years played 331 League games for the Blues. He was an inspiring skipper in succession to Ron 'Chopper' Harris, and always played the game for club and country with tremendous enthusiasm and energy. Appointed Chelsea manager in 1975, he steered the club back to the First Division in 1976–77 and then sensationally quit just eight weeks later because he was unhappy with the terms of his new contract. Always a strong-willed, single-minded man, McCreadie upped sticks and moved to the United States, where he managed Memphis Rogues. He later earned his living as a painter and decorator.

Joe McDONALD ☆☆☆
Born: Blantyre, 10 February 1929
English clubs: Sunderland, Nottingham Forest
Position: Left-back
Caps won while in England: 2 (of 2)

Signed from Falkirk for £6,000 in 1953, Joe McDonald was a strong and cultured left-back who became a key defensive member of Sunderland's Bank of England team. He won his two caps with Scotland while at Roker Park in 1956, and two years later joined Nottingham Forest at the start of the season in which he helped them win the FA Cup by beating Luton Town at Wembley. He played 137 League games for Sunderland and 109 for Forest.

Ted MacDOUGALL ☆☆☆☆
Born: Inverness, 8 January 1947
English clubs: Liverpool, York, Bournemouth, Manchester United, West Ham, Norwich, Southampton, Blackpool
Position: Striker
Caps won while in England: 7 (of 7)

'Nine-goal wonder' Ted MacDougall became an overnight sensation in an FA Cup tie against Margate in 1971, a game that was to change his life. He scored nine of the Bournemouth goals in an amazing 11–0 victory, at last living up to the potential he had shown while an apprentice at Liverpool before being released to start his League career with York City. 'SuperMac' joined Tommy Docherty's tartan army at Old Trafford, but could not hit it off with The Doc and after just six months moved on to West Ham. He had been at Upton Park only nine months when John Bond, once his manager at Bournemouth, persuaded him to join him at Norwich City in December 1973. It was while at Carrow Road that he won his seven Scottish caps. MacDougall netted 51 goals in 112 League games for the Canaries, memorably linking up with his old Bournemouth and York sidekick Phil Boyer. By the time he retired in 1980 he had found the net 256 times in 535 League games for seven clubs, taking his final shots as player-manager at Blackpool after stopping off on the south coast at Southampton and Bournemouth for a second time. His most prolific period was in the first of two stops at Bournemouth when he rattled in 103 goals in just 146 League games. He sold his sports shop business in Bournemouth in 1985 and emigrated with his French-Canadian wife to Canada, where he became a wealthy property developer. He retained his interest in football with a series of coaching videos for the international market, and on visits to the UK was a regular at the Bournemouth club where he cemented himself in the land of footballing legend.

James McFADDEN ☆☆
Born: Glasgow, 14 April 1983
English club: Everton
Position: Forward
Caps won while in England: 3 (of 6)

Old-timers rub their eyes and wonder if they are dreaming when they see Jamie McFadden in action for Everton and Scotland. He is a throwback to the way free-spirited Scots used to play, with beautiful close control, deceptive changes of pace, and improvisation that can baffle team-mates as much as opponents. Goodison manager David Moyes had to beat off competition from Celtic, Rangers and Preston to land McFadden from Motherwell for £1.25 million in September 2003. He blossomed under the tuition of Terry Butcher at Motherwell, and was given the freedom to use his natural ball-playing skills down the left wing. Efforts will be made to turn him into more of a team player, but those who like to see individualists will hope his inventive mind is not too stifled by blinkered coaching. It is at the feet of players like McFadden and Fletcher that Scotland just might have a bright future.

Frank McGARVEY
Born: Glasgow, 17 March 1956
English club: Liverpool
Position: Striker
Caps won while in England: 2 (of 7)

Here's one for the trivia quizzes – which player was capped twice by Scotland while with an English club for which he never kicked a ball? Step forward Frank McGarvey, who spent a year with Liverpool in 1979–80 after joining them from St Mirren for £250,000. He did not fit into manager Bob Paisley's plans, and he sold him on to Celtic in 1980 for £275,000 without once selecting him. McGarvey had the last laugh by banging in 113 goals in 268 League matches for Celtic before returning to where he had started, with St Mirren. The lack of stars alongside McGarvey's name is not a misprint. That's how big an impact he made on English club football!

Mark McGHEE ☆☆☆☆
Born: Glasgow, 20 May 1957
English clubs: Newcastle, Reading
Position: Striker
Caps won while in England: 0 (of 4)

As a player, Mark McGhee made his name with Celtic and Aberdeen, mixed with two short stays at Newcastle where he showed just flashes of his finishing skills. He also moved abroad to ply his trade with SV Hamburg. McGhee went

to the top of the mountain for advice before switching to a managerial career. He talked to Sir Alex Ferguson, his manager during successful goal-hunting days at Aberdeen. Armed with guidance from the Guv'nor, he started as a player-manager with Reading, taking them to their highest ever League placing before accepting the job of Leicester City manager. He had hardly got his feet under the Leicester desk when he found Wolves making an offer he could not refuse. Like so many before him, he was beaten at Molineux by the ghosts of Wolves' past. In November 1998 he left the Midlands club for a flirtation with television punditry before climbing back on board the managerial merry-go-round with Millwall, guiding them to the Second Division and the First Division play-offs in his first two seasons. He was sacked by Millwall in October 2003 following a disappointing start to the new season, and was immediately snapped up as the new boss of Brighton.

John McGINLAY ☆☆☆☆
Born: Inverness, 8 April 1964
English clubs: Shrewsbury, Bury, Millwall, Bolton, Bradford City
Position: Striker
Caps won while in England: 14 (of 14)

Patience is clearly a virtue with John McGinlay. He spent years in football's relatively obscure regions with Nairn County in the Highland League, then at

Yeovil Town, played in New Zealand and then came home to Elgin City, who sold him to Shrewsbury Town for £25,000 in 1989. Then he beavered away with Bury and Millwall before Bolton gave him a platform on which to show his talent. He became known as 'Super John' at Bolton, where goals started to flow with regularity – 87 in 192 League appearances. In 1996–97 he did more than anybody to blast Bolton into the Premiership, with 24 goals that made him the First Division's leading marksman. His remarkable rise from football's shadowlands reached its peak in his 30th year, when he won the first of fourteen Scottish caps that came in a rush. Bradford City paid £650,000 for him in November 1997, but a sequence of painful injuries virtually ended his days at the top of the hill. On his way down he played briefly for Oldham and Cincinnati Riverhawks in the United States. Then it was back into the non-League world where he had spent his formative football years, learning the management ropes with first Gresley Rovers and then Ilkeston Town.

John McGOVERN ☆☆☆☆☆
Born: Montrose, 28 October 1949
English clubs: Hartlepool, Derby, Leeds, Nottingham Forest, Bolton
Position: Midfield
No full caps

It seems astonishing that a player of the quality and character of John McGovern, who won every club medal in sight, was ignored by the Scottish selectors apart from a couple of Under-23 call-ups. If they had listened to Brian Clough he would have had a cupboardful of caps. McGovern seemed almost handcuffed to Clough. Wherever Cloughie and his right-hand man Peter Taylor went they took McGovern with them like a talisman. He was with Clough at Hartlepool, Derby County, Leeds United and Nottingham Forest. He collected a League championship medal at Derby and Forest, skippered the back-to-back European Cup winners and also two League Cup-winning teams. McGovern made up for a shortage of eye-catching flair with his grit and determination, and brought bite and balance to all the Clough-team midfield engine rooms. He finished his playing days while doubling up as manager at Bolton, and later worked as assistant manager to Peter Shilton at Plymouth and to Archie Gemmill at Rotherham. As a fifty-something in the new millennium, he kept in touch with the game as a respected broadcaster on BBC Radio Nottingham.

QUOTE: 'I was so proud to captain that Forest team. We were written off as not having a chance in Europe, but proved everybody wrong by winning two successive European Cup finals. We had tremendous all-round strength and the balance of the team was just right – plus, of course, we had a management team that knew just how to motivate us.'

Alan McINALLY ☆
Born: Ayr, 10 February 1963
English club: Aston Villa
Position: Striker
Caps won while in England: 8 (of 8)

Alan McInally played just 59 League games for Aston Villa, including nine as a substitute, between scoring assignments with Celtic and Bayern Munich. A powerfully built striker who could make his presence felt in the penalty area, he started his career with his local club Ayr United, scoring 32 League goals for them in 93 matches. At Celtic he found the net seventeen times in 65 League games, and his eighteen goals for Villa persuaded Bayern Munich to part with £1.1 million for him in June 1989. Following his retirement, he became a popular pundit with the Sky Sports team.

Dave MACKAY ☆☆☆☆☆
Born: Edinburgh, 14 November 1934
English clubs: Tottenham, Derby,
Swindon Town
Position: Midfield/central defence
Caps won while in England: 18 (of 22)

See Part One for his full career details.

Bobby McKINLAY ☆☆☆☆
Born: Lochgelly, 10 October 1932
English club: Nottingham Forest
Position: Centre-half
No full caps

Ask any centre-forward who was hunting goals in the Football League in the 1950s and 1960s and they will tell you that Bobby McKinlay was as good a centre-half as there was in the game. The Scottish selectors must have been wearing blinkers to have missed him. Signed from Bowhill Rovers in 1951, he gave Forest loyal service for nineteen years while putting together the impressive club record of 614 League appearances. He was the rock around which the Forest defence was built in their FA Cup-winning year of 1959. It was fitting that at the end of his playing career he should become a prison officer, because he had kept centre-forwards under lock and key across two decades.

QUOTE: 'It would have been nice to have played for my country, but I was happy to give all my energy to Forest. We had a great club spirit, and I enjoyed every moment of my career. The highlight of course was winning the FA Cup. There was not a lot of money to be earned in those days, but we could not have played any harder had they been paying us ten times as much.'

William (Billy) McKINLAY ☆☆☆

Born: Glasgow, 3 December 1964
English clubs: Blackburn, Leicester
City, Bradford City, Preston
Position: Midfield
Caps won while in England: 15 (of 29)

A schools, youth and Under-21 inter-national, Billy McKinlay was well established in the full Scotland team by the time he joined Blackburn Rovers from Dundee United for £1.75 million in 1995. There was an early shock for him at Ewood Park when new manager Ray Harford made it clear that he did not fit into his plans, and he spent much of his time risking splinters on the substitute's bench. He was at last given a regular place in the Rovers midfield when Tony Parkes took over as caretaker-manager in 1996–97. The Blackburn supporters immediately warmed to him when they saw how energetically he worked in his position just in front of the back line of the defence, winning the ball with thunderclap tackles and then triggering counter-attacks with careful distribution. He was back on frustrating substitute duty when Brian Kidd took over the managerial reins and went on a series of loan moves that took in Leicester City, Bradford City, Preston and Clydebank. He returned to Leicester in the summer of 2002, volunteering to play for no wages while the club sorted out their financial crisis, and he became a regular in the side that battled its way back to the Premiership. Discovered as a teenager when playing for Hamilton Thistle, McKinlay won fifteen of his Scottish caps while playing for Blackburn.

Robert McKINNON ☆

Born: Glasgow, 31 July 1966
English clubs: Newcastle, Hartlepool, Carlisle
Position: Left-back
Caps won while in England: 0 (of 3)

Robert (Rab) McKinnon could not crack it at top level in England, despite a sweet left foot. He had trials at Manchester United and Leeds and was given one outing by Newcastle before cementing himself in the Hartlepool defence. He played 189 League games for the 'Pool in two spells. It was after a £150,000 move to Motherwell in 1991–92 that he won his three caps. His travels on the football roundabout also took him to Twente Enschede, Hearts and Carlisle. It had been quite an adventure for the defender who laid the foundations to his career with Rutherglen Glencairn, and ended the journey back home in Scotland with Clydebank. He captained Clydebank before hanging up his boots at the age of 35, and continued to keep in touch with the game on scouting missions for his old Dutch club Twente Enschede.

Andy McLAREN ☆☆☆
Born: Larkhall, 24 January 1922
English clubs: Preston, Burnley,
Sheffield United, Barrow
Position: Inside-forward
Caps won while in England: 4 (of 4)

Another of the players who lost his best years to the war, Andy McLaren joined Preston from Larkhill Thistle in 1939 but did not start his League career until 1946. He had Tom Finney and Bill Shankly as team-mates, and won his four caps in the immediate post-war years as an inside-forward who could make and take goals. McLaren found the net 29 times in 69 League appearances for Preston, played briefly for Burnley and Sheffield United and had his passing-out parade at Barrow, where he netted an impressive 52 goals in 155 League games.

John McLEOD ☆☆☆
Born: Edinburgh, 23 November 1938
English clubs: Arsenal, Aston Villa
Position: Winger
Caps won while in England: 0 (of 4)

Here's another one for the collectors of trivia – who scored Arsenal's first goal in European competition? Step forward John McLeod, who netted in the ninth minute of an Inter-Cities Fairs Cup tie against Staevnet of Denmark in Copenhagen in September 1963 (Arsenal destroyed the Danish part-timers 7–1

and managed to lose the second leg at Highbury 3–2!). McLeod had arrived at Highbury from Hibernian for £40,000 in the summer of 1961 when he was a current Scottish international and expected to roast English full-backs with his lightning-fast raids down the right wing. But he was never the same force in England as he had been in Scotland, and new Arsenal manager Billy Wright quickly unloaded him to Aston Villa for £35,000 after he had scored 23 goals in 101 League games for the Gunners. McLeod was dangerous when cutting in from the touchline and unleashing powerful cross shots. His scoring instinct brought him sixteen goals in 125 League appearances for Villa before playing for Mechelen in Belgium and, finally, Raith Rovers. He returned to the Midlands to work in insurance, and later retired to his homeland.

Frank McLINTOCK ☆☆☆☆☆
Born: Glasgow, 28 December 1939
English clubs: Leicester, Arsenal, QPR
Position: Midfield/central defender
Caps won while in England: 9 (of 9)

More than anybody, Francis (Frank) McLintock was responsible for Arsenal winning the League championship/FA Cup double in 1970–71. His generalship brought authority to the defence and his driving leadership inspired the entire team. The author owns up to being biased about McLintock because he was a good pal in his Highbury days, but even neutrals would have seen that he was the shining light that lifted the Gunners out of the shadows of their haunting past. McLintock had been a buccaneering right-half when Billy Wright bought him from Leicester City for £80,000 in 1964. He was an energetic member of the Leicester City team beaten in the FA Cup finals of 1961 and 1963. Many wondered about the wisdom of manager Bertie Mee and coach Don Howe persuading him to switch to centre-half, but he proved that by intelligent positional play he could dominate at the heart of the defence despite a lack of real power in the air. In his veteran days, he helped Queen's Park Rangers to runners-up place in the First Division in 1975–76. Footballer of the Year in 1971, he was rewarded with a meagre nine caps by Scotland. He should have had a cartload. If anybody was going to make an outstanding manager, we were all convinced it would be McLintock, who talked tactics in his sleep. Yet things did not work out for him when he was holding the managerial reins with Leicester or Brentford. He was George Graham's assistant at Millwall, and everybody was surprised when he did not follow his friend back to Highbury. He became a successful players' agent and had a string of business interests. These days he keeps in touch with the game as an omniscient pundit with the Sky Sports team.

QUOTE: 'I lost five times at Wembley before the double year and had got to hate the place, and I would have pulled it down years before the bulldozers moved in! But winning the double and clinching it with the win against Liverpool in the FA Cup final at Wembley made up for much of the heartache. The strength of our Arsenal team was that we had a great team spirit, were well organised by coach Don Howe and we had a nice mixture of strength and skill.'

Gordon McQUEEN ☆☆☆☆☆
Born: Kilwinning, 26 June 1952
English clubs: Leeds, Manchester United
Position: Central defender
Caps won while in England: 30 (of 30)

Legendary Leeds manager Don Revie knew a great Scot when he saw one. He picked Gordon McQueen from the relative obscurity of St Mirren in 1972 as a successor at centre-half to The Giraffe, Jack Charlton. McQueen felt quite at home when he arrived at Elland Road because he found himself one of seventeen Scots on the staff! He was a snip at £30,000, with Celtic and Tottenham both beaten in the race to sign him. His father, Tommy, had been a goalkeeper with Hibs and Accrington Stanley, and Gordon started between the sticks before realising his height and power was better utilised in the middle of the defence. McQueen quickly cemented himself into the Leeds back line, and in his first season the team put together an undefeated run of 29 matches. He was a tower of strength when they won the League championship in 1973–74 and reached the European Cup final the following season. There was an almost endearing rawness about the giant, 6ft 3in McQueen, and he would lollop out of position like a playful lion cub, but few people could master him in the air and for such a big man he had exceptionally quick recovery powers and he was deadly in set-piece situations. To this day Leeds fans find it hard to forgive him for following fellow Scot Joe Jordan across the Pennines to Old Trafford in 1978 for what was then a record £495,000. He formed a perfect tandem team at Manchester United with Aberdonian Martin Buchan, McQueen the chalk to Buchan's cheese. He played in losing and winning FA Cup teams, and in 1979–80 got on the score sheet nine times as United chased Liverpool to the League championship in runners-up place. He added thirteen international caps to the seventeen he won while at Leeds. Injuries started to handicap him, and this allowed Kevin Moran and Paul McGrath to stake claims to the central defensive positions. After leaving Man United in 1984 he played for a year in Hong Kong, where he contracted typhoid fever that led to complications that nearly cost him his life. The Big Man battled back, and he later moved into management with Airdrieonians and coached at his original club St Mirren before joining his old Man United team-mate Bryan Robson as reserve team coach at Middlesbrough. He has brightened many an STV and Sky football match with his intelligent comments as a studio expert.

QUOTE: 'Billy Bremner used to say that I had joined the best post-war British team when I went to Leeds, and when we were at our peak I would say he was right. It all came apart when Don Revie left to manage England, and my transfer request did not go down well with the Leeds supporters. But the club made a massive profit from my move to Manchester United, where I thoroughly enjoyed playing alongside Mr Cool Martin Buchan. We were a perfect balance for each other.'

Neil MARTIN ☆☆☆
Born: Tranent, 20 October 1940
English clubs: Sunderland, Coventry, Nottingham Forest, Brighton, Crystal Palace
Position: Centre-forward
Caps won while in England: 1 (of 3)

It is part of Hibernian footballing legend how Neil Martin was about to quit the game to become a long-distance lorry driver when manager Walter Galbraith persuaded him to move from Queen of the South to Easter Road. Martin was now on the road to soccer fame, and his game flourished under a new Hibs manager called Jock Stein and then Jock's successor Shankly – not Bill, but his brother Bob. Martin was a veritable goal machine, including in his 53 League goals for Hibs seven hat-tricks, four times going on to score four goals. Particularly powerful in the air, he is one of the few players to have scored more than a century of goals both north and south of the border. He moved to Sunderland for £40,000 in 1965, and on his travels through England – sans lorry – he netted 104 League goals with Sunderland (38), Coventry (40), Nottingham Forest (28) and Brighton (8). It had been an eventful long haul.

Don MASSON ☆☆☆☆
Born: Banchory, 26 August 1946
English clubs: Middlesbrough, Notts County, QPR, Derby
Position: Midfield
Caps won while in England: 17 (of 17)

It took Scotland a long time to wake up to the fact that they had a fine midfield general playing among the English. Don Masson was almost 30 before he got his first international call in 1976, and then won seventeen caps in a flurry. His measured passes gave shape and purpose to Middlesbrough, Notts County, Queen's Park Rangers and Derby before he closed his 600-match tour back at Meadow Lane, where he later became manager of the Notts County sports complex. He had started out with Middlesbrough juniors in 1963, leaving behind a queue of disappointed Scottish clubs who would

liked to have signed him. He and his Derby midfield partner Bruce Rioch were the main motivators of the Scotland team that qualified for the 1978 World Cup in Argentina. He will have sad memories of his final international appearance, a World Cup finals match against Peru in which he missed from the penalty spot with what was usually his reliable right boot. Masson later became landlord at the Gallery Hotel in Nottingham.

Dominic MATTEO ☆☆☆☆
Born: Dumfries, 28 April 1974
English clubs: Liverpool, Sunderland, Leeds
Position: Central defender
Caps won while in England: 6 (of 6)

One of the most versatile defensive players in the English League, Dominic Matteo has been desperately unlucky with injuries that have punctuated his career. He is an intelligent player with the sort of vision and anticipation that keeps him a thought and a deed ahead of the opposition. Matteo – Dom to all his mates – got an excellent grounding as a youth player at Anfield before making his breakthrough into the first-team. He had established himself in the first-team, primarily at left-back, when his injury problems started. After a short loan spell at Sunderland, he returned to challenge for his place at Liverpool and was used in a variety of positions. At the start of the 2000–01 season he made a

£4.75 million move to Leeds, manager David O'Leary nodding the deal through despite a medical report that revealed knee problems. He forged a solid partnership in the Leeds back line with Rio Ferdinand, and when Rio moved on to Manchester United became club captain and the central defender around whom the Leeds defence was built. He elected to be considered for Scotland's senior side after playing for England at youth, 'B' and Under-21 levels, but after six full caps declared his international career over because he was keen to protect his delicate physique. New Leeds manager Terry Venables needed him more than ever when Jonathan Woodgate was allowed to leave Elland Road, and then Peter Reid inherited him in the desperate last weeks of the 2002-03 season. Matteo battled through injury problems to give Leeds much-needed defensive stability in the successful battle against the threat of relegation.

Kenny MILLER ☆☆☆
Born: Edinburgh, 23 December 1979
English club: Wolves
Position: Striker
Caps won while in England: 3 (of 5)

Kenny Miller made up for the disappointment of not establishing himself at Ibrox by becoming a goal-scoring hero at Molineux. He joined Wolves from Rangers after walking away from his dream of becoming a Gers idol. The single-minded striker made his decision to leave Rangers less than two years after his £2 million arrival from Hibs. Ironically, it was Alex McLeish who sold him to Rangers and things might have worked out differently for him if he had still been at Ibrox when McLeish took over as manager. He quickly became accepted by the Wolves fans as the man who could help shoot them to the Premiership. Scottish team boss Berti Vogts gave him the highest possible praise when he likened him to German scoring legend Gerd Muller. His goals were vital in the Wolves climb to the Premiership via the 2002–03 play-offs.

Bobby MITCHELL ☆☆☆☆
Born: Glasgow, 16 August 1924
English club: Newcastle United
Position: Outside-left
Caps won while in England: 2 (of 2)

It seems laughable that a wizard of a winger like Billy Mitchell could collect only two international caps. He became one of the Tyneside gods after moving to Newcastle from Third Lanark in 1949, and mesmerised defences with his intricate skills while setting up goals for such deadly finishers as 'Wor' Jackie Milburn and George Robledo. The Bobby Dazzler, as the newspapers dubbed him, was no slouch in front of goal himself, and he netted 113 goals in 408 appearances for the Magpies. He was a major force in Newcastle's three

FA Cup-winning teams of the 1950s, and in his last appearance at Wembley scored a superb second goal in the 3–1 dismantling of Manchester City. The Glaswegian, who could have opened an envelope with his magical left foot, later ran two pubs in his adopted hometown of Newcastle before his death in 1968. Geordie fans of a certain age will argue that it's a black-and-white case that he was one of the all-time great wingers. Only the Scottish selectors seemed to disagree.

Willie MOIR ☆☆☆☆

Born: Aberdeen, 19 April 1922
English clubs: Bolton, Stockport County
Position: Inside-forward
Caps won while in England: 1 (of 1)

It was while playing wartime football for the RAF Kirkham team in Lancashire that Willie (or Billy) Moir was signed by Bolton. He rewarded their enterprise by scoring 118 goals in 325 League matches in the immediate post-war period when the Wanderers were really firing on all cylinders. He was one of those compact, perfectly balanced inside-forwards who seemed to roll off a Scottish conveyor belt. His control was faultless and he packed a powerful and accurate shot. He had a prolific partnership with Nat 'The Lion of Vienna' Lofthouse that decimated First Division defences, making many of Nat's goals with precise passes and

always looking to be on the end of the England centre-forward's knock-downs. Lofty and Moir scored the goals that gave Bolton a 2–1 half-time lead against Blackpool in the famous 'Matthews final' of 1953. Willie, who was Bolton club captain before Lofthouse, left Burnden Park in 1955 and wrapped up his splendid career with two seasons at Stockport, scoring 26 goals in 70 League games and then managing the club until 1960.

Bobby MONCUR ☆☆☆☆

Born: Perth, 19 January 1945
English clubs: Newcastle, Sunderland, Carlisle
Position: Central defender
Caps won while in England: 16 (of 16)

A born leader, Bobby Moncur was one of Newcastle's finest captains and he also skippered his country with distinction. He was a tough-tackling centre-back who took no prisoners, yet managed to look elegant while flattening opponents during a seventies era when the game was much more physical than now. Perhaps the strongest part of his game was an ability to read situations quickly and then be in the best position to deal with them ahead of the opposition. Anybody who was on Tyneside in 1969 will never forget his contribution to the Inter-Cities Fairs Cup victory. He not only played like a Trojan in defence, but also scored three goals over the two-leg final against

Ujpest Dosza. In 296 League matches for Newcastle he scored just three times, and he equalled this output in a final that ended a barren run for the Magpies. He had won Scottish youth international honours at centre-forward and left-back but it was the centre of defence that suited him best of all and from where he could help orchestrate what was happening ahead of him. He swapped the black-and-white stripes for the red-and-white of deadly rivals Sunderland after playing his last match for Newcastle in the disappointing 3–0 FA Cup final defeat at Wembley in 1974. He helped the Wearsiders to promotion in 1975–76 and was voted their player of the season. Moncur, an intelligent and personable man, seemed ready-made for management, but he enjoyed only limited success at Carlisle United, Hearts, Plymouth, Whitley Bay and Hartlepool. Always a surprising character, he extended his interest in sailing to running a yacht charter business based in Newcastle. He was the ideal man to skipper the yacht. He keeps close to football as a radio broadcaster and a match-day host at St James' Park. **QUOTE:** 'I will never forget the explosion of joy that greeted our Fairs Cup victory in 1969. Supporters had been waiting for a long time for something to happen, and the Fairs Cup gave them what they wanted. It took me some time to establish myself in the Newcastle first-team, and at one stage I was very close to being transferred to Norwich. The deal fell through, and I stayed at Newcastle for the best years of my career.'

Willie MORGAN ☆☆☆☆
Born: Glasgow, 2 October 1944
English clubs: Burnley, Manchester United, Bolton, Blackpool
Position: Winger
Caps won while in England: 21 (of 21)

A George Best look-alike, Willie was also in the Best mould as a winger. He was whippet fast, had excellent close control, and he was always being compared to the Irish genius, particularly when he joined him in the attack at Old Trafford. He first came to prominence with Burnley, coming up through their junior ranks and scoring nineteen goals in 183 League games. Morgan joined Man United for £117,000 three months after they won the European Cup in 1968. Over the next six seasons he scored 25 goals in 285 League appearances, and was so pleasing on the eye, on the wing or in midfield, that the United supporters voted him their player of the year in both 1970 and 1971. He got on famously with his fellow Glaswegian Tommy Docherty when he first took over as manager at Old Trafford, but they then had the mother and father of a fall-out and The Doc sold him back to Burnley in 1975. They continued to battle from long range through legal eagles and finished up facing each other in court. It was all very messy and caused a lot of anguish for two likeable but stubborn men. Morgan later played for Bolton and Blackpool to take his total League appearances to 623, and he also experienced football in the United States with Minnesota. He was always intelligent in the use of his money, investing in a chain of laundrettes and a sports shop in Altrincham, where he continues to live while running a marketing and promotions business.

QUOTE: 'I have so many memories, but one that sticks out is of a match I played early in my career for Burnley on Boxing Day 1963. It was in the First Division against Matt Busby's Manchester United. I scored two goals and Andy Lochhead netted four. They were my first goals at the top level against the club who were to give me the best years of my career.'

Jackie MUDIE ✰✰✰✰
Born: Dundee, 10 April 1930
English clubs: Blackpool, Stoke, Port Vale
Position: Inside-forward
Caps won while in England: 17 (of 17)

The third of the famous Blackpool 'M-Squad' – along with Matthews and Mortensen – John (Jackie) Mudie joined the Seasiders from Stobswell Juniors at the age of seventeen in 1947. Over the next thirteen years he scored 143 goals in 320 League matches. He was a brilliant two-footed marksman, a handful for any defence in either inside-forward position or as leader of the attack despite, at 5ft 6in, lacking the usual height of a centre-forward. Mudie was close friends with Matthews, with whom he teamed up again at Stoke and then at Port Vale, where he became team manager while Sir Stanley was general manager. When he left Port Vale in 1967 after two years in charge he concentrated on building up his successful painting and decorating business in the Potteries district. Jackie, who found the net nine times in seventeen successive international appearances, died in 1992.

George MULHALL ✰✰✰✰
Born: Falkirk, 8 May 1936
English club: Sunderland
Position: Outside-left
Caps won while in England: 2 (of 3)

A darting left winger with an accurate cross and a powerful shot, George Mulhall was spotted by Aberdeen while playing for Kilsyth Rangers. His performances for the Dons from 1955 to 1962 attracted continual interest from English clubs, and it was Sunderland who moved in to capture him with a £20,000 cheque in September 1962. He won one cap with Aberdeen and two with Sunderland, all three for matches against Northern Ireland. Mulhall was a great favourite at Sunderland with his trickery and marksmanship, which brought him 55 goals in 253 League games. He moved to South Africa in 1969, and became captain of Cape Town City. On his return to the United Kingdom in 1971, he managed Halifax, Bolton and

Bradford, and went back to The Shay in 1994, first as youth team coach, then as manager again before becoming director of football and, later, chief scout.

Frank MUNRO ☆☆☆
Born: Broughty Ferry, 25 October 1947
English club: Wolves
Position: Central defender
Caps won while in England: 9 (of 9)

Disillusioned when Chelsea let him go after a trial as a centre-forward, Francis (Frank) Munro returned home in 1962 and started his professional career with Dundee United. Aberdeen bought him for £10,000 in 1966, and he had the distinction of scoring the first ever Dons goal in Europe. He gave such an outstanding performance for the Dons against Wolves in a summer tournament in the United States in 1968 that Molineux manager Ronnie Allen bought him for £55,000. He switched from centre-forward to centre-half, and developed into one of the most solid and reliable defenders in the League. He made 371 appearances for Wolves, scoring eighteen goals, before moving back to Scotland in 1976 for a short stay. Munro then went Down Under to Australia, playing for Hellas and taking short-term coaching assignments with Albion Rovers, Hamlyn Rangers and Kellor Austria. In 1989 he came home and worked as a salesman for a garden furniture company. At the age of 45 he suffered a severe stroke, was forced to give up work and subsequently needed the aid of a stick to walk.

Bobby MURDOCH ☆☆☆
Born: Rutherglen, 17 August 1944
English club: Middlesbrough
Position: Midfield
Caps won while in England: 0 (of 12)

Lisbon Lion Bobby Murdoch won respect on both sides of the border for his dignified demeanour on and off the pitch. He was a magnificent midfield marshal for the Celtic team that monopolised Scottish football under Jock Stein. Murdoch, who supplied skill and force in equal measures, was voted Scottish Football Writers' Player of the Year in 1969. He moved south to Jack Charlton's Middlesbrough in 1973 when his best was just behind him, and he still had enough left in the tank to drive Boro to promotion to the First Division, working in the midfield engine room alongside young Graeme Souness. It was the inspired idea of Jock Stein to switch Murdoch from a striker's role to a scheming function at right-half. He thrived on the extra responsibility, and his powerful long-range shooting made him a menace to goalkeepers. It was his shot that Steve Chalmers deflected into the Inter Milan net for Celtic's winning goal in the 1967 European Cup final. The former sheet-metal worker spent nine years at Ayresome Park as player, coach and manager between 1973 and 1982. He became a match-day 'meeter and greeter' at Celtic Park after a pub business went sour on him, and he was continually battling with ill health, sadly dying in Glasgow at the age of 56 in 2001. He will always be remembered as an outstanding footballer and a fine human being.

Gary NAYSMITH ☆☆☆
Born: Edinburgh, 16 November 1978
English club: Everton
Position: Defender
Caps won while in England: 11 (of 18)

Primarily a left-back, Gary Naysmith has also been effective as a left-sided midfielder for Everton. Walter Smith knew all about his potential from his days in charge at Rangers, and he brought him south to Goodison from Hearts for £1.75 million in October 2000, just pipping Coventry manager Gordon Strachan for his signature. Naysmith has been unlucky with injuries, and had recently recovered from an ankle problem when Liverpool powerhouse Steven Gerrard, in a moment of recklessness, caught him with a two-footed tackle during the Merseyside derby. He was highly thought of at Hearts, where he made 121 League and Cup appearances after being loaned out to Whitehill Welfare while waiting for his first-team chance. Naysmith won the first seven of his Scottish caps while at Tynecastle. He overcame knee ligament problems

following an operation, and was a steadying influence in both the Everton and Scotland defence in the 2002–03 season. He lost his usual level-headed way during the 2003 Merseyside derby at Goodison, and he was sent off after being shown a second yellow card. This was out of character for a disciplined and dedicated player.

Pat NEVIN ☆☆☆☆
Born: Glasgow, 6 September 1963
English clubs: Chelsea, Everton, Tranmere
Position: Winger
Caps won while in England: 28 (of 28)

Inspired by his schoolboy idol Jimmy Johnstone, Pat Nevin tried to follow in his hero's footsteps at Parkhead but was told he was too small. He gave up thoughts of a career in professional football until coming under the influence of Craig Brown at Clyde, who encouraged him 'to dribble like Jimmy'. It was the start of twenty years on the football roundabout, during which he played nearly 750 games. He abandoned a degree course to join Chelsea, and struck up a prolific partnership with Kerry Dixon. After scoring 36 goals in 193 League games, he had disagreements with the Chelsea management and moved to Everton in a £925,000 deal in 1988. His ability to run at top speed with the ball seemingly tied to his feet – Jimmy Johnstone style – made him a menace to the tightest defences.

Everton liked to use him as a substitute, bringing him on to use his speed and trickery when games needed retrieving. He played 109 League games for Everton, 28 of them as a substitute. Intelligent on and off the pitch, he became the chief spokesman for the players as chairman of the Professional Footballers' Association. He continued his career with Tranmere, Kilmarnock and Motherwell, later becoming director of football at Fir Park. His 28 caps with Scotland were won over a span of eleven years. He is now an estimable member of the media, giving considered opinions as a broadcaster and writer. Among his works is a book entitled *In Ma Head, Son!* with psychologist Dr George Sik. It was about what goes on in the mind of a footballer. Pat usually managed to win the mind games on the football pitch.

Charlie NICHOLAS ☆☆☆
Born: Glasgow, 30 December 1961
English club: Arsenal
Position: Striker
Caps won while in England: 13 (of 20)

Known as 'Cheeky Charlie' Nicholas at Celtic, he became labelled 'Champagne Charlie' after being signed for £650,000 by Arsenal manager Terry Neill in the summer of 1983. He was just 21 and not properly matured, and he got scorched by the publicity searchlight as he lived life to the full on the London celebrity circuit. Nicholas had wonderfully natural gifts, the ability to turn a half chance into a goal in the blinking of an eye, and power to go with his grace. What he didn't have was the self-determination to give 100 per cent concentration and dedication to his football. Charlie, a born entertainer and electric personality, wanted to *enjoy* life away from the strict disciplines of football, and he happily went along with the Fleet Street desire to feature him as much on the fashion and gossip pages as in the sports sections. His two goals against Liverpool in the 1987 Littlewoods Cup final at Wembley proved that he could perform on the biggest of stages, but his general play lacked the sort of consistency that new Highbury manager George Graham demanded. With Arsenal, he showed only erratic glimpses of the wonder play that brought him more than 50 goals for Celtic in 1981–82. The North Bank at Highbury loved Charlie, and identified with his swaggering and at times precocious play. But he could not fit into the George Graham team pattern, and was sold to Aberdeen in 1988 for £400,000. He had contributed 54 goals in 184 League appearances for Arsenal. By normal standards that was not a bad output, but Charlie was something special and this fell below what was expected of him. He rediscovered some of his old magic with The Dons, and finished back with Celtic in 1990. So it had come a full circle for the former apprentice car mechanic, and he was back where it had all started and where he will always have a permanent place in the land of legend. He is now a bright broadcaster (one of the few apart from the likes of Sue Barker to wear a diamond stud in his ear), and he is also an outspoken newspaper columnist, who would no doubt have some strong things to say if he saw a young Charlie Nicholas not making the most of his God-given talent.

QUOTE: 'Yes, I did make some mistakes at Arsenal, but the press greatly exaggerated my London lifestyle. I was a conscientious trainer, and did my best on the football pitch but in a team in which individualism was not exactly encouraged. Whenever I meet Arsenal fans they are always very warm to me, so I must have pleased them with my performances.'

Steve NICOL ☆☆☆☆☆

Born: Irvine, 11 December 1961
English clubs: Liverpool, Notts County, Sheffield Wednesday, West Brom
Position: Full-back/midfield
Caps won while in England: 27 (of 27)

After laying the foundations with Ayr United, Steve Nicol built an illustrious career at Liverpool, where he was a powerhouse of a player across a span of 467 matches from 1981 to 1995. Whether at full-back or as the midfield anchor-man, Nicol was Mr Reliable in defence and breathed defiance and determination for both his club and country. He was a major player in the Liverpool side that won four League championships, three English FA Cup finals, and reached two European Cup finals – with the peak moment a victory against Roma in the 1984 final. After extra playing and coaching experience with Notts County, Sheffield Wednesday and West Brom, Nicol headed for the United States, where he first coached Boston Bulldogs and was then, in November 2002, named head coach of the New England Revolution after being voted US soccer Coach of the Year. A class act on both sides of the Atlantic.

John O'HARE ☆☆☆☆

Born: Dumbarton, 24 September 1946
English clubs: Sunderland, Derby, Leeds, Nottingham Forest
Position: Centre-forward
Caps won while in England: 13 (of 13)

Along with fellow Scots Archie Gemmill and John McGovern, John O'Hare followed Brian Clough on the glory trail. When Cloughie became manager of Derby in 1967, he remembered the young Scot who had replaced him in the Sunderland attack after injury had finished his career at Roker Park. He made him his first signing, paying £23,000 to take him to the Baseball Ground and to rescue him from what had become a miserable existence at Sunderland. O'Hare's subtle style of playing was not appreciated by the Roker fans, who had grown accustomed to the straight-forward, no-nonsense goal-hunting of Clough. The burly, broad-shouldered O'Hare was a centre-forward who liked to come from deep, tricking rather than battering his way through defences. Cloughie paired him with a quick and decisive partner in Kevin Hector, and together they shot Derby to the Second and First Division championships. O'Hare found the net 65 times in 248 League appearances and made many more goals with his intricate skills and his ability to hold on to and shield the ball while team-mates found space for themselves to receive a pass. When Tommy Docherty brought him back into the international fold for the fourth of his thirteen caps, he described O'Hare as 'the finest target man in football, with more skill in his little toe than I had in my entire body'. He followed Clough to Leeds for what was a stuttering seven months taking in just seven games, and then joined up with him again at Nottingham Forest. He made a considerable making-and-taking goals contribution to Forest's League championship, first European Cup and League Cup triumphs before playing in the United States with Dallas and then going non-League with Belper Town and managing Ockbrook in the Midlands. O'Hare later ran a pub, worked with a sales firm and then used his sharp brain as stock controller with a Derby motor dealership.

QUOTE: 'The tightening of the rules by referees helped my game because I liked to shield the ball, and defenders used to hack at me from behind to try to get at it. I had a style of my own that was not always appreciated by some of the fans, but my team-mates knew that I was deliberately holding the ball so that they could get into better positions.'

Brian O'NEIL ☆
Born: Paisley, 6 September 1972
English clubs: Nottingham Forest, Derby County, Preston
Position: Midfield/defender
Caps won while in England: 1 (of 6)

A succession of injuries handicapped Brian O'Neil when he returned to the English scene with Derby County after two years' defensive duty for Wolfsburg in Germany. Derby were in dire financial straits and he was allowed to move on a free transfer to Preston in 2003 after just seventeen League appearances for the Pride Park club. Equally at home whether in the centre of the defence or playing an anchorman role in midfield, O'Neil had spent six seasons with Celtic before travelling the football roundabout with Nottingham Forest (on loan), Aberdeen and Wolfsburg. His career with Derby got off to the worst possible start when he was clattered by the redoubtable Roy Keane in the first minute of his debut against Manchester United. It left him with a knee injury and from then on he was always struggling for fitness and eventually had to have a cartilage operation. Preston manager Craig Brown, who knew all about his pedigree, was so pleased with his performances that he gave him a two-and-a-half-year contract.

Alex PARKER ☆☆☆☆
Born: Irvine, 2 August 1935
English clubs: Everton, Southport
Position: Full-back
Caps won while in England: 1 (of 15)

Rock solid at right-back, Alex Parker made his name as a dependable defender at Falkirk, where he won fourteen of his Scottish caps and was a mainstay in the team that won the Scottish Cup in 1957. Everton agreed to buy him in 1958 but had to wait until he completed a National Service assignment in Cyprus. He was followed into the Goodison team by 'Golden Vision' Alex Young, and they gave a mixture of Scottish steel and skill to the Everton team that won the League championship in 1962–63. Parker played 198 League games for the Merseysiders before moving on to Southport, where he had a spell as manager at the end of his playing career. He crossed the Irish Sea for some club management combined with running 'The Swinging Sporran' pub. It was then home to Scotland as landlord of another pub, this time in Gretna Green.

Derek PARLANE ☆☆
Born: Helensburgh, 5 May 1953
English clubs: Leeds, Manchester City, Swansea, Rochdale
Position: Striker
Caps won while in England: 0 (of 12)

It was clear that dashing Derek Parlane had left his best behind him at Rangers when he joined Leeds for £160,000 in March 1980. He had been a goal-scoring machine at Ibrox, playing a major role in helping them win two championships, three Scottish FA Cups and two Scottish League Cup triumphs. Parlane struggled to settle to the pace of the English game and failed to live up to expectations at Elland Road, particularly as he found himself being continually compared to his manager Allan Clarke, who was a goal-scoring legend at Leeds. He became a have-boots-will-travel player after scoring just ten goals in 50 League appearances for Leeds. His adventures took him on the road to Hong Kong, Manchester City, Swansea, Belgium, Rochdale, Airdrie and finally, in 1988, to Macclesfield Town. A conscientious and intelligent man, he found his niche as a sportswear salesman in the north-west and became the high-powered sales manager for Reebok UK.

Tommy PEARSON ☆☆
Born: Edinburgh, 6 March 1913
English club: Newcastle
Position: Winger
Caps won while in England: 2 (of 2)

Tommy Pearson's career was interrupted by the Second World War just as he was at his peak as a quick, darting outside-left. He joined Newcastle in 1933 following a trial period with Hearts and after shining in junior football with Murrayfield Athletic and Rosslyn Juniors. Pearson netted 46 goals in 212 League games for the Magpies either side of the war, and won his two Scottish caps in 1947 at the age of 34 and in his last season with Newcastle United. He made his international debut in the number 11 jersey in the 1–1 draw against England at Wembley, and then five weeks later in May 1947 won his second cap in the 2–1 defeat by Belgium in Brussels. Tommy died in 1999, aged 86.

Jackie PLENDERLEITH ☆
Born: Bellshill, 6 October 1937
English club: Manchester City
Position: Centre-half
Caps won while in England: 1 (of 1)

Jackie Plenderleith was at the heart of the defence for the accomplished Hibernian side that dominated Scottish football in the late 1950s with their Famous Five forward line. Ironically, he won his one and only cap after a move to Manchester City in 1960 when he was struggling to find the drive that made him such a formidable force with Hibs. He played in the 5–2 victory over Northern Ireland as the selectors searched for a successor in the number 5 shirt to Bobby Evans. The selectors preferred Billy McNeill in the next game – the infamous 9–3 thrashing by England! Plenderleith came from the football hotbed of Bellshill and laid the foundations to his career with Armadale. He was a strong and solid defender for Hibs, but cracks showed in his game when he moved to Maine Road. Injuries and a loss of form restricted his input to just 41 League games in three seasons.

Gerry QUEEN ☆☆
Born: Glasgow, 15 January 1945
English clubs: Crystal Palace, Leyton Orient
Position: Striker
No full caps

Gerry Queen was a gift to the headline writers when he joined Crystal Palace from Kilmarnock in the summer of 1969. 'Queen Tripped at the Palace' was pretty typical. A neat, upright and decisive forward, he scored 24 goals in 108 League appearances. He was unable to attract the Scottish selectors in an era when his rivals for the attacking roles included such luminaries as Denis Law and Kenny Dalglish. There will be many Palace fans and also those at Orient, where he spent four productive years, who will confirm that he was as close as you can get to international class without getting the – so to speak – royal acclamation.

John QUIGLEY ☆☆☆
Born: Glasgow, 28 June 1935
English clubs: Nottingham Forest, Huddersfield, Bristol City, Mansfield Town
Position: Striker
No full caps

A schemer with an eye for goal, Johnny Quigley joined Nottingham Forest from Ashfield Juniors in 1957 and gave excellent service to the Midlands club over the next seven years. He scored 51 goals in 236 League games for Forest, and created many more with intelligent passes after making openings with clever ball control. It was his semi-final goal that clinched an FA Cup final place for Forest in 1959, and he collected a winners' medal against Luton. He dropped deeper into midfield later in his career and let the ball do the work while playing for Huddersfield, Bristol City and Mansfield. The highlight of his three-year stay at Mansfield Town was a 3–0 FA Cup fifth-round victory over the full-strength Hurst-Moore-Peters West Ham team in 1968–69. He gave England skipper Bobby Moore a torrid time, and witnesses of his hugely competitive performance wondered why he had never been rewarded with a Scotland cap.

Alex RAE ☆☆☆
Born: Glasgow, 30 September 1969
English clubs: Millwall, Sunderland, Wolves
Position: Midfield
No full caps

Graeme Souness managed to break Alex Rae's heart without going near him on a football pitch. He was one of a cluster of youth players cleared out of Ibrox when Souness took over as Rangers manager. He picked himself up, dusted himself down and found himself a place with Falkirk. After three seasons at Brockville Park, Millwall manager Bruce Rioch came in for him in 1990 and he quickly won a reputation at The Den as a tenacious and competitive midfielder who could win the ball, make use of it and score goals. Sunderland manager Peter Reid noticed this all-round ability, and took him to the North-East for £1 million in 1996. He played a prominent part in helping to push Sunderland to promotion to the Premiership before being sidelined by a tendon injury. When he regained full fitness, Wolves came in for him and he moved to Molineux for £1.2 million in September 2001. At the end of his first season, the Wolves supporters voted him their Player of the Year. His aggression brought him six yellow cards as he linked up in midfield with Paul Ince to drive Wolves back to the Premiership in 2002–03.

Tommy RING ☆
Born: Glasgow, 8 August 1930
English clubs: Everton, Barnsley
Position: Winger
Caps won while in England: 0 (of 12)

A left winger of pace and guile, Tommy Ring had his finest hours with Clyde. He remains their most-capped player, winning his twelve caps when exceptional players of the calibre of Billy Liddell and Willie Ormond were among his rivals for the number 11 shirt. Clyde supporters will always remember him for the winning goal he scored against Celtic in the 1955 Scottish Cup final. His peak years were behind him when he joined Everton for one season in 1960, scoring six goals in 27 League appearances before moving on to Barnsley for his final shots in England.

Bruce RIOCH ☆☆☆☆
Born: Aldershot, 6 September 1947
English clubs: Luton, Aston Villa, Derby, Everton, Birmingham, Sheffield United, Torquay United
Position: Midfield
Caps won while in England: 24 (of 24)

Capped under the heritage ruling, Bruce Rioch was the first English-born captain of Scotland. He had an educated left foot, and a blistering shot that he often unleashed from his midfield command post. The son of a professional soldier, Rioch had a military bearing on the pitch. He was tall and upright like a guardsman and bossed the midfield with a confidence bordering on arrogance. He first came to prominence when scoring 24 goals in 44 League games on his way to a Fourth Division championship medal with Luton in 1967–68. Tommy Docherty took him to Aston Villa along with his brother, Neil, for £110,000, and he helped them reach the 1971 League Cup final. He won a League championship medal with Dave Mackay's Derby in 1974–75, and had a season at Everton before returning to Derby, who by then were under the command of The Doc. It was an unhappy reunion, Docherty famously transfer-listing both Scotland skipper Rioch and his team-mate Don Masson three months before the 1978 World Cup finals. After a disappointing World Cup that saw the end of his international career, Rioch had brief loan spells with Birmingham and Sheffield United before a stint in the United States with Seattle Sounders. In 562 League games he scored 129 goals, many of them of the spectacular variety that rivalled even Peter Lorimer's thunderbolts for power. He came back to England from Seattle to play for Torquay, the club with which he started an eventful managerial marathon that took in assignments at Middlesbrough, Millwall, Bolton, Arsenal, QPR (as assistant to Stewart Houston who had been his assistant at Highbury), Norwich City and Wigan Athletic.

Paul RITCHIE ☆☆☆

Born: Kirkcaldy, 21 August 1975
English clubs: Bolton, Manchester
City, Walsall
Position: Defender
Caps won while in England: 5 (of 9)

Satisfaction and frustration have come to Paul Ritchie in equal amounts during defensive service on both sides of the border. He joined Hearts from Links United in 1992 and over the next eight years established himself so well at Tynecastle that he won the first four of his international call-ups. A quick and tenacious tackler with a finely tuned left foot, he brought his pace and commitment on loan to Bolton in 1999. He had just cemented himself in the Wanderers defence with 21 first-team games when he was invited to join Rangers. Ritchie jumped at the chance but in six months at Ibrox did not get a kick in the first-team. Manchester City brought the languishing defender back into the English League, and just as he thought he had come out of his nightmare he was put out of action by pelvic and groin problems. He was sent to Paris for treatment from the specialist who works with the French national team, and on his return to Maine Road impressed new manager Kevin Keegan with his enthusiasm and energy. But injury prevented him from making a consistent challenge for the number 3 shirt vacated by the retiring Stuart Pearce, and he went off on another loan spell to Harry Redknapp's buoyant Portsmouth team. He played seven League matches for promotion-pushing Pompey before next taking his boots on loan to Derby County and then to Walsall on a free transfer.

David ROBERTSON ☆

Born: Aberdeen, 17 October 1968
English club: Leeds United
Position: Full-back
Caps won while in England: 0 (of 3)

A stylish left-back with Aberdeen and then Rangers, David Robertson was signed by new Leeds manager George Graham for £500,000 in 1997. He had just entrenched himself in the Leeds defence when he suffered a severe knee injury that necessitated an operation. During his lay-off he started to study coaching, and he moved back to Scotland as player-coach at Montrose. A strong-minded character, his international career was cut short after three matches following a disagreement with then manager Craig Brown. Injury meant he made just 26 League appearances at Leeds in four years of torment. In 2003 he took his first step on the managerial ladder as boss of Elgin City.

Jimmy ROBERTSON ☆☆☆
Born: Glasgow, 17 December 1944
English clubs: Tottenham, Arsenal,
Ipswich, Stoke, Walsall, Crewe
Position: Winger
Caps won while in England: 1 (of 1)

Flying Jimmy Robertson was one of that rare breed who managed to win the hearts of the supporters at both Tottenham and their deadly North London rivals Arsenal. He had first shown his pace on the wing and considerable right-footed shooting power when a teenager at Cowdenbeath. In 1964, after scoring eighteen goals in 52 appearances for St Mirren, he moved south to join a Tottenham team that Bill Nicholson was rebuilding after a sensational start to the decade with the League and Cup double. Robertson netted 25 goals in 157 League games for Spurs, with his main job to provide crosses for the G-men partners Jimmy Greaves and Alan Gilzean. His high spot was the first goal in the 1967 FA Cup final at Wembley that helped Tottenham to a 2–1 victory over Chelsea. He moved to Arsenal in 1968 in a straight swap for David Jenkins. While the teenage prodigy from Bristol sunk almost without trace at Tottenham, Robertson pleased the Highbury fans with his positive running and controlled crosses. It was the arrival of Peter Marinello that signalled the end of his Arsenal experience in 1970, and he played at the back end of his career with Ipswich, Stoke, Walsall and Crewe. He left football and joined a computer insurance company in Staffordshire, later becoming a member of the Task Force Group.

John ROBERTSON ☆☆
Born: Edinburgh, 2 October 1964
English club: Newcastle
Position: Striker
Caps won while in England: 0 (of 16)

Newcastle fans got barely a fleeting glimpse of the striking powers that turned John Robertson into a legend at Hearts. He scored a remarkable 310 goals in 719 appearances in two spells for the Edinburgh club, sandwiching an unsatisfactory move from Tynecastle to Tyneside for £700,000 in 1988. He stayed just eight months at Newcastle, failing to find the net in twelve League games before returning to his favourite hunting ground at Hearts in a £650,000 deal. He lifted his Hearts League scoring record to 214 goals and then went off in a new direction as coach at Livingston. On Boxing Day 2002, he was unveiled as the new manager of Inverness Caledonian Thistle.

John ROBERTSON ☆☆☆☆☆
Born: Uddingston, 20 January 1953
English clubs: Nottingham Forest,
Derby
Position: Winger
Caps won while in England: 28 (of 28)

John Robertson, the original Fat Boy Slim, could have stepped out of the *Come Dancing* school of footballers. He would glide past full-backs with a slow-slow-quick-quick-slow gait that left much quicker defenders baffled as to how they had missed their tackles. Throughout his career, Robertson had weight problems that continually earned him caustic comments from manager Brian Clough. But Cloughie, who inherited him when he took over as Forest manager in 1975, knew that he was a diamond of a player who needed careful polishing. He took him off the transfer list, switched him from wing-half to left wing, and he and his partner Peter Taylor helped him develop into, arguably, the finest outfield player in the full-of-flair Forest team that won the League championship and back-to-back European Cups. It was Red Robbo who scored the goal that retained the European Cup with a 1–0 victory over Kevin Keegan's Hamburg in 1980. A year earlier, his pinpointed cross was headed home by Trevor Francis for the winning goal in the European Cup final against Malmo. Robertson joined Forest from Drumchapel Amateurs after gaining Scottish Schoolboy and Youth international honours as a left-half.

Much to Cloughie's undisguised disgust, Robertson followed Peter Taylor to Derby County in 1983, for a £135,000 fee set by a tribunal. The move did not work out the way Robertson had hoped, mainly because of a recurring knee problem. After a cartilage operation, he returned to Forest on a free transfer in August 1985 but he was carrying extra pounds and was unable to find any of the old magic. He drifted into non-League soccer with Corby Town, Stamford and Grantham, and later became a publican and then an insurance consultant. Martin O'Neill brought him back into the football fold, first as a scout and then he promoted his former Forest club colleague to assistant manager. His goals output for Forest was 61 in 384 League games, and he made many more for team-mates. As well as his smooth-as-silk skill, Robertson will be remembered – particularly by Liverpool – for his accuracy from the penalty spot. It was his penalty that beat Liverpool in the 1978 League Cup final replay, and he scored from the spot in each leg of the 1980 League Cup semi-final against the Merseysiders. Deadeye Robbo was also on the spot for Scotland, with four of his nine goals in 28 internationals coming from penalties. This included two in a World Cup qualifier against Israel, and the winner against England at Wembley in 1981. No wonder the fans were saying, 'It's not over 'til the fat man scores.'

QUOTE: 'My best memory has to be scoring the only goal of the match in the 1980 European Cup final. Everybody was waiting for me to cross the ball, but I thought I might as well have a go myself. I will never forget the looks of shock and horror on the faces of the Hamburg players as the ball hit the back of the net.'

with his younger brother, James, who was also a Scottish international, who played for Hibs, Newcastle, Crystal Palace and Falkirk. Alex, the wing wizard, died in 2001 aged 64.

Alex SCOTT ☆☆☆☆
Born: Falkirk, 22 November 1936
English club: Everton
Position: Winger
Caps won while in England: 5 (of 16)

Whether in the blue of Rangers, Everton or Scotland, Alex Scott was a Blue Flash on the wing, beating full-backs with pace and skill and then putting over inch-perfect centres or firing in fierce cross shots. Taking over on the Rangers right wing from Ibrox legend Willie Waddell, he managed to fill the great man's boots and helped Rangers to four Scottish League titles, the League Cup twice and the Scottish Cup. He then brought his dribbling and scoring skills to Goodison, when he won League championship and FA Cup winners' medals. His 108 goals in 331 matches was a high scoring ratio for a winger, and he added five more in his sixteen appearances for Scotland when he had to compete with Jimmy Johnstone and Willie Henderson for the number 7 shirt. He shared the Rangers' record of twelve European goals until Ally McCoist rewrote the record books in 1996–97. He returned north of the border from Everton in 1967 to play for Hibernian and then Falkirk. Following his retirement, he went into business

Jimmy SCOULAR ☆☆☆☆☆
Born: Livingston, 11 January 1925
English clubs: Portsmouth, Newcastle, Bradford Park Avenue
Position: Wing-half
Caps won while in England: 9 (of 9)

Ask any Football League professional plying his trade in the 1940s and 1950s who was the hardest tackler he ever faced and the name Jimmy Scoular will not be far from his lips. Scoular the Scowler looked as if he had been quarried out of the Livingston pavements where he grew up. He was the epitome of rugged, with a strong, square jaw, heavy eyebrows, legs like tree trunks and a tackle that was out of the Hammer House of Horror. Portsmouth discovered him playing for Gosport Borough near to his HMS *Dolphin* base as a wartime engineer. He played for Pompey in the immediate post-war years, when they won back-to-back League championships, and the half-back line he formed with Jack Froggatt and Jimmy Dickinson was as good a defensive combination as any in the land. Scoular had so much stamina opponents must have wondered if he had an extra lung, and his passing was accurate for distances up to 50 yards. He had just one weakness – a tinderbox temper that continually landed him in trouble with referees. Scoular won his nine caps with Pompey at a time when Anglos came at the back of the queue with the Scottish selectors. He was transferred to Newcastle in 1953 to take over from the great Magpies skipper Joe Harvey, and he collected the FA Cup in 1955. At 35, he became player-manager of Bradford Park Avenue. Then in June 1964 he started a nine-year stint as manager of Cardiff City. He later scouted for Aston Villa, Wolves and managed Newport before leaving football for jobs in the jewellery trade and the chemical industry. Scoular finally retired to Dinas Powys, near Cardiff, and died in 1998 at the age of 73.

Bill SHANKLY ☆☆☆☆☆
Born: Glenbuck, 2 September 1913
English clubs: Carlisle, Preston
Position: Wing-half
Caps won while in England: 5 (all pre-war)

See Part One for his full career details.

Graeme SHARP ☆☆☆☆
Born: Glasgow, 16 October 1960
English clubs: Everton, Oldham
Position: Striker
Caps won while in England: 12 (of 12)

One of the most underrated strikers in the game, Graeme Sharp often took a back seat at Everton to glory goal-hunters like Andy Gray and Gary Lineker. But shrewd observers knew that it was Sharp who was providing the ammunition with his deft touches, clever positioning and skill in holding the ball while team-mates found space. A handful for any defence on the ground, he was also a master of the airways and he continually won possession in deadball situations and nodded it down to the feet of colleagues. The influence of Andy Gray seemed to rub off on him and he became much more physical after a quiet start to life at Goodison. He joined Everton rather than Aston Villa from Dumbarton for a bargain £120,000 in 1980, and developed into the finest target man in the First Division. His play was not always appreciated by the spectators, but the players knew who was making the attack tick when Everton won the FA Cup in 1984 and the League championship in 1984–85 and 1986–87. It is a mystery how he won only a dozen Scottish caps. Oldham manager Joe Royle, an ex-Evertonian who knew a thing or three about centre-forward play, signed him for £500,000 in 1991. Handicapped by a recurring back problem that hurried him into retirement, Sharp took over as manager at Oldham after Royle had 'gone home' as boss at Goodison. He resigned in 1997 after three years in the Boundary Park hot seat, and later returned to Everton in a PR capacity, working closely with the fans who, in retrospect, realise what an exceptional player he was.

QUOTE: 'I was lucky to have players of the quality of Andy Gray and Gary Lineker to play alongside. That Everton team of the 1980s had just the right balance between skill and strength, and there was not a weakness anywhere. Some of the football we played was out of this world.'

Duncan SHEARER ☆☆

Born: Fort William, 28 August 1962
English clubs: Chelsea, Huddersfield, Swindon, Blackburn
Position: Striker
Caps won while in England: 0 (of 7)

When Duncan Shearer was appointed assistant manager to Steve Paterson at Aberdeen in December 2002 he was returning to the club where he had been a top-flight marksman after failing to set the world alight in England. Chelsea let him go in 1985 after he had made just two League appearances, and he then battled to make an impact in the lower divisions with Huddersfield and Swindon. His 78 goals in 159 League games with Swindon inspired Blackburn to pay £800,000 for him in 1991, but he struggled to impress new Ewood Park boss Kenny Dalglish and after just six games he was sold on to Aberdeen for £500,000. His direct attacks on goal were an immediate success at Pittodrie and he became their leading scorer and won the first of his caps when he was into his thirties. Shearer was warmly welcomed back to

Aberdeen when he and Steve Paterson took over the managerial reins after working together with success at Caledonian Thistle.

Ronnie SIMPSON ☆☆☆☆

Born: Glasgow, 11 October 1930
English club: Newcastle
Position: Goalkeeper
Caps won while in England: 0 (of 5)

Ronnie Simpson's career notes read like something out of a *Roy of the Rovers* yarn. This son of a former Rangers captain was just fourteen when he turned out for Queen's Park against Clyde at Hampden Park in the last year of the war, the youngest ever player in a senior Scottish game. Many years later he added an extraordinary twist to his tale. At 36, he became the oldest man to keep goal for Scotland, and just to make it even more memorable this in a game when the Scots whooped to a 3–2 victory over reigning World Cup winners England in their citadel of Wembley. In between his youngest and oldest feats he established himself as a goalkeeping hero on both sides of the border. Simpson spent five years as an amateur with Queen's Park and was in the Great Britain squad for the 1948 London Olympics. He turned professional with Third Lanark in 1950 and had only been with them for six months when Newcastle bought him for what was then a record fee for a Scottish goalkeeper of £8,750. He was a magnificent last line of defence for the Geordies, collecting FA Cup winners' medals in 1952 and 1953. After 262 League games for Newcastle, they decided his best was behind him and sold him to Hibernian in October 1960 for £2,100. Many agreed with the Newcastle assessment that Ronnie's reflexes were not what they were, and the evidence was there for all to see when he had to pick the ball out of his net six times in his Easter Road debut against, wait for it, Celtic! A new manager arrived at Hibs in the shape of Jock Stein, who did not fancy the veteran Simpson one bit. They had an angry disagreement and Stein sold Simpson to Celtic, who wanted him as reserve cover. Just six months later Stein followed Simpson to Celtic, and the rest – as they say – is history. 'Simmie' was Celtic's goalkeeper throughout most of their glorious domestic reign of the 1960s, and he was one of the unforgettable Lisbon Lions who collected a European Cup winners' medal in 1967. He was already 34 when he moved to Parkhead, but went on to make 184 appearances between the posts for Celtic. The strength of his game was his safe handling, excellent positioning and rapid reflexes that often got him out of trouble after failing to collect crosses at the first time of asking. These days, retired Ronnie is a much-in-demand after-dinner speaker to whom it is well worth lending an ear or two. He certainly has a story to tell.

QUOTE: 'Jock Stein and I did not see eye to eye at Hibernian, but we grew to respect each other at Parkhead. It was extraordinary what that Celtic team achieved, and I was so proud to be part of it all when most people thought I had returned to Scotland with retirement in mind.'

Jackie SINCLAIR ☆☆☆
Born: Culross, Fife, 21 July 1943
English clubs: Leicester, Newcastle, Sheffield Wednesday, Chesterfield
Position: Winger
Caps won while in England: 1 (of 1)

Starting out with the Blairhall Colliery team, John (Jackie) Sinclair was thrust into the limelight by no less a manager than Jock Stein. He gave him his first big break in 1960 when performing minor miracles at Dunfermline. A fast, decisive left winger with good finishing instincts, Sinclair travelled the English football escalator with Leicester City (50 goals in 103 League appearances), Newcastle (six in 43 games), and Sheffield Wednesday (fourteen in 101). He also had a loan spell with Chesterfield. His most memorable moments came in European competition, first of all with Dunfermline at the age of nineteen. He scored two goals in the 6–2 vanquishing of Valencia in a Fairs Cup tie in 1962–63. Six years later he played in both legs of the final against Ujpest Dosza to help Newcastle win the Fairs Cup. Sinclair won his only

Scotland cap while with Leicester City – a 1–0 defeat by the exceptional Eusebio-inspired Portugal team that was having its final warm-up match before the 1966 World Cup finals. He later moved to the Scottish village of Dollar, and took a job as a golf club steward in Dunfermline.

Jim SMITH ✩✩✩
Born: Glasgow, 20 January 1947
English club: Newcastle United
Position: Midfield
Caps won while in England: 3 (of 4)

Nicknamed 'Jinky' because of his dribbling runs from deep midfield positions, Jim Smith first came to prominence as a swaggering, enter-taining showman with Aberdeen. Newcastle were so taken with him that they paid out a £100,000 fee for the first time to take him to Tyneside in the summer of 1969. The Geordie fans loved his Jim Baxter-style showboating skills, but did not see nearly as much of him as they would have liked because of serious injury problems. He was finally forced to retire after 129 League games. A self-confessed gambler, he blew all his money and became a taxi-driver in Newcastle until having to give up driving because of ill health. He was a wonderfully talented player, who deserved better luck – both on the football field and in the betting shop.

Graeme SOUNESS ✩✩✩✩✩
Born: Edinburgh, 6 May 1953
English clubs: Tottenham, Middlesbrough, Liverpool
Position: Midfield
Caps won while in England: 40 (of 54)

See Part One for his full career details.

David SPEEDIE ✩✩✩
Born: Glenrothes, 20 February 1960
English clubs: Barnsley, Darlington, Chelsea, Coventry, Liverpool, Blackburn, Southampton, Birming-ham, West Brom, West Ham, Leicester
Position: Striker/midfield
Caps won while in England: 10 (of 10)

On and off the pitch, David Speedie liked to keep on the move. He was a bundle of energy, who harried, harassed and niggled defenders with his perpe-tual-motion performances. His transfers were so frequent that he must have been on first-name terms with the removal men. Speedie, who had a fiery temper to match his red hair, was continually in trouble with referees. Brought up in Yorkshire, he started his career with Barnsley and arrived at Chelsea via Darlington in 1982. He struck up a winning partnership at Stamford Bridge with Kerry Dixon, scoring 47 goals in 162 League games. Next stop Coventry, where he scored 31 goals in 132 League matches until falling out with manager Terry Butcher. Kenny Dalglish made him one of his last signings for Liverpool, and he scored six goals in just twelve League appearances. The Liverpool fans would have considered the £675,000 fee money well spent when he scored two goals in the Merseyside derby against Everton. He next teamed up with Mike Newell at Blackburn, and together they powered Rovers to promotion as founder members of the new Premier League. But Speedie did not play for Rovers in the Premiership. He was on his travels again, this time to Southampton in part exchange for a young centre-forward called Alan Shearer. This brought him back in harness with Kerry Dixon, but they were nothing like as successful as in their Chelsea days and after only eleven League appearances he was off on loan assignments with Birmingham, West Brom and West Ham before taking his final shots at Leicester. After hanging up his much-travelled boots, he became a players' agent. His temper was still on a short fuse when, in his forties, he was briefly banned from playing for Coventry in the Masters six-a-side indoor tournament!

he won thirteen of his fourteen Scotland caps. He found the net 36 times in 103 League games while at Stamford Bridge, providing good value for the £450,000 paid to Rangers. Spencer was a virtually unknown player at Ibrox, and had been on loan to Morton and to a Hong Kong club. Knee and ankle injuries and a virus held up his career after a £2.5 million transfer to Queen's Park Rangers in 1996, and after sixteen months at Loftus Road he got caught up in a farce of a move to Everton. First of all it was on a loan, and then there was protracted haggling over a fee before Howard Kendall got his man for £1.5 million. Over a full frustrating year Spencer managed just nine games before an unimpressed Walter Smith let him go on loan and then full time in a £500,000 move to Motherwell, where his brother-in-law Billy Davies was player-manager. In 2001 he moved with his wife and family to Colorado, where he has become Rapids' club captain and leading marksman, running on to the passes of Colombian master Carlos 'Wild Hair' Valderrama.

John SPENCER ☆☆☆
Born: Glasgow, 11 September 1970
English clubs: Chelsea, QPR, Everton
Position: Striker
Caps won while in England: 14 (of 14)

Feisty and totally committed to every game in which he plays, John Spencer had his peak seasons at Chelsea where

Ian ST JOHN ☆☆☆☆☆
Born: Motherwell, 7 June 1938
English clubs: Liverpool, Coventry, Tranmere
Position: Centre-forward/midfield
Caps won while in England: 15 (of 21)

There is a generation growing up who think of Ian St John as the straight man in the Saint and Greavsie double act. They do not realise that he was one of the most talented attacking players ever to come out of Scotland, who had an even more impressive double act on the pitch with Liverpool goal-hunter Roger Hunt. He was the front man of what Bill Shankly saw as the Scottish spine running through the Liverpool team, from Tommy Lawrence in goal, through Ron Yeats in the centre of defence, Willie Stevenson as a defensive anchorman in midfield and up to St John. The Saint was equally potent whether leading the attack or coming through from a deep position as a support striker. He arrived at Anfield from Motherwell in 1961 for what was then a club record fee of £37,500. The major English clubs were alerted to his goal-scoring powers when he topped the Motherwell hit list three times in his first four seasons, including a hat-trick in under three minutes against Hibernian in 1959. Shanks saw the signing of St John, followed soon after by Ron Yeats, as the start of the Red Revolution. The Saint quickly proved himself an artist of a centre-forward, holding his line together with intelligent positional play, neat flick passes and spring-heeled heading. He was such a hero at Anfield that when a local church displayed a poster asking, 'What would you do if Jesus returned among us?' somebody scrawled the answer, 'Move St John to inside-left.' The Saint collected a Second Division championship medal in his first season at Anfield, League

championship medals in 1964 and 1966, and memorably scored the extra-time winning goal in the 1965 FA Cup final against Leeds with an extraordinary header when he corkscrewed his body to reach a ball that was going behind him. Capped 21 times by Scotland, he netted nine international and 178 League goals. He later played for Coventry and Tranmere, had a spell in South Africa, and managed Portsmouth before kicking off an enormously successful broadcasting career. Television (in the opinion of the author) dropped Saint and Greavsie far too early. They can still be heard together in a brilliant after-dinner double act, and the Saint runs a string of youth coaching camps.

QUOTE: 'Anfield was an exciting place to be when Shanks was breathing fire into the players and the supporters. You could warm your hands on his enthusiasm, and we were all ready and willing to run through brick walls for him. Every time I see a replay of my goal that clinched our FA Cup final victory over Leeds in 1965 I wonder how I managed to score. The game was into extra-time and I was feeling knackered. My socks were rolled down to my ankles because of cramp, and we were beginning to think a replay was on the cards. A centre from Ian Callaghan was going behind me, but somehow I managed to twist my body and get my head to it. When the ball went in I think they could hear the Wembley cheers all the way back at Anfield! It was a moment that will live with me for ever.'

Billy STEEL ☆☆☆☆
Born: Denny, 1 May 1923
English club: Derby County
Position: Winger
Caps won while in England: 14 (of 30)

A maker and taker of remarkable goals, jet-heeled Billy Steel struck an amazing deal when he agreed to join Derby County from Morton in 1947 for a then British record £15,500. He was allowed to commute from Scotland to play for Derby, who were desperate to beat a queue of clubs for his signature after he had starred for Scotland against England in a 1–1 draw at Wembley. He gave an outstanding individual performance that earned him a prestige place in the Great Britain team against the Rest of Europe at Hampden, a showpiece game in which he scored a wonder goal from 20 yards. Steel, who had briefly been on the books of Leicester City and St Mirren before joining Morton, produced many scintillating performances for Derby over the next three seasons, during which he scored 27 goals in 109 matches and also managed to fit in fourteen international appearances. He was a gymnastic fitness fanatic, and one of his favourite tricks in training was to walk the length of the pitch on his hands. A man of little patience, he was continually at loggerheads with the Derby directors over his travelling to and from Scotland, and it became obvious that he was keen to return north of the border. Dundee had the financial clout of a wealthy impresario called George Anderson, and they smashed the British transfer record in 1950 to take the flamboyant Steel to Dens Park for sums variously reported between £18,500 and £23,500. He rattled in 46 goals in 131 League and Cup games for Dundee, and helped them become the first club to win two successive League Cup finals. Steel was a single-minded man who would not suffer fools gladly or otherwise, and he often gave team-mates the sharp end of his tongue if they did not meet his perfectionist standards. He could explode in anger, often caused by the deficiencies of his own players. For a man who stood only 5ft 6in tall, he was surprisingly strong in the air and an aggressive and committed competitor. His fiery nature earned him the unwanted record of being the first Scottish player sent off in an international match during a roughhouse of a game against Austria in Vienna in 1951. An Austrian supporter dressed in traditional lederhosen and heavy boots kicked him up the backside as he walked towards the dressing-room after he had been sent off following a clash with a defender. It took five policemen to stop an enraged Steel 'doing a Cantona' on the spectator! Throughout his career he made a close study of journalism, and at 31 – troubled by a recurring ankle injury – he surprisingly emigrated to the United States. Steel played and wrote about soccer in the States and eventually became a newspaper executive in California before his death in 1982 at the age of 59.

Colin STEIN ☆☆
Born: Linlithgow, 10 May 1947
English club: Coventry City
Position: Centre-forward
Caps won while in England: 4 (of 21)

Colin Stein created transfer history in 1968 when Rangers made him the first £100,000 player to move from one Scottish club to another. He had been building a reputation at Hibernian as a centre-forward of not only some style but also of much substance. Everton matched the Rangers offer, but Stein preferred to stay in Scotland. He had laid the foundation to his career at Armadale Thistle, where his all-action style of play was a throwback to the old-style centre-forwards. When he arrived at Ibrox, he lived up to his reputation with a procession of fine goals. There were times when his eagerness to please took him beyond the boundaries of propriety, and he was given his marching orders four times in fifteen months. On New Year's Day 1971 he had to come to terms with an appalling tragedy in which he unconsciously played a part. His late equaliser in the Auld Firm match against Celtic triggered a chain of events that led to 66 spectators being crushed to death on Stairway 13 at Ibrox. The tragedy cut deep with the brilliant young footballer, but he has always kept his silence and out of respect for the victims has never discussed the incident. After playing a leading role in helping Rangers win the

European Cup Winners' Cup in 1972, he moved to Coventry City in a deal valued at £130,000 that took Quentin Young to Rangers in part exchange. Stein scored 22 goals in 83 appearances for the Sky Blues, but was a shadow of the player who had looked the complete centre-forward at Hibs and Rangers. Stein returned to Rangers after two years, struggling to recover his old bustling, defence-dismantling style. There was one big moment of glory left. It was his headed goal for the Gers at his old hunting ground of Hibernian that clinched the 1975 League championship and ended Celtic's run of domestic dominance. In 206 appearances for Rangers Stein scored 97 goals. His ten goals for Scotland included four in one match against Cyprus in 1969. When he left football, Colin quietly returned to his hometown of Linlithgow, where he made a living as a joiner while, with his wife, following their hobby of bowls. Both became international-class players.

Jimmy STEPHEN ☆☆☆
Born: Fettercairn, 23 August 1922
English clubs: Bradford Park Avenue, Portsmouth
Position: Full-back
Caps won while in England: 2 (of 2)

Jimmy Stephen moved from Johnshaven in Aberdeenshire to Bradford Park Avenue in August 1939, just two weeks before war was declared. He made such a good impression in wartime services football that he was selected to captain Scotland in their first post-war international. It should have been one of the greatest days of his life when he led the Scots out against Wales at Wrexham, but it all turned sour for him when he unwittingly scored an own goal in a 3–1 defeat. A solid, hard-tackling full-back who was equally secure on either flank, he played 94 League games for Bradford and then joined Portsmouth as they were putting together the team that won two successive League championships. He played exactly 100 League games in four years at Fratton Park. His only other cap came in 1947, again against Wales and this time at Hampden Park. The Scots were beaten 2-1.

Willie STEVENSON ☆☆☆
Born: Leith, 26 October 1939
English clubs: Liverpool, Stoke City, Tranmere Rovers
Position: Wing-half
No full caps

Another player mysteriously missed by the Scottish selectors, Willie Stevenson had won Scottish League and Cup medals with Rangers when he was dropped into the reserves. He was so disillusioned that he packed his bags and emigrated to Australia! Bill Shankly knew all about his talent, and he got in touch with him Down Under and persuaded him to come back to continue his career with Liverpool. Stevenson, a cultured and stylish wing-half in the best Scottish traditions, settled into the Anfield team to complete one of the great Liverpool half-back lines, with Gordon Milne and Ron Yeats. His smooth movements masked a steely determination to win the ball, and once he had it he would use it with imagination to trigger many of the counter-attacks that were a Liverpool speciality. He was a major force in the championship teams of 1964 and 1966, and the 1965 FA Cup-winning side. After 188 First Division games for the Reds he later played for Stoke City and Tranmere. On his retirement he started a contract cleaning business in Macclesfield, and keeps in touch with Anfield through the former players' association. Australia must seem further away than ever!

David STEWART ☆☆
Born: Glasgow, 11 March 1947
English clubs: Leeds United, West Brom, Swansea
Position: Goalkeeper
Caps won while in England: 1 (of 1)

Understudy to fellow-Scot David Harvey for much of his time at Leeds, David Stewart came into his own in the 1974–75 season when Billy Bremner skippered the Yorkshire club to the European Cup final in Paris. He played 55 League matches in all for Leeds before moving to Swansea via West Bromwich Albion. Stewart was a safe, unspectacular goalkeeper who won seven Under-23 caps while playing for Ayr United, for whom he played 157 League games before his move to Elland Road in 1972. After finishing with Swansea in 1980 he had two years in Hong Kong before returning to Wales to work as a goldsmith. He could then claim to be goldfingers – after all, he did save a penalty in his only appearance for Scotland against East Germany in 1978.

Jim STEWART ☆☆
Born: Kilwinning, 9 March 1954
English club: Middlesbrough
Position: Goalkeeper
Caps won while in England: 1 (of 2)

Goalkeeper Jim Stewart completed the full circle when he joined Kilmarnock in 2002 as the Killie full-time goal-keeping coach, including his 6ft 3in son Colin under his wing. Jim had started out with Kilmarnock in 1968, and then moving to Middlesbrough nine years later. It was with Killies that he won his first Scottish cap in 1977, and his second followed while he was at Ayresome Park. He played 34 League games for Boro before moving back to Scotland with Rangers. In a career stretching to 500 games, he also kept goal for St Mirren and Partick Thistle. Stewart became a Ministry of Defence policeman on his retirement, working with Kilmarnock on a part-time basis until persuaded to take the goalkeeper coaching job on a permanent basis.

Michael STEWART ☆
Born: Edinburgh, 26 February 1981
English club: Manchester United
Position: Midfield
Caps won while in England: 3 (of 3)

Michael Stewart brings into focus the dilemma facing Scotland manager Berti Vogts. He has been selected for full international duty with barely a glimpse of first-team football as a springboard for playing for his country. He is clearly an exceptional prospect, but is having to run before he can walk because of the scarcity of top-quality Scottish profes-sionals. Stewart is a competitive and skilful midfielder who has often sat on the Man United bench, covering for the midfield masters. The flame-haired youngster has had a handful of excur-sions at first-team level, and Sir Alex Ferguson rates him highly. United signed him straight from his school in Edinburgh in competition with Rangers. Stewart has been given a thorough grounding in the United youth and reserve teams, but it is hardly the right preparation for the international arena. He was briefly loaned to Royal Antwerp and then Nottingham Forest, and he made four first-team appearances for United in the 2002–03 season, once in the team that regained the Premiership title. The best is yet to come for this talented young man.

Ray STEWART ☆☆☆☆
Born: Perth, 7 September 1959
English club: West Ham United
Position: Full-back
Caps won while in England: 10 (of 10)

West Ham supporters thought so highly of Ray Stewart that they voted him the greatest Hammers right-back of all time. He endeared himself to them with a procession of perfect performances across an eleven-year stay at Upton Park during which he played 345 League games. Stewart was one of the deadliest penalty takers ever to step foot on to a pitch, and he scored 75 of the 86 penalties he took for the Hammers. In the 1981–82 season alone, he netted thirteen penalties! He joined West Ham from Dundee United in 1979, and while at Upton Park earned ten international caps. Stewart was not the quickest of full-backs, but he had good powers of recovery, a telling tackle and good passing ability. As his penalty record reveals, he had an excellent temperament and was never ever fazed. He returned home to Scotland and started a managerial career with Livingston and then took charge at Stirling. His two years at Stirling were disappointing and he was out of the game following the sack in April 2002, but was back in the fold in the New Year of 2003 as manager of Forfar Athletic.

Robbie STOCKDALE ☆☆☆
Born: Redcar, 30 November 1979
English club: Middlesbrough
Position: Defender
Caps won while in England: 5 (of 5)

Another Scottish international who spotlights the problems of finding home-grown talent. Robbie Stockdale is a Yorkshireman who has been drawn into Scotland's net because he has Scottish grandparents. Berti Vogts selected him after he had made his international debut for England Under-21s! He was struggling to win a first-team place during Bryan Robson's reign as Middlesbrough manager, and he went to Sheffield Wednesday on loan. His determined and enthusiastic defensive work appealed to new Boro boss Steve McClaren, and he became a regular on the team sheet at the Riverside Stadium. Injuries handicapped his progress, and he slipped out of the international squad.

Gordon STRACHAN ☆☆☆☆☆
Born: Edinburgh, 9 February 1957
English clubs: Manchester United, Leeds, Coventry
Position: Midfield
Caps won while in England: 50 (of 50)

There have been few players in modern times to match Gordon Strachan for thinking on their feet. As he has proved as a battle-worn manager, he is a born tactician and this used to be obvious to witnesses of his distinguished playing career. With his red hair, impish humour and perpetual-motion style of play, he stood out like a searchlight in a blackout for club and country. He was a super skipper for Alex Ferguson's surprising Aberdeen team, and then gave Manchester United midfield drive and direction after Ron Atkinson had taken him to Old Trafford in return for a fee of £600,000. It was a transfer that had a touch of Monty Python about it, with FC Cologne announcing that Strachan had signed for them. Strachan headed for Manchester rather than Germany and in 1985 collected an FA Cup winners' medal to go with the cupboardful of prizes he had collected at Aberdeen. The only area where he was erratic was from the penalty spot, missing as many as he scored but still having the character to step up and take the kicks at critical times. When Alex Ferguson followed him to Old Trafford everybody thought they would rekindle the fire they had started at Aberdeen, so it was a major surprise in March 1989 when he was allowed to move to Leeds for £300,000. It was the Ferguson view that the Strachan engine was no longer firing on all cylinders. He proved his old boss hopelessly wrong by giving six stupendous years to Leeds, including an amazing 1991–92 campaign when he inspired his new club to the League championship, a short head in front of his old club. Meantime, he had assured himself legendary status at home in Scotland where his 50th and final cap in

1992 earned him a place in the Scottish Hall of Fame. Ron Atkinson signed him again, this time for Coventry as manager in waiting. He poured himself into his new role as boss of the Sky Blues, almost willing them to stay up during what were annual struggles for survival. Strachan won many battles but finally lost the war, yet his first experience in management had given him the taste for more punishment. He took charge of Southampton in October 2001, and in no time at all had them playing football that was both functional and flowing. In his first full season in charge at St Mary's he steered Southampton to a very respectable eighth place in the Premiership and to the FA Cup semi-final. Gordon has a tongue that can be comical or caustic, depending on his mood, but he is never anything less than interesting to listen to. **QUOTE:** 'I have so many rich memories of my playing career. The outstanding ones, I suppose, are the European triumph at Aberdeen early in my career and the League championship at Leeds near the end. Both were so unexpected by even the closest observers of the game.'

Neil SULLIVAN ☆☆☆☆
Born: Sutton, 24 February 1970
English clubs: Wimbledon, Crystal Palace, Tottenham
Position: Goalkeeper
Caps won while in England: 28 (of 28)

After eleven years with Wimbledon punctuated by a brief loan spell at

Crystal Palace, Neil Sullivan arrived at White Hart Lane for what most people expected to be a wind-down period to his career as second fiddle to England international goalkeeper Ian Walker. Manager George Graham had other ideas, and Sullivan became his firm number one choice. Qualifying for Scotland under the heritage ruling, Sullivan won his first sixteen caps while with Wimbledon. He is a courageous shot stopper who never minds diving in where the boots are flying, and he makes up for occasionally suspect positioning by using his rapid reflexes and physical strength to get himself out of trouble. Following the departure of Ian Walker to Leicester, USA international Kasey Keller came into Glenn Hoddle's squad and Sullivan had to relinquish his place as first-choice 'keeper after an injury received while on international duty for Scotland sidelined him in 2002.

Paul TELFER ☆☆☆

Born: Edinburgh, 21 October 1971
English clubs: Luton Town, Coventry City, Southampton
Position: Midfield
Caps won while in England: 1 (of 1)

New Southampton manager Gordon Strachan knew the sort of player he wanted to give the Saints a touch of class and a feel of steel in the midfield. He turned to a player he had helped create in his own image – Paul Telfer, who followed him to St Mary's from Coventry in a free transfer under the Bosman ruling. He had been much more expensive when he arrived at Coventry from Luton in 1995 for £1.5 million, having developed through the youth team at Kenilworth Road. Telfer was reunited with his former Sky Blues team-mate Paul Williams at Southampton, and they dovetailed neatly into the Strachan scheme of things. Capped for Scotland by Craig Brown, Telfer is solid and reliable in any of the midfield positions. He lacks the flair that always lit up his manager's play, but brings similar energy and drive to the team.

Ian URE ☆☆☆

Born: Ayr, 7 December 1939
English clubs: Arsenal, Manchester United
Position: Centre-half
Caps won while in England: 3 (of 11)

In 1963, Arsenal manager Billy Wright paid what was then a world record fee for a centre-half of £62,500 to bring John (Ian) Ure to Highbury from Dundee. Ure had been outstanding in Dundee's recent run to the European Cup semi-finals, but a strike of players at Dens Park had left him rusty and he got off to a nightmare start to his new life in London. He had striking Scandinavian looks and was tall and leggy, so he could hardly hide as he stumbled around the middle of the Arsenal defence like a blind man in a maze. Billy Wright kept faith with him and he gradually settled down to show the form that had earned him his first eight caps at Dundee. The pressure of trying to shore up the leaking Arsenal defence manifested itself in losses of temper that brought him four dismissals, including an extraordinary one at Old Trafford in 1967 when he and Denis Law – a friend with whom he roomed on Scottish international duty – were sent off for fighting each other. Frank McLintock, another Scotland international team-mate, was bought from Leicester to play at right-half to his centre-half, but just as they were slotting in together Ure was put out of action by a knee injury that called for a cartilage operation. He battled his way back into the team, only to be part of an Arsenal side that suffered a humiliating 3–1 League Cup final defeat by Third Division Swindon at Wembley in 1969. Soon after, he had a furious bust-up with Gunners manager Bertie Mee because he was told to wear a different number shirt, about which he had a superstition. In August 1969, Manchester United manager Wilf McGuinness put him out of his Arsenal misery by taking him to Old Trafford in an £80,000 deal. They were shambolic days at Man United, and Ure did not have the happiest of times before injury forced his retirement after just 47 League games. An intelligent, intense and outspoken man, Ure followed a young manager called Alex Ferguson into the East Stirling hot seat for a year, and then coached in Iceland before turning his back on football in 1997. He became a social worker,

specialising in counselling inmates at the notorious Low Moss prison.

Tommy WALKER ☆☆
Born: Livingston Station, 26 May 1915
English club: Chelsea
Position: Inside-forward
Caps won while in England: 0 (of 20)

Tommy Walker's distinguished career bridged the Second World War, starting and finishing with Hearts and with service to Chelsea in between. A schemer-scorer, he netted 23 goals in 97 League matches while at Stamford Bridge for three seasons in the immediate post-war years. He returned to Hearts, taking his League goals haul for them to 103 before guiding them through their 1950s golden era. As Hearts manager, he lifted two League championships, four League Cups and a Scottish FA Cup. He was acknowledged as one of the first gentlemen of football, and was rewarded with an OBE in 1960 for his services to the game. He later served as Dunfermline secretary and manager of Raith Rovers.

Ian WALLACE ☆☆☆
Born: Glasgow, 23 May 1956
English clubs: Coventry City,
Nottingham Forest, Sunderland
Position: Striker
Caps won while in England: 3 (of 3)

It was feared that Ian Wallace's career was over when he was hauled from a wrecked car with a damaged eye. This was soon after Coventry City had bought the red-haired striker from Dumbarton for £40,000 in the summer of 1976. But he made a full recovery, and he was Coventry's leading marksman for his first three seasons at Highfield Road. His progress was watched closely by Nottingham Forest manager Brian Clough, who was sufficiently impressed to pay £1.25 million for him in October 1980. Strong in the air for a man who stood only just over 5ft 7in, Wallace's strength was an ability to turn a half chance into a goal with electric speed and positive finishing power. He was rarely able to live up to his early potential at Forest and after scoring 36 goals in 134 League games was allowed to move to Brest in France for £40,000. Within a year he was back in England for a season with Sunderland, and then played for Maritimo in Portugal in 1986 before moving to Australia. He broke a leg while playing for club side Croatia and switched to a coaching role and had a spell in charge at the Dumbarton club where he had been a goal-plundering hero in the 1970s.

John WARK ☆☆☆☆
Born: Glasgow, 4 August 1957
English clubs: Ipswich, Liverpool, Middlesbrough
Position: Midfield
Caps won while in England: 29 (of 29)

John Wark has the blue blood of Scotland mixed with the blue blood of Ipswich, a club where he had three successful spells as a player. He scored more than 200 League and Cup goals for Ipswich, an incredible contribution from a player whose main role was in midfield and, at the closing seasons of his career, in the back line of the defence. The way he combined with Dutch masters Frans Thijssen and Arnold Muhren in the Ipswich engine room was one of the most fascinating features of the 1980–81 season, when Bobby Robson's Ipswich captured the UEFA Cup and Wark the Players' Player of the Year award. He joined Ipswich as an apprentice in 1974, and it was ten years later that Liverpool manager Joe Fagan persuaded him to move to Anfield as a £450,000 replacement for Graeme Souness, who was bound for Sampdoria. He won many admirers at Anfield with his midfield marauding before a broken leg robbed him of some of his dynamic power. He returned to Ipswich after four years and 42 League and Cup goals in 108 games for Liverpool. His memorable moments at Anfield included two League championship medals and a hat-trick against Polish side Lech Poznan in a European Cup tie at Anfield. After two seasons back at Ipswich he had a 31-match stop-off at Middlesbrough before 'going home' to Portman Road in a player-coach role. Since his retirement he has scouted for Gordon Strachan, and performs hospitality duties for the Ipswich club he served so well.

David WEIR ☆☆☆
Born: Falkirk, 5 October 1970
English club: Everton
Position: Central defender
Caps won while in England: 10 (of 37)

David Weir had a full and fruitful career in Scotland before his move south to Everton. He defended with defiance for Falkirk and then Hearts, triggering the interest of Rangers manager Walter Smith, who twice tried to take him to Ibrox. It was third time lucky for Smith when he finally got his man after taking charge at Everton. Weir, who played for Celtic Boys, put his professional career on hold while studying for four years at Evansville University in the United States, returning to Scotland in 1992 to sign for Jim Jefferies at his hometown club Falkirk. Both Everton and Liverpool were keen to sign him after he had emerged at Hearts as one of the most dependable defenders in the UK, showing command in the air in both penalty areas, plus strength in the tackle and good distribution. He chose to sign for Everton rather than Liverpool because he had so much respect for Walter Smith and his right-hand man Archie Knox. Able to play in almost any of the defensive positions, his versatility was fully utilised by Walter Smith until he settled in at the heart of the defence in a rock-solid partnership with fellow Scot Richard Gough. Walter Smith's successor David Moyes continued to put his faith in the Gough-Weir tandem

team and then paired Weir with Alan Stubbs. Weir's caps collection with Scotland would be considerably more had he not informed Berti Vogts that he did not want to be considered for future matches after the team manager publicly criticised his performance in a best forgotten match against the Faroe Islands. His fierce competitive spirit makes him ideal captain material, and it twice spilled over during the 2002–03 season and he was shown two red cards. The sort of powerful man you want on your side rather than against you.

John WHITE ☆☆☆☆☆
Born: Musselburgh, 17 March 1937
English club: Tottenham
Position: Midfield
Caps won while in England: 18 (of 22)

John White was taken from us at his peak when he was struck by lightning while sheltering under a tree during a solo round of golf in 1964. He was 27 and recognised by the professionals in the game as one of the finest play-makers in Europe. John had scored 40 goals in 183 appearances for Tottenham after joining them from Falkirk in 1959 for a bargain price £20,000. He had been capped 22 times by Scotland, and was an ever-present for Super Spurs in their double year of 1960–61. His passes helped Spurs retain the FA Cup in 1962, and the following year he was a member of the first British side to win a major European trophy when

Tottenham brought home the Cup Winners' Cup. In his youth he had been turned down by both Rangers and Middlesbrough as being too small, but he quickly showed his frail appearance was misleading when starting his career with Alloa Athletic and then Falkirk. Bill Nicholson bought him following a two-line whip from Dave Mackay and skipper Danny Blanchflower, who had both seen him playing for Scotland. He took time to settle to the pace of English League football, but once attuned he became one of the finest schemers in the game. It was his ability off the ball that made him such a phenomenal player, and his habit of turning up unseen in the best possible positions earned him the apt nickname, 'The Ghost of White Hart Lane'. He would pop up from out of nowhere just when he was needed most to make a pass or collect the ball. John had the gift of being able to give the exact weight to the ball so that it would arrive where and when it was wanted. He had the energy to run all day and could cut a defence in half with just one cunningly placed ball. Danny Blanchflower was the brains of that great Tottenham team, Dave Mackay the heart and John White the eyes. Together they formed one of the great club midfield trios of all time. Jimmy Greaves said of him: 'When I joined Tottenham in 1961 all the talk was of Blanchflower, Mackay, Bobby Smith and Cliffie Jones. John White rarely got a mention. But I quickly found out that he was the man who quietly made the team tick. Time and again it was his positioning and passing that opened the way to goal. If there had been the same TV analysis of goals then as there are now, you would have found John being credited with dozens of assists.'

Derek WHYTE ☆☆☆
Born: Glasgow, 31 August 1968
English club: Middlesbrough
Position: Central defender
Caps won while in England: 6 (of 12)

After seven years and more than 200 first-team games for Celtic, Derek Whyte brought his defensive discipline south to Middlesbrough in a £950,000 transfer. It was then Boro's record fee, and Whyte proved himself worth every penny as, in his first season, he played a storming part in helping them to promotion to the Premiership. He became club captain and a leader on and off the pitch during five years of marvellous service to the North-East club. His coolness under pressure and ability to find a team-mate with a well-delivered ball from a packed penalty area helped give Middlesbrough stability and counter-attacking ammunition. He returned to Scotland in December 1997, taking over as skipper of Aberdeen and later moving home to Glasgow to give his leadership powers to Partick Thistle.

Gareth WILLIAMS ☆☆☆
Born: Glasgow, 12 December 1981
English club: Nottingham Forest
Position: Midfield
Caps won while in England: 5 (of 5)

Coming up through the Forest ranks from his days as a trainee, Gareth Williams blossomed and prospered as he grew accustomed to the pace of first-team football. Capped by Scotland at youth and Under-21 level, the Scot with Welsh roots quickly proved he had an old head on his shoulders to go with young legs that carried him up and down from defence to attack with great alacrity. He matured so rapidly that he was trusted with the captaincy in his early twenties, and led by example with storming performances from his midfield command post. Essentially a team player, he brings colleagues into the game with intelligently placed passes and hustles and harasses the opposition when Forest are not in possession. He was a regular in the Nottingham Forest side that challenged for promotion to the Premiership in 2002–03, falling at the heartbreak play-off hurdle.

Alex WILSON ☆☆☆
Born: Buckie, 29 October 1933
English club: Portsmouth
Position: Full-back
Caps won while in England: 1 (of 1)

Alex Wilson was a full-back from the old school who tackled like thunder and was expert at jockeying wingers, pushing them out towards and often over the touchline in the days when football was very much a game of physical contact. He joined Portsmouth from his local junior club Buckie Rovers in 1950 and became part of the furniture at Fratton Park. He played more than 400 League and Cup matches for Pompey in fifteen years of loyal service. His one Scotland call-up by the selectors came at right-back in a 2–1 victory against Finland in Helsinki in 1954 when he was barely established in the Portsmouth first-team.

Ian WILSON ☆☆☆
Born: Aberdeen, 27 March 1958
English clubs: Leicester, Everton, Derby County, Bury, Wigan
Position: Midfield
Caps won while in England: 5 (of 5)

A former Aberdeen and Dundee youth player, Ian Wilson began to draw the scouts when he moved to Highlands club Elgin City. It was Leicester City who got in first and persuaded him to move to Filbert Street in 1979 in a £30,000 deal.

He made such an impressive impact in more than 300 League and Cup appearances for the Foxes that new Everton boss Colin Harvey bought him in September 1987 for £300,000. It was smart business by Leicester, who had squeezed the best out of the willing midfield workhorse before selling him on at a huge profit. He won three of his five caps with Everton, but was never totally settled at Goodison, where he found himself understudy to the inventive Kevin Sheedy. After risking splinters as a perpetual substitute at Everton, he moved to Turkish club Besiktas, where his neat passes helped them win two League and Cup doubles in a row. Wilson returned to England two years later to play for Derby County, Bury and Wigan. He was always a thinking footballer and applied his mind to coaching, working on a regular basis with Highlands club Peterhead in between assignments in Japan and Turkey. Wilson then took on the job of preparing Peterhead for life in the Scottish Football League and proved himself a motivational manager in their new world.

Bob WILSON ☆☆☆☆☆
Born: Chesterfield, 30 October 1941
English club: Arsenal
Position: Goalkeeper
Caps won while in England: 2 (of 2)

As the author is a personal friend of Bob Wilson, there might be some bias creeping in. At his absolute peak between 1970 and 1972, there have been few goalkeepers in his class. He was just a fingertip behind the three kings Gordon Banks, Peter Shilton and Pat Jennings, and even they might have had to bow the knee to him in Arsenal's double year of 1970–71, when he was absolutely magnificent. There was only one real error, when he left his near post unguarded to allow Steve Heighway to shoot a Liverpool equaliser in the 1971 FA Cup final. But Charlie George got him out of trouble with a brilliant extra-time winner, which was only fitting because it was Bob who had discovered him while coaching at a Holloway school. Wilson had the unusual distinction of playing schools football for England and winning two full caps with Scotland, when Tommy Docherty made him the first player to qualify because of the heritage ruling. Bob's dad was Scottish and he grew up in Chesterfield in a Scots-speaking household. He has had to endure endless leg-pulling because his middle name is Primrose, following the Scottish tradition of taking his mother's surname. Oh yes, Bob is Scottish to the core. Billy Wright signed him for Arsenal, persuading him to give up a teaching career to become a full-time goalkeeper after amateur experience with Wolves. He made an erratic start to his professional life, but nobody worked harder at his game and after five seasons he established himself as first-choice goalkeeper. Wilson was the only defender to appear in every single one of Arsenal's 64 matches during that memorable double year. He developed good positional sense, had a safe pair of hands and was brave beyond the call of duty. Even while playing he had the good sense to realise he would need another career, and he started taking a close interest in broadcasting. On his retirement he became an excellent anchorman for the BBC *Football Focus* programme, then switching to ITV to give them expert screen service before bowing out in 2002. He has always kept closely involved with Arsenal as a highly respected coach, including England's David Seaman among his disciples. Bob is a born teacher, and his goalkeeping academy has produced a conveyor belt of well-schooled keepers who are made to realise that theirs is a specialist position that requires specialist knowledge. Greavsie would say that he should have found a few more Scottish pupils, but the author could not possibly comment. Tragedy darkened the lives of Bob and his wife Megs when they lost their daughter, Anna, after a long fight with cancer, and they have since devoted much of their time to raising money for a charity set up in memory of the lovely Anna. You can find out full details here: www.willowfoundation.org.uk

QUOTE: 'The double year was so special because just two years earlier we had been humbled at Wembley by Swindon in the League Cup final. That was our all-time low, but we proved there was enormous character running through the team in the way that we came back to shut up all the critics. It goes without saying that the success of that Arsenal side of the early 1970s was down to teamwork, with Frank McLintock an outstanding captain, Don Howe an inspirational coach, and Bertie Mee proving that top management is about delegation. I was so proud to be selected for Scotland because I know it meant so much to my father.'

George WOOD ☆☆☆
Born: Douglas, Lanarkshire, 26 September 1952
English clubs: Blackpool, Everton, Arsenal, Crystal Palace, Cardiff, Hereford
Position: Goalkeeper
Caps won while in England: 4 (of 4)

A former stonemason, George Wood chiselled an excellent career for himself in England after a £7,000 move in 1972 from East Stirling to Blackpool at the age of 19. He played 495 League games during goalkeeping assignments for the Seasiders (117 games), Everton (103), Arsenal (60), Crystal Palace (192), Cardiff (67), Blackpool again (15) and Hereford (49). Big, blond and brave, Wood gave his peak performances at Goodison and Highbury, and was so outstanding at Arsenal that for several months in 1982 he kept the one and only Pat Jennings out of the team after the Irishman had been sidelined by an injury. Never totally accepted by the demanding Arsenal fans, he lost his place back to Jennings after he had been controversially suspended for a so-called professional foul on Aston Villa's Peter Withe. There was as much gamekeeper as goalkeeper about George, and he later became an ornithologist with the Glamorgan Wildlife Trust while also managing non-League Inter Cardiff.

Tommy WRIGHT ☆☆☆
Born: Clackmannan, 20 January 1928
English clubs: Sunderland, Oldham
Position: Utility forward
Caps won while in England: 3 (of 3)

A versatile forward who was at his most lethal on the right wing, Tommy Wright joined Sunderland's 'Bank of England' side for £9,000 from Partick Thistle in 1949. He could more than hold his own in the all-star Sunderland forward line, and despite being out on the wing for much of the time managed to reach double figures with his goals output in four separate seasons. He was carried off with an appalling leg injury when he was 24, and doctors said he would never play again. But he proved them all wrong and was Sunderland's top scorer the following season. He scored 52 League goals in 170 matches for the Wearsiders, and won his three Scottish caps in 1952–53 when the likes of Willie Waddell, Lawrie Reilly and Gordon Smith were competing for the number 7 shirt. He had another short session in England with Oldham after playing for East Fife.

Ron YEATS ☆☆☆☆☆
Born: Aberdeen, 15 November 1937
English clubs: Liverpool, Tranmere
Position: Centre-half
Caps won while in England: 2 (of 2)

It was Bill Shankly who lit the flame to the Red Revolution at Liverpool, and it was Ron Yeats who was the chief torch bearer. Shanks bought him from Dundee United for £30,000 in 1962, and the author was among the sportswriters invited by Shankly to 'come and walk around him . . . the man's a colossus.' The Shanks spin convinced us (and opposing centre-forwards) that Yeats was at least seven foot tall. In actual fact he was 6ft 2in, but certainly gave the impression of being a much bigger obstacle while standing like a man-mountain in the middle of a Liverpool defence that was so dominant in the early 1960s. An inspiring skipper, the former slaughterman from Aberdeen led Liverpool up from the Second Division as champions, and was a major force in their League title-winning teams of 1963–64 and 1965–66 and he collected the FA Cup in 1965. It is quite astonishing that he won only two Scottish caps, and it gives a false impression of his ability. He was a tough and traditional centre-half in the days just before they became known as central defenders. Big Ron, king of the airways and surprisingly nimble on his feet for such a 'colossus', left Anfield in

1971 for playing and managing adventures with Tranmere Rovers, and later Stalybridge Celtic and Barrow. He had outside interests in haulage and catering businesses, and eventually returned 'home' to Anfield as chief scout.

QUOTE: 'Bill Shankly used to make me feel ten feet tall! We had some great times under him, and the one day I will never ever forget was when I became the first Liverpool skipper to lift the FA Cup. The fans treated us like gods, and I could have sailed back to Liverpool on the champagne that was being offered.'

Alex YOUNG ☆☆☆☆☆
Born: Loanhead, 3 February 1937
English clubs: Everton, Stockport County
Position: Centre-forward
Caps won while in England: 2 (of 8)

Never has a footballer been better nicknamed than Alex Young – the Golden Vision of Goodison. Eight Scotland caps is a nonsense for a player who could charm his way through defences with gliding skills that were a gift to him from the footballing gods. He was a centre-forward from the now-you-see-me-now-you-don't school, ghosting through from deep positions and bringing his team-mates into the action with cleverly chipped or deadly diagonal passes that could cut defences open at the heart. He had been hero-worshipped at Hearts for six years, and Goodison fans soon found out why when he moved to

Everton for a laughable £40,000 in 1960. His value in today's market? Let's start the bidding at £20 million . . . and over there a man has his hand raised and has bought him for £30 million. It's Sir Alex Ferguson stepping into this dream scenario, himself a former centre-forward during the Young years who appreciated just what a genius of a player he was. Near the end of his days at Goodison, Young was dropped by manager Harry Catterick in favour of a sixteen-year-old prodigy called Joe Royle. Police had to come to Catterick's rescue when irate Everton supporters threatened to lynch him for dropping their idol. To see Young and Welsh international Roy Vernon working in tandem in the Everton attack was to see football at its best, and together they helped to propel the club to the League championship in 1962–63. Three years later Young was in the Everton team that beat Sheffield Wednesday in the 1966 FA Cup final. He hung up his golden boots in 1968 after scoring 77 goals in 228 League games, and fleetingly tried managing with Irish club Glentoran before caressing the ball for one last time as a player with Stockport County. Young then went home to Edinburgh to run a wholesale business. It had been quite an adventure since leaving the coal mines behind to become a full-time professional footballer with Hearts, where in six years he won two Scottish championship medals, and winners' medals in the League Cup and Scottish Cup. Those who saw him at his peak would not believe that he had come up from the coal mines. Surely, this was a man who had come down from Mount Olympus.

Willie YOUNG ☆☆☆
Born: Edinburgh, 25 November 1951
English clubs: Tottenham, Arsenal, Nottingham Forest, Norwich, Brighton, Darlington
Position: Central defender
No full caps

'Wild Willie' Young would have won a hat-rack full of caps but for getting involved in the infamous Copenhagen bar incident in 1974 that led to him being suspended along with four established Scottish internationals. He was an Under-23 international at the time, just waiting for the nod for a place in the senior side. But the selectors would not trust him following the alcohol-fuelled controversy. After 187 solid appearances for Aberdeen, he travelled the England soccer circuit with Tottenham (54 League games), Arsenal (170), Nottingham Forest (59), and finally, while battling with injuries, Norwich City (5), Brighton (4) and Darlington (4). Terry Neill liked him so much that he bought him twice, as manager at Highbury and then White Hart Lane. Yet it was typical that Willie – always an earthquake waiting to happen – should fall out with a man who had shown such faith in him, and he moved on to Forest after a mega

disagreement with Neill. A redhead with a fiery temper to match, Young was not the most subtle of players and his managers would have their hearts in their mouths as he clattered into opponents with tackles that were agricultural in their execution. Goodness knows where the recipients had their hearts! Willie was always exciting to watch, and with a little more polish on the ground to go with his aerial power he could have developed into one of the great centre-halves, but he was too reckless and incident-prone for the taste of the more squeamish among us. The game was a lot less colourful when he sheathed his sword and took over a picturesque country pub on the outskirts of Nottingham.

Tommy YOUNGER ☆☆☆☆
Born: Edinburgh, 10 April 1930
English clubs: Liverpool, Stoke, Leeds
Position: Goalkeeper
Caps won while in England: 16 (of 24)

A safe rather than spectacular goalkeeper, Tommy Younger won two Scottish League championships with his hometown Hibernian club before joining Liverpool for £9,000 in 1956. Weighing in at just over 15 stone, he was a giant presence on the Liverpool goal-line and centre-forwards would think twice before taking him on in shoulder-barging duels in the days when goalkeepers were not protected by referees. A fact for trivia hunters: he is the only Liverpool goalkeeper to have played at centre-forward for the Reds. He went off injured during a 1957 game against Derby County, and – in what were pre-substitute days – he later rejoined the game at the head of the attack. He was Scotland's goalkeeper in the 1958 World Cup when his performances lacked their usual consistency and reliability, and he never played international football again. He later had spells as player-manager of Falkirk, and kept goal for Stoke and Leeds as well as trying his luck in Toronto. He was assistant manager at both Stoke and Leeds, and then returned home to Edinburgh, where he became a director of the Hibs club with which he had started on his great adventure. Greatly respected throughout the game, he became president of the Scottish Football Association, an office he held on his untimely death at the age of 53 in 1984.

The Dream Team

A tartan army of visitors to my website at www.macsoccer.co.uk selected their favourite post–war Anglo–Scots so that, based on the votes received, I could piece together a Dream Team.

This is a breakdown of the Top Ten votes received for each position, with the support given in percentage terms (I give the English team with which each player has been most associated).

GOALKEEPERS

Jim Leighton (Man United)	28%
Andy Goram (Oldham Athletic)	14%
Bob Wilson (Arsenal)	12%
Bill Brown (Tottenham)	11%
David Harvey (Leeds)	9%
Tommy Younger (Liverpool)	7%
Ronnie Simpson (Newcastle United)	6%
George Farm (Blackpool)	4%
Neil Sullivan (Wimbledon)	3%
Jim Herriot (Birmingham City)	2%
Others	4%

FULL-BACKS

Willie Donachie (Man City)	26%
David Hay (Chelsea)	16%
Eddie McCreadie (Chelsea)	14%
Frank Gray (Leeds)	9%

George Burley (Ipswich)	8%
David Weir (Everton)	6%
Arthur Albiston (Man United)	4%
Tommy Gemmell (Nottm Forest)	3%
Willie Cunningham (Preston)	3%
Ray Stewart (West Ham)	2%
Others	9%

CENTRAL DEFENDERS

Alan Hansen (Liverpool)	27%
Gordon McQueen (Man United)	12%
Frank McLintock (Arsenal)	11%
Colin Hendry (Blackburn)	9%
Ron Yeats (Liverpool)	8%
Martin Buchan (Man United)	7%
Bobby Moncur (Newcastle)	6%
Kenny Burns (Nottm Forest)	4%
Richard Gough (Tottenham)	3%
John Wark (Ipswich)	2%
Others	11%

DEFENSIVE MIDFIELD

Billy Bremner (Leeds)	21%
Graeme Souness (Liverpool)	16%
Dave Mackay (Tottenham)	13%
Steve Nicol (Liverpool)	11%
Jimmy Scoular (Man City)	9%
Tommy Docherty (Preston)	8%
Bruce Rioch (Derby)	7%
Craig Burley (Chelsea)	6%
Scot Gemmill (Nottm Forest)	4%
Stuart McCall (Everton)	2%
Others	3%

CREATIVE MIDFIELD

Jim Baxter (Nottm Forest)	26%
Bobby Collins (Leeds)	12%
Gary McAllister (Leeds)	11%
Pat Crerand (Man United)	10%
Archie Gemmill (Nottm Forest)	9%
Gordon Strachan (Leeds)	8%
John White (Tottenham)	7%
Asa Hartford (Man City)	6%
Charlie Cooke (Chelsea)	5%
George Graham (Arsenal)	2%
Others	4%

WINGERS

Billy Liddell (Liverpool)	18%
Jimmy Johnstone (Sheff United)	16%
John Robertson (Nottm Forest)	15%
Peter Lorimer (Leeds)	12%
Willie Henderson (Sheff Wed)	9%
Graham Leggat (Fulham)	8%
Tommy Hutchison (Man City)	7%
Willie Johnston (West Brom)	6%
Pat Nevin (Everton)	4%
Willie Morgan (Man United)	2%
Others	3%

STRIKERS

Kenny Dalglish (Liverpool)	52%
Denis Law (Man United)	41%
Others	7%

The favourite formation in all the teams selected was 4–4–2, with Kenny Dalglish and Denis Law being selected as twin striking partners in more than ninety per cent of the submitted sides.

This is how the Dream Team would line up:

LEIGHTON

HAY   McQUEEN   HANSEN   DONACHIE

BREMNER   SOUNESS   MACKAY   BAXTER

DALGLISH   LAW

Sir Alex Ferguson was the choice as manager, selected just ahead of Sir Matt Busby and Bill Shankly. Dave Mackay collected most votes as captain.

Thank you to everybody who voted. Sweet dreams!

The '200' Club

The following Scottish-born footballers have each played more than 200 post-war Football League games for a single English club. (I've also included selected major players who have made 190 or more appearances.) An asterisk indicates a full Scottish international. The list includes substitute appearances.

Key:
G: Goalkeeper; FB: Full-back; D: Defender; CD: Central defender; CH: Centre-half; M: Midfield; WH: Wing-half; IF: Inside-forward; W: Winger; F: Forward

Player	Club	Position	Seasons	Games	Goals
Henry Adamson	Notts County	WH	1946–55	233	5
Charlie Aitken	Aston Villa	D	1959–75	561	14
George B Aitken	Workington	CH	1953–59	262	3
George G Aitken*	Sunderland	M	1951–58	245	3
Arthur Albiston*	Man United	FB	1974–87	379	6
Ian Alexander	Bristol Rovers	FB	1986–93	291	6
Jim Allan	Swindon	G	1971–83	371	0
John Anderson*	Leicester	G	1948–59	261	0
Sandy Anderson	Southend	FB	1950–62	452	8
Owen Archdeacon	Barnsley	W	1989–96	233	23
Jim Bain	Swindon	W	1947–53	235	40
Stuart Balmer	Charlton	CD	1990–97	227	8

Player	Club	Position	Seasons	Games	Goals
Bill Baxter	Ipswich	WH	1960–71	409	21
Jimmy Baxter	Barnsley	IF	1945–52	222	54
	Preston	IF	1952–59	245	65
Bob Beattie*	Preston	IF	1937–53	264	49
Bobby Bell	Watford	FB	1957–64	268	2
Willie Bell*	Leeds	FB	1960–67	204	15
John Benson	Torquay	FB	1964–70	240	7
Jack Bertolini	Brighton	WH	1958–65	258	12
Ian Black*	Fulham	G	1950–57	263	1
Adam Blacklaw*	Burnley	G	1956–67	318	0
Jim Bowie	Oldham	M	1962–72	333	37
John Boyle	Chelsea	M	1964–73	198	10
Billy Bremner*	Leeds	M	1959–76	586	90
Frank Brennan*	Newcastle	CH	1946–55	318	3
Ian Britton	Chelsea	W	1971–81	263	33
Chic Brodie	Brentford	G	1963–70	199	0
Murray Brodie	Aldershot	M	1970–82	460	84
Frank Brogan	Ipswich	W	1964–70	203	58
Mike Brolly	Grimsby	W	1976–82	254	27
Alistair Brown	West Brom	F	1972–83	279	54
Bobby Brown	Workington	FB	1956–67	419	2
Bill Brown*	Tottenham	G	1959–66	222	0
Bill Brown	Grimsby	FB	1951–57	265	1
Sandy Brown	Everton	FB	1963–71	209	9
Alex Bruce	Preston	F	1975–83	301	135
Tommy Bryceland	Norwich	IF	1962–70	254	49
Martin Buchan*	Man United	CD	1971–83	376	4
Bill Buchanan	Barrow	FB	1949–55	242	0
John Buchanan	Cardiff	M	1974–81	231	54
George Burley*	Ipswich	FB	1973–85	394	6
Frank Burns*	Preston	FB	1973–80	273	0
Tommy Cahill	Barrow	FB	1955–64	283	3
Colin Calderwood*	Swindon	CD	1985–93	330	20
Bobby Cameron	QPR	IF	1950–59	256	59

Player	Club	Position	Seasons	Games	Goals
Alan Campbell	Charlton	M	1965–70	198	28
Jock Campbell	Charlton	FB	1946–57	255	1
Jim Cannon	Crystal Palace	CD	1971–87	571	30
Willie Carr*	Coventry	M	1967–75	252	33
	Wolves	M	1975–81	237	21
David Carroll	Wycombe	M	1988–02	302	40
Gordon Chisholm	Sunderland	CD	1978–85	197	10
John Christie	Southampton	G	1951–59	197	0
Colin Clarke	Oxford United	CD	1965–78	444	23
Steven Clarke*	Chelsea	D	1987–97	330	7
Jim Cochrane	Darlington	FB	1975–80	223	5
Jim Collins	Brighton	IF	1962–66	201	44
Eddie Colquhoun*	Sheff United	CD	1968–77	363	21
Bob Conroy	Bury	FB	1955–62	217	2
Charlie Cooke*	Chelsea	M	1966–77**	299	22
Tony Coyle	Stockport	W	1979–86	219	28
Tommy Craig*	Sheff Wed	M	1969–74	214	38
Campbell Crawford	Exeter	FB	1967–73	234	3
Graeme Crawford	York City	G	1977–80	235	0
Pat Crerand*	Man United	M	1963–70	304	10
Joe Crozier	Brentford	G	1937–48	200	0
Bob Cumming	Grimsby	W/FB	1974–87	365	58
Gordon Cumming	Reading	M	1969–77	295	51
George Cummings	Aston Villa	FB	1935–48	210	0
Willie Cunningham*	Preston	FB	1949–63	440	3
Kenny Dalglish*	Liverpool	F	1977–89	355	118
Andy Davidson	Hull City	FB	1952–67	520	18
Angus Davidson	Scunthorpe	M	1969–76	321	45
Alex Dawson	Preston	F	1961–67	197	114
Tommy Deans	Notts Co	FB	1949–55	239	0
John Dick*	West Ham	F	1953–62	326	153
Tommy Docherty*	Preston	M	1949–58	324	5
Willie Donachie*	Man City	FB	1968–79	351	2
Neil Dougall	Plymouth	IF	1949–58	274	26

Player	Club	Position	Seasons	Games	Goals
Colin Douglas	Doncaster	M/D	1981–92	404	53
Ian Drummond	Bournemouth	FB	1949–55	265	1
Jim Dudley	West Brom	WH	1948–59	285	9
Willie Duff	Charlton	G	1956–63	213	0
Dally Duncan*	Derby	W	1932–46	261	63
Jimmy Dunn	Leeds	FB	1947–59	422	1
Joe Dunn	Preston	CH	1951–60	223	2
Jim Elder	Colchester	WH	1950–54	199	15
Allan Evans*	Aston Villa	CD	1977–89	380	51
Dave Ewing	Man City	CH	1949–62	279	1
George Farm*	Blackpool	G	1948–59	561	1
Ewan Fenton	Blackpool	WH	1947–59	203	20
Bobby Ferguson*	West Ham	G	1967–79	240	0
Harry Ferrier	Portsmouth	FB	1946–53	241	8
Malcolm Finlayson	Millwall	G	1948–56	230	0
Hugh Fisher	Southampton	M	1967–77	302	7
Alex Forbes*	Arsenal	WH	1948–56	217	20
Bill Forbes	Preston	WH	1949–56	192	7
Duncan Forbes	Colchester	CD	1961–68	270	2
	Norwich	CD	1968–80	295	10
John Fowler	Colchester	FB	1955–67	415	5
Bill Frame	Leicester	FB	1933–49	220	0
Doug Fraser*	West Brom	D	1963–71	257	8
Jimmy Frizzell	Oldham	IF/M	1960–69	317	56
Jimmy Gabriel*	Everton	WH	1960–67	256	33
	Southampton	WH	1967–72	192	25
Archie Gemmill*	Derby	M	1970–77	261	17
Scot Gemmill*	Nottm For	M	1990–99	245	21
Tommy Gibb	Newcastle	M	1968–75	199	12
Alex Gibson	Notts Co	CH	1959–68	347	10
Davie Gibson*	Leicester	IF	1962–70	280	41
John Gilchrist	Millwall	FB	1961–68	279	10
Don Gillies	Bristol City	F/D	1973–80	200	26
Alan Gilzean*	Tottenham	F	1964–73	343	93

Player	Club	Position	Seasons	Games	Goals
Jimmy Gordon	Middlesbrough	WH	1945–53	241	3
John Gorman	Carlisle	FB	1970–76	229	5
Gerrie Gow	Bristol City	M	1969–80	375	48
Arthur Graham*	Leeds	W	1977–83	223	37
George Graham*	Arsenal	M	1966–72	227	59
Jackie Graham	Brentford	M	1970–79	374	38
Davie Gray	Bradford City	WH	1948–55	242	13
Eddie Gray*	Leeds	W/M	1965–83	455	52
Frank Gray*	Leeds	FB	1971–84	332	27
John Grogan	Mansfield	CH	1947–51	201	0
Bryan Gunn*	Norwich City	G	1986–97	391	0
Gary Hamilton	Middlesbrough	M	1983–91	229	25
Peter Handyside	Grimsby	D	1992–2001	199	4
Alan Hansen*	Liverpool	CD	1977–89	434	8
John Hardie	Bradford PA	G	1963–70	265	0
John Harris	Chelsea	D	1945–56	326	14
Jim Harrower	Accrington	FB	1954–60	246	2
Asa Hartford*	West Brom	M	1967–74	214	18
David Harvey*	Leeds	G	1982–84**	349	0
Danny Hegan	Ipswich	M	1963–68	207	34

(Danny was born in Coatbridge, but chose to play for Northern Ireland.)

Player	Club	Position	Seasons	Games	Goals
Jackie Henderson*	Portsmouth	CF	1950–57	217	70
Stewart Henderson	Brighton	FB	1965–73	198	1
John Hendrie	Middlesbrough	W	1990–96	192	44
Colin Hendry*	Blackburn	CD	1987–98**	337	34
David Herd*	Man United	CF	1961–68	202	114
George Herd*	Sunderland	IF	1961–69	278	47
John Hewie*	Charlton	D	1951–65	495	37
Tom Higginson	Brentford	WH	1959–69	388	15
Bobby Hill	Colchester	IF	1955–64	240	20
Dave Hilley	Newcastle	IF	1962–67	194	31
Dennis Hollywood	Southampton	FB	1962–71	234	4
Bobby Hope*	West Brom	M	1960–72	336	33
Stewart Houston*	Man United	FB	1973–79	205	13

Player	Club	Position	Seasons	Games	Goals
Bill Hughes	York City	W	1951–61	349	55
Billy Hughes*	Sunderland	F	1966–77	287	74
Tommy Hutchison*	Coventry	W/M	1972–80	314	24
Archie Irvine	Doncaster	M	1969–75	228	16
Sammy Irvine	Shrewsbury	M	1972–78	207	18
Joe Jakub	Bury	M/D	1980–88	265	27
Alex Jardine	Millwall	FB	1950–57	299	25
Fred Jardine	Luton	FB	1961–71	220	9
Tommy Johnston	Notts Co	M/W	1948–56	267	88
Willie Johnston*	West Brom	W	1972–79	207	18
Hugh Kelly*	Blackpool	WH	1945–59	429	5
John Kelly*	Barnsley	W	1945–52	217	25
Bobby Kennedy	Man City	FB	1961–69	219	9
Bobby Kerr	Sunderland	M	1966–79	368	56
Joe Kiernan	Northampton	M	1963–71	308	13
Ian King	Leicester	CH	1957–66	244	6
Jake King	Shrewsbury	FB	1971–82	306	20
John Kirton	Stoke	WH	1935–52	219	2
Denis Law*	Man United	F	1962–73	309	171
Tommy Lawrence*	Liverpool	G	1962–71	306	0
Sam Lawrie	Charlton	W	1956–62	193	70
Jimmy Leadbetter	Ipswich	W/M	1955–64	344	43
Walter Lees	Watford	CD	1968–75	226	10
Graham Leggat*	Fulham	F	1958–67	254	127
Billy Liddell*	Liverpool	F	1939–60	495	216
Jimmy Logie*	Arsenal	IF	1939–54	296	68
Peter Lorimer*	Leeds	W/M	1962–85	526	168
Gordon Low	Bristol City	WH	1961–68	205	12
Gary McAllister*	Leicester	M	1985–90	201	46
	Leeds	M	1990–96	231	31
Tony McAndrew	Middlesbrough	CD	1973–85	313	15
Tom McAnearney	Sheff Wed	WH	1951–65	352	19
Lou Macari*	Man United	F	1973–84	329	78
Don McCalman	Bradford PA	CH	1959–66	297	5

Player	Club	Position	Seasons	Games	Goals
Brian McClair*	Man United	F/M	1987–98	355	88
John McCormick	Crystal Palace	CH	1966–72	194	6
Eddie McCreadie*	Chelsea	FB	1962–73	331	4
Billy McCulloch	Stockport	D	1945–54	309	4
Iain McCulloch	Notts Co	W	1978–83	215	51
Stan McEwan	Blackpool	CD	1974–82	214	24
John McGinlay*	Bolton	F	1992–97	192	87
John McGovern*	Derby	M	1968–74	190	16
	Nottm For	M	1975–82	253	6
Ally McGowan	Wrexham	FB	1953–64	408	2
Tommy McGuigan	Hartlepool	IF	1950–57	325	75
Alex McIntosh	Carlisle	FB	1949–54	227	4
Dave McIntosh	Sheff Wed	G	1947–58	293	0
Angus Mackay	Exeter	F	1947–55	257	78
Dave Mackay*	Tottenham	M/D	1959–68	268	42
Iain McKechnie	Southend	G	1966–73	255	0
Bobby McKinlay	Nottm For	CH	1959–69	614	9
Bob McKinnon	Hartlepool	FB	1986–91	247	7
John McKinven	Southend	W	1960–69	286	62
Ross MacLaren	Swindon	M/D	1988–94	197	9
Scott MacLaren	Carlisle	G	1948–54	262	0
Tommy McLaren	Port Vale	M	1967–76	333	28
Joe McLaughlin	Chelsea	CD	1983–89	220	5
Alistair McLeod	Blackburn	W	1956–60	193	47
George McLeod	Brentford	W	1958–64	207	20
Frank McLintock*	Arsenal	M/CD	1964–72	314	26
Jim McNab	Sunderland	M	1957–67	285	13
	Preston	M	1967–73	224	6
Neil McNab	Man City	M	1983–90	221	16
Peter McNamee	Peterborough	W	1960–65	192	60
Ken McNaught	Aston Villa	CD	1977–83	207	8
David McNiven	Bradford City	F	1977–83	212	64
Ian McParland	Notts Co	F	1980–89	221	69
John McPhee	Blackpool	WH	1962–70	259	15

Player	Club	Position	Seasons	Games	Goals
Ken Malcolm	Ipswich	FB	1954–62	274	2
Danny Malloy	Cardiff	CH	1954–61	225	1
Dick Malone	Sunderland	FB	1970–77	236	2
Arthur Mann	Notts Co	FB	1972–79	253	21
Dennis Martin	Carlisle	W	1967–70	275	48
Eric Martin	Southampton	G	1967–74	248	0
Les Massie	Huddersfield	F	1955–66	334	100
Don Masson*	Notts Co	M	1968–74	274	81
George Meek	Leeds	W	1952–60	195	19
Colin Meldrum	Reading	LB	1962–69	266	8
Ally Millar	Barnsley	M	1971–80	289	17
Ian Miller	Blackburn	W	1981–89	268	16
Bobby Mitchell*	Newcastle	W	1949–60	367	95
Willie Moir*	Bolton	IF	1945–55	325	118
Bobby Moncur*	Newcastle	CD	1962–73	296	3
John Moore	Luton	CD	1965–72	274	13
Willie Morgan*	Burnley	W	1961–75**	196	19
	Man United	W	1968–74	238	25
Jackie Mudie*	Blackpool	IF	1947–61	320	143
Tommy Mulgrew	Southampton	IF	1954–62	293	90
George Mulhall*	Sunderland	W	1962–68	253	55
George Mulholland	Bradford City	FB	1953–60	277	0
Steve Mungall	Tranmere	D/M	1979–95	512	13
Frank Munro*	Wolves	CD	1968–76	296	14
Rod Munro	Brentford	FB	1946–52	199	0
Scott Murray	Bristol City	M	1997–2003	225	46
Neil Myles	Ipswich	WH	1949–59	223	15
Kit Napier	Brighton	CF	1966–72	256	84
Hugh Neill	Carlisle	FB	1961–68	247	2
Pat Nevin*	Chelsea	W	1983–88	194	36
	Tranmere	W	1992–96	201	30
Malcom Newlands	Workington	G	1952–59	251	0
Steve Nicol*	Liverpool	M/D	1982–94	343	36
George O`Brien	Southampton	IF	1959–66	244	154

Player	Club	Position	Seasons	Games	Goals
John O`Hare*	Derby	F	1967–74	248	65
Ian Ower	Workington	G	1963–67	199	0
Alex Parker*	Everton	FB	1958–65	198	5
Sandy Pate	Mansfield	FB	1967–77	413	2
Matt Patrick	York City	W/M	1946–53	246	47
Tommy Pearson*	Newcastle	W	1933–47	212	46
George Peden	Lincoln	FB	1967–73	225	14
John Porteous	Plymouth	WH	1949–56	215	13
Ian Porterfield	Sunderland	M	1967–77	230	17
George Potter	Hartlepool	FB	1971–76	213	4
Bill Punton	Norwich City	W	1959–66	219	24
John Quigley	Nottm For	IF	1957–65	236	51
Alex Rae	Millwall	M	1990–96	218	63
Douggie Reid	Portsmouth	IF	1946–55	308	129
Mark Reid	Charlton	FB	1985–90	211	15
Tom Ritchie	Bristol City	F	1971–81	321	77
Bobby Roberts	Leicester	M	1963–70	229	26
Ally Robertson	West Brom	CD	1969–86	506	8
Eddie Robertson	Bury	FB	1955–63	196	5
George Robertson	Plymouth	FB	1950–63	359	2
John Robertson*	Nottm For	W	1970–83	387	61
Bill Robertson	Chelsea	G	1946–60	199	0
Alan Ross	Carlisle	G	1963–78	466	0
Bob Ross	Brentford	M	1966–72	292	58
Bobby Ross	Grimsby	M	1965–70	212	18
George Ross	Preston	FB	1960–72	386	3
Bill Russell	Doncaster	FB	1979–85	244	15
Bill Rutherford	Darlington	WH	1952–59	253	3
Alex Scott	Carlisle	FB	1950–55	200	4
Jimmy Scoular*	Portsmouth	WH	1945–53	247	8
	Newcastle	WH	1953–60	247	8
Stewart Scullion	Watford	W	1966–71	225	30
Bobby Seith	Burnley	WH	1952–59	211	6
Bill Shankly*	Preston	WH	1933–48	296	13

Player	Club	Position	Seasons	Games	Goals
Graeme Sharp*	Everton	F	1979–91	322	111
John Shaw	Bristol City	G	1975–84	295	0
Ronnie Simpson*	Newcastle	G	1951–59	262	0
Colin Sinclair	Darlington	F	1971–76	203	59
John Sjoberg	Leicester	D	1960–73	335	15
Bernie Slaven	Middlesbrough	F	1985–93	307	119
Gavin Smith	Barnsley	W	1946–53	257	35
Jim Smith	Preston	D	1955–69	314	13
Charlie Sneddon	Accrington	CH	1953–60	213	3
Graeme Souness*	Liverpool	M	1978–83	247	38
Alex Spark	Preston	CD	1966–75	225	6
Ian St John*	Liverpool	F/M	1961–71	336	95
Jackie Stewart	Birmingham	W	1948–54	203	54
Ray Stewart*	West Ham	FB	1979–90	345	62
Jim Stirling	Southend	CH	1950–59	218	2
Gordon Strachan*	Leeds	M	1989–95	197	37
Gerald Sweeney	Bristol City	M/FB	1971–82	406	22
Tony Taylor	Crystal Palace	FB	1968–74	195	8
Paul Telfer*	Coventry	M	1995–2001	191	6
Jim Thomson	Burnley	D	1968–76	297	3
Ken Thomson	Stoke	CH	1952–59	278	6
Hugh Tinney	Bury	FB	1966–72	238	3
John Walker	Reading	IF/WH	1957–64	297	24
Keith Walker	Swansea	M/WH	1989–97	269	9
Jock Wallace	Blackpool	G	1934–48	235	0
Joe Wallace	Shrewsbury	WH	1954–62	337	3
Colin Walsh	Charlton	W	1986–95	242	21
John Wark*	Ipswich	M/D	1974–96***	539	135
Charlie Watkins	Luton	WH	1948–54	218	16
Archie Whyte	Oldham	CH	1950–55	234	0
John Whyte	Bradford City	FB	1950–56	236	2
Alex Wilson*	Portsmouth	FB	1951–66	352	4
Ian Wilson*	Leicester	M	1979–87	285	17
Ray Wilson	West Brom	FB	1964–75	232	3

Player	Club	Position	Seasons	Games	Goals
Ron Wilson	Port Vale	FB	1963–70	264	5
Tom Wilson	Millwall	CH	1961–67	201	15
Bobby Wood	Barnsley	WH	1951–64	338	41
George Wood*	Crystal Palace	G	1983–87	192	0
Charlie Wright	Charlton	G	1966–71	195	0
Ron Wylie	Notts Co	IF/M	1950–58	227	35
	Aston Villa	IF/M	1958–64	196	16
Ron Yeats*	Liverpool	CH	1961–71	358	13
Ramon Yeoman	Middlesbrough	WH	1958–64	210	3
Alex Young*	Everton	CF	1960–68	228	77

**In two spells at the club   ***In three spells at the club